# CONVERSION;

ITS

# THEORY AND PROCESS,

## PRACTICALLY DELINEATED.

BY REV. THEO. SPENCER.

If any man will come after me, let him deny himself, and take up his cross, and follow me.—MATT. xvi. 24.

NEW YORK:
PUBLISHED BY M. W. DODD,
CORNER SPRUCE STREET AND CITY HALL SQUARE.
1854.

FOUNDRY OF S. ANDRUS AND SON,
HARTFORD.
W. C. Armstrong, Typographer.

# PREFACE.

THE chief objects of the following work are to enlighten the honest inquirer in relation to his duty to God, to encourage the believer in faith and hope, and to aid the churches in advancing the work of grace in their congregations. The writer is deeply impressed with the responsibility of attempting to guide immortal souls into the right paths, but the providence of God seems so evidently to have "laid a necessity upon him," that he dares not shrink from the duty. In discharging it, he has endeavored to present the cardinal evangelical doctrines without formality, and merely as the exigencies of his subject demanded; and while he has avoided dry theological discussions and every thing merely theoretical, he has not hesitated to develop every important principle which was adapted to his designs, even at the hazard of being considered too particular by the ignorant or indolent.

In the earlier period of his ministry he was much disheartened by the absence of that precision of instruction in relation to the sinner's duty to Christ which is so indispensable to his intelligent discharge of it, and consequently to his final salvation. In every other branch of science such accuracy is attainable, and indeed is a peculiar beauty in the legal and other professions; and it seemed evident that the Scriptures intended it should be acquired on this most important of all subjects also. The many discouraging apostasies which followed his own and others' instructions, finally determined the writer to devote himself to a study of the position, exigencies, and capabilities of impenitent and regenerate mind, the truths that were adapted to its various frames, and the ways of the Holy Spirit with the hearts of men so far as they were revealed or were discoverable from the impressions produced by him. The results of such investigations, pursued for more than a quarter of a century, during which he has conversed with thousands of careless persons, convicted sinners, or doubting Christians, are now presented to the reader. While engaged in them, he has never knowingly suffered his opinions to be influenced by fancy, or by the power of mere authority except that of divine revelation, which has always been absolute with him; but he has endeavored to elucidate the teachings of the Scriptures by developing facts and principles as they exist in the actual workings of the human mind.

The majority of those who have intellectually received the Holy Scriptures, and who have enjoyed its instructions, (for whom this work is intended, to the exclusion of the caviler and the sceptic,) have at some periods indulged hopes of heaven more or less confidently, and which have proved to be more or less transient. To meet the necessities of such, the writer has commenced with an investigation of various grounds of hope; these should be critically examined also by every reader, whether he is avowedly destitute of a hope in Christ, or whether he entertains one in the validity of which he is confident; for a knowledge of them is indispensable to an intelligent perusal of the remainder of the work. May the Most High condescend to make it conducive to his own glory in turning sinners to righteousness, and in preparing many of his children for a more useful service here, and for a joyous passage through the dark valley of death to the blessedness of his holy and heavenly kingdom!

UTICA, N. Y., 1854.

# CONTENTS.

## CHAPTER I.

### ANALYSIS OF VARIOUS RELIGIOUS EXPERIENCES



## CHAPTER II.

### ELEMENTS OF MORAL CHARACTER IN GENERAL.

## CHAPTER III.

### ELEMENTS OF HOLY CHARACTER.

PAGE.



## CHAPTER IV.

### ELEMENTS OF UNHOLY CHARACTER.

PAGE.



CHAPTER V.

MORAL CHARACTERISTICS OF THE EXERCISES BEFORE ANALYZED.



CHAPTER VI.

OBSTACLES TO THE SINNER'S PROGRESS.

## CHAPTER VII.

### OBSTACLES TO THE SINNER'S PROGRESS.



## CHAPTER VIII.

### DEVELOPMENT OF RIGHT MORAL PRINCIPLES.



## CHAPTER IX.

### ASSURANCE.

# Conversion;

## ITS THEORY AND PROCESS,

### PRACTICALLY DELINEATED.

## CHAPTER I.

### ANALYSIS OF VARIOUS RELIGIOUS EXPERIENCES.

*Pastor*. WILL you please communicate to me your present views and feelings in relation to your religious prospects?

*Inquirer*. I am not aware of possessing any very peculiar feelings, beyond a general desire to secure my salvation. Some years ago I indulged a hope of pardon and acceptance in Christ; but my subsequent inconsistent feelings and conduct have almost entirely destroyed my confidence in its validity. Whenever I attempt to revive it, or to recall the evidences on which it was founded, I am sure to be disappointed; and when I endeavor to abandon that hope, and seek one more substantial and permanent, I find that it clings to my heart in spite of all I can do, making me merely repeat efforts long since tried, and leaving me in the same state in which I began.

*P.* I presume that, at those times, you strive for feelings which you find yourself unable to summon; and that you search for some evidences of acceptance which you cannot acquire, notwithstanding all your prayers and labors. There is a cloud before your mind, whose darkness you cannot penetrate; and an insensibility of heart to be overcome, which your efforts seem only to increase; and you are left at a loss what to do?

*I.* Such are precisely the difficulties with which I have had to contend. When I address myself to the duties of religion, I find that I do not know *how to begin right*, and cannot discover how to give my heart to God. When I reflect that my former hope may be invalid, the apprehension seizes my soul that I may be eternally lost on account of this ignorance. This is dreadful; and if you will extricate me from this danger, you shall have my best thanks.

*P.* Under the guidance and blessing of the Holy Spirit, to whom is to be ascribed all the power and praise, I will show you clearly what hindrances lie in your path, and how they are to be removed; and will explain what your duty is, and how to enter upon it. In order to accomplish this, however, your uninterrupted attention must be devoted to the subject, and you must determine to follow the advice hereafter given so far as you are convinced of its propriety.

*I.* I will do so without hesitation.

*P.* We know not but that your hope may be valid; but if we would ascertain its true character beyond a doubt, recourse must be had to the period when it was first embraced. We are required to examine ourselves whether we are in the faith (2 Cor. 13:5); and to ascertain the validity of our hope with precision, we must take a retrospection of the rise or inception of those principles on which it was originally founded, when they stood alone, or uncombined with those other exercises which tend to impair a clear perception of them. Such an investigation, if carefully conducted, will be productive of no false security, and will be entirely safe. Indeed, without it, it is doubtful whether you can abandon your hope, if it is invalid. You are well aware that your mere resolutions to dismiss it, are of no account; and that, if it is ill-founded, it must be rejected before you can embrace a good one. And by means of such a scrutiny alone can you reach a certain knowledge that it is a valid one, and so enjoy the comforts of an assured hope.

*I.* I shall be pleased to observe that course; but must depend on you to propose questions upon such points as are necessary to be inquired into.

*P.* I will do so. In pursuing our conversations, we shall first investigate your early exercises. We will next examine the great principles of Christianity, in order to ascertain what God would have us become. We will next develop those characteristics of the natural heart which he requires us to abandon. Then, by comparing your own exercises with these principles and characteristics, you can decide with entire certainty upon their character before God. The mind will then be in a position to perceive and to remove the various obstacles to your progress; and the precise point of your duty in turning to God will become intelligible. Afterwards, many subjects of importance to the well-being of the soul, will come up for our investigation.

*I.* Your proposed course is highly reasonable and satısfactory. But can I depend upon my recollections? My heart is deceitful above all things.

*P.* The deceitfulness of the heart does not interfere with our memory of past events. It consists in a disposition to believe every thing we deem good for ourselves, and to disbelieve in whatever we do not like. It is seen also in that infatuation which, under a hope of impunity, drives men along in sin, against the dictates of their conscience and the threatenings of God. Against these you should guard.

*I.* I am anxious to proceed.

*P.* I presume that you always respected religion, and desired to embrace it before you died?

*I.* Certainly. When I was a mere child, I was accustomed to pray, read my Bible, and do many other things in order to please God, and have him love me.

*P.* Why did you wish to have him love you?

*I.* Because then he would pardon my sins and receive me into everlasting peace.

*P.* I suppose you always understood and regarded religion as designed for your good?

*I.* Yes.

*P.* As you grew older, did you become convinced that you was a sinner, and that it would be right and just in God to cast you off for ever?

*I.* I did. And such convictions of conscience produced remorse, and deepened my desires to obtain relief by embracing a hope of salvation.

*P.* You knew that God had a right to claim your love and service, and the consciousness that you did not render them produced such fears and anxieties?

*I.* Yes.

*P.* During the various times when you were thus partially awakened, what did you attempt in order to become a Christian?

*I.* I tried to secure a hope.

*P.* How did you expect to succeed?

*I.* By obtaining some new feelings or change of heart, which would be an evidence of my pardon and acceptance.

*P.* In order to which, you endeavored to please God by reforming your conduct, and by prayer and the use of all the means which appeared to have been successful in other cases?

*I.* Yes. I made many mental efforts to feel and act right.

*P.* Why did you desire salvation?

*I.* For the same reason that all mankind desire it—to be delivered from perdition, and to enjoy eternal peace.

*P.* Did you not, at times, desire to be delivered from sin, because it was indispensable to a good hope?

*I.* Yes; I always knew it was indispensable.

*P.* We will use the term salvation in this sense for the present; as indeed we must, if we would comprehend one another, since it is the only one in which the impenitent understand it. Did you not often intermit your efforts?

*I.* Yes. Either I would become satisfied prematurely, or would fail in effecting a change. I believed Christ was willing, but could not find the right way to go to him; and then would suspend my endeavors until a more favorable opportunity. After indulging for a season in worldliness and sin, my desires for salvation would revive.

*P.* You mentioned that you had once indulged a hope in Christ. Was it at an early age?

*I.* Yes. Circumstances, not necessary to be detailed, revived my desires. The more I reflected, the deeper were my anxieties to get religion; while the more I endeavored to love God, the more insensible to his goodness and holiness my feelings became. I feared it would prove to be the last offer of grace, and I became willing to renounce the world and every thing else that hindered my salvation, and determined never to give up seeking religion.

*P.* Did you not become again discouraged, and suspend those efforts for the time being?

*I.* No. I had many fears, but was persuaded there was some right way to be saved; and I persevered until I found it, as I then hoped.

*P.* What resolution did you at last form relative to serving God?

*I.* Having tried every other way in vain, I finally concluded that, whether my evidences came immediately or gradually, I would obey the Lord in the best way I could.

*P.* Did you hope, at the time, that you might be accepted and pardoned for Christ's sake?

*I.* I did. I hoped it would prove the right way, provided I should persevere in it. It would have been very irrational to take any course which I had good reason to believe would result in no benefit.

*P.* Previous to this resolution you had not possessed love to God?

*I.* Certainly not; for if I had, I should have enjoyed a hope of pardon before then.

*P.* It was your desire to secure your future safety

and peace, or your salvation, that made you form that resolution?

*I.* Yes. I also thought it would be right, and resolved to serve the Lord, come what might.

*P.* That is, you *knew*, as always before, that it was the right of God to claim your service and love, and that it was your duty to render them; but you was induced to form that resolution, by the desire to secure your salvation, and also by the desire to take that step as the *right way* to please God and effect it.

*I.* Yes, that explains it precisely. Still, I did not expect salvation by my own strength, but only through the mercy of Christ. I think that, before, I depended too much on my own efforts to become good; but then I depended altogether on Christ for pardon and acceptance.

*P.* Immediately on forming that resolution, did you feel relieved from your load of anxiety, and become calm and composed under the hope that you had at last taken the right way to be accepted, and that you might be enabled to persevere in it?

*I.* I did.

*P.* Was not this a new state of feeling, and did it not encourage you to believe that you had already succeeded, in some measure, in getting an evidence of acceptance?

*I.* Yes. And my feelings increased to much pleasure, at the joyful thought.

*P.* And was not this pleasure so new and eventually so strong, as to induce the full belief that you had succeeded, and that the Spirit had given these feelings as a witness of your pardon, and acceptance, and title to hope in Christ; and did you not then hope in him for pardon and happiness?

*I.* Such were precisely my views and feelings. After some hesitation, lest my good prospects might prove deceptive, I could no longer resist the force of such evidences, but embraced a hope in the pardoning mercy of Christ.

*P.* And did you not then exercise much pleasure and gratitude toward Christ for his friendship and goodness?

*I.* I did, and it confirmed my hope in him. And then a view of his kindness in dying for me, and in preserving me so long while his enemy, in pardoning and loving me, and of the secret pleasure I took in him therefor, and the knowledge that I must endure to the end to be saved, made me renew the resolution to serve him the remainder of my days; and it seemed a pleasure to do so.

*P.* Did you feel willing to leave yourself in the hands of God, to be at his disposal?

*I.* Yes. Always before God out of Christ had been a consuming fire, and I feared to be in his hands because I knew he would punish me. But now I felt that he was reconciled, and I could safely leave myself at his disposal, hoping for his favor only through Christ. Still, the Saviour was in all my thoughts.

*P.* Although your thoughts, and consequently your affections, were thus chiefly on him, I suppose you still *approved* of the strict holiness and rigid justice of the Father, even though you hoped to escape from their stern demands by means of Christ; while your *love* was called forth toward Christ for his matchless goodness and grace?

*I.* Yes; and I could take pleasure in the Father for the gift of such a precious Saviour.

*P.* After indulging these feelings, did not a view of your past sins produce sorrow and regret that you had been so ungrateful to Christ?

*I.* I felt that my conduct had been so unkind and ungrateful, that I could hardly forgive myself the wrong they had done my Saviour.

*P.* Your feelings being chiefly attracted toward Christ as a Saviour, I suppose you had not acquired those exercises toward a God of holiness and justice which Job describes: "Wherefore I abhor myself, and repent in dust and ashes." That is, while you disapproved of sin against the Father, you did not then condemn yourself to a deserved perdition as justly exposed to his justice, nor loathe and abhor yourself on account of your moral deformity and as fitted only for destruction, nor hate yourself as too vile to hope and too odious to be accepted?

*I.* While I felt self-condemned for my past course of ungrateful conduct, it was with hope in Christ, and pleasure in his goodness and mercy. Of course, with such pleasant feelings, I could not entertain those you have described; nor have I supposed that new converts ever indulge in such gloomy views as Job expresses.

*P.* You knew that sin was forbidden; but did not your anxiety to preserve those evidences of acceptance, and to avoid displeasing God, and forfeiting his favor and your salvation, as well as a sense of its ingratitude, induce you to resolve to avoid sin thereafter?

*I.* Yes; and it was then a positive pleasure to do any thing which appeared to be necessary to sustain my hope in the mercy of Christ.

*P.* Did you not, at first, take pleasure in converts and older Christians because of their amiable dispositions, engaging manners, congeniality of feeling and pursuits, friendly interest in your welfare, as well as from their being the friends of Christ, bound to the same heaven as yourself, and whose example, conversation and prayers encouraged you to hope and persevere in the ways of salvation?

*I.* Yes; such considerations made me strongly at tached to some particular individuals.

*P.* As you became more familiar with religious feelings, did not the strictness and rigid principles and conduct of some older Christians become somewhat repulsive?

*I.* I found so little to sympathize with in some of them, that their society afforded me little or no pleasure, to say the least; and this made me prize those more with whom I could have feelings in common.

*P.* Did you not, at first, feel a strong interest for the conversion of your friends and others?

*I.* I desired their salvation from eternal misery above every other thing which they could attain; and on this account, as well as to continue in the line of duty myself, I tried to influence some of them to secure a hope of eternal life. My own pleasure in the hope of pardon, naturally led me to desire the same for them; my own deliverance induced me to sympathize with their deplorable state and prospects; and I also disapproved of their ingratitude to their heavenly Benefactor.

*P.* Did you not take much satisfaction in secret and social prayer, when your hope was strong and your prospects bright? Did you not then enjoy it, because it was the medium of expressing and indulging your pleasure in the mercy of Christ, and of seeking those spiritual aids by which your evidences were to be preserved, and your eternal safety and peace insured?

*I.* Yes; you have described my feelings correctly.

*P.* Did you not, at such times, take pleasure in reading the Scriptures, in order to obtain the information necessary to make your salvation sure? and did you not love to search out and apply to yourself the precious promises which they contained?

*I.* Yes; in connection with the general information it furnished, such were the sources of my enjoyment in perusing the word of God.

*P.* Did you not then pursue the duty of self-examination, in order to ascertain your present evidences, to revive those which had drooped, and to secure others? When these were satisfactory, your pleasure in the duty was the greatest; but when, for any reason, they were the reverse, it afforded you no enjoyment?

*I.* Yes; it seemed an indispensable duty in order to preserve my evidences, and I therefore observed it for a while.

*P.* Did you not also aid in promoting the various objects of benevolence in which Christians were engaged, and in sustaining and extending the influence of the gospel?

*I.* Of course. It was reputable and praiseworthy to engage in such objects; it gratified my sympathies for the welfare of others, and it seemed a duty to Christ, not to be dispensed with, if I would persevere and be saved.

*P.* Did you contemplate, at that time, making a public profession of religion by uniting with the Church?

*I.* I wished to do so, but was afraid. My friends urged it as a duty, if I would preserve the favor of Christ; but a secret reluctance to such a committal induced me to postpone it, until my feelings had so much abated, that I not only lost the desire to make a profession of religion, but was glad that I had not so pledged myself. I have since, however, very much regretted the omission, under the belief that a public acknowledgment of Christ would have withheld my steps from backsliding, and relieved me from many subsequent troubles.

*P.* Did your evidences eventually decline?

*I.* They did, almost entirely. For some time after I embraced that hope, I felt quite happy in my glorious prospects, and in my Saviour. At times, doubts of my acceptance would occur; but I was enabled to recall and deepen my evidences, and then all would be pleasant again. After some months, however, I lost my joys in religion; and the world, with its pleasures and pursuits, became far too attractive and engrossing.

*P.* I suppose that, as the subject lost its freshness and power by familiarity, you became less careful to preserve those evidences, and less watchful over your thoughts, feelings, and deportment; temporal affairs gradually usurped a prominent place in your mind; business infringed more and more upon your private and public duties; conscience made you uneasy by its reproofs; and fears took the place of pleasure, when you thought of your salvation. When you resorted to your closet, it was more to quiet conscience and to allay those fears, than to enjoy your first love; your purposes, there renewed, failed to renew your hope with its evidences; until these duties seemed to have lost their efficacy, and they became therefore unattractive, and sometimes tedious, and were performed more seldom than before.

*I.* Alas, it was very much as you describe. By my wickedness and neglect, my evidences were mostly lost. I had expected to have "no more conscience of sin," but

I became so self-condemned, that it seemed of little use to make further efforts at that time. Finally, I came to resume my former worldly feelings in a great degree, and to neglect many duties which, I was well aware, were incumbent on me. I was a sadder man at times, if not a wiser.

*P.* When your hope thus failed, your religious pleasures vanished with it; just as they were excited and were high, when your hope existed and was bright? From which you can perceive that your religious feelings proceeded entirely from your hope.

*I.* Of course they did; and I lost them when it faded away.

*P.* While you were in this hopeless state, did you feel willing to be in the hands and at the disposal of the Father?

*I.* Of course not, for I could not then go to him with a hope in Christ. To have gone any other way, would be to meet the very destruction I wished to avoid.

*P.* Having failed to find that continued enjoyment in religion which you anticipated, you have since endeavored to derive pleasure from the world and its pursuits?

*I.* Such has been far too much the case. I have made many efforts since to go to Christ in a right way, and to do my first work over again; but have never been favored with such decided evidences as I at first received.

*P.* Have you, at any time since, entirely abandoned that hope?

*I.* No, not entirely. The recollection that I once possessed such new and happy feelings, about which I cannot be mistaken, has always afforded me some consolation and encouragement in the greatest extremities.

If, as I suppose, they were the gift of the Spirit, I must have been converted then; but my subsequent conduct contradicts the fact; so that I am encouraged, or discouraged, as I contemplate the one or the other.

*P.* Have you since enjoyed any partial return of those evidences?

*I.* My desire of salvation has been as strong as ever, though dormant at times. On occasions of peculiar religious interest in the community, I have been aroused to seek my future peace, have renewed my efforts, and have regained some of those former exercises, though not in such power and freshness. But after a while they would die away again, and leave me more miserable than before. I am almost discouraged.

*P.* Is it still, when you deliberately contemplate the subject, your strongest desire to secure your eternal safety and peace?

*I.* Yes, in the proper way. It is the chief anxiety of my heart; for "What is a man profited if he shall gain the whole world, and lose his own soul? or what shall a man give in exchange for his soul?"

*P.* For the sake of further information, I will now delineate the modes adopted by several other classes of persons to accomplish the same object. You will observe that while all agree with you in pursuing their future safety and peace as the ultimate object of their desires, and while all acquire a hope thereof, with its pleasures and other results, as has been detailed in your own experience, each adopts different means therefor. A very short description, just sufficient to enable you to compare your experience with theirs, if it is not already fully perceived, must suffice; and we will not now pause either to approve or to condemn any of the courses specified.

*A.*, in dwelling upon his condition and prospects, feels much alarm, and becomes convinced that he has greatly sinned against God; and his anxiety to secure his salvation grows more and more strong. These feelings he regards as those which the Spirit gives, to be cultivated until they ripen into full evidences of his acceptance. With a view to his securing a hope of eternal safety and peace, he endeavors to deepen his desires by reflecting upon the pains of perdition, and to generate love to Christ by dwelling upon his past goodness and his present willingness to save him, if he goes to him in the right way. He determines, perhaps, to mortify his pride and humble himself before God, by acknowledging that he is a self-ruined sinner, unable in his own strength to secure salvation, and that he is therefore unmeritorious of his favor. In order the more effectually to accomplish his purpose, he endeavors to cleanse his heart, to relinquish every outward sin, to engage in whatever duties may seem suitable to aid him in his object, and to imitate the example of those who had previously succeeded. Perhaps he resorts to meetings for prayer, presents himself as an inquirer after salvation, and mingles with those who are made the subjects of special prayer. He becomes more encouraged as he proceeds, until, aware of the right of God to dispose of him as he will, he considers that he can now go to him sincerely and safely; and, placing his hope on Christ for acceptance, he resolves to give himself up to God. In the belief that he has now gone to him in the right way, he feels relieved and pleased. Having now attained the relief he so much desired, and his other feelings being so new and pleasant, he believes that these are the evidences needed, and is encouraged to hope that he has been accepted by Christ. He thinks he is now converted, and has obtained religion and rejoices in a hope of eternal safety and peace.

*B.* is suffering under adverse fortunes, the loss of friends, or other afflictions, or is becoming aged, so that the world is losing its attractiveness. He realizes the value of eternal happiness in some degree, and contrasts the "pleasures which are for evermore" with the fleeting and frivolous enjoyments of time, and determines to forsake the latter for the former; or, as he would express it, to give up all for Christ, through whom alone he can hope to receive pardon and peace. In the belief that he has now complied with the duty required, he hopes in Christ, and rejoices in his happy prospects.

*C.* believes that Christ died in a special sense for the elect, and that, if his sins were punished in him, his own salvation will be sure; and he also considers that faith in him consists in simply believing, on the mere assertion of the fact, that Christ died for him in particular, and that he is able and willing to save him. With a view to secure his salvation, and under pungent feelings of conviction, perhaps, he believes that his sins were punished in Christ, and that he will save him. This conclusion produces relief; and his expectations being thus far answered, he feels more encouraged and persuaded that he is accepted in Christ. This, in its turn, produces new and happy feelings, which he receives as the witness of the Spirit. He consequently becomes more confirmed in the belief that he is one of the elect, and joy in Christ fills his heart. The desire to render his salvation sure by persevering to the end, and the pleasure the confidence of doing so will afford him, induce him to resolve to obey Christ thereafter; and he rejoices in a Saviour found.

*D.* is disposed toward the Campbelite views of religion. He considers that, in order to secure his future safety and peace, he should believe the gospel, as he would believe any historical facts; that on making a profession of such belief, he should be baptized, which he thinks is equivalent to the regeneration required in the Scriptures; that, on being so baptized, he will receive remission of sins and the Holy Spirit; and that, as a consequence of the gift of the Spirit, he will have a pure heart and a good conscience. With a view to a hope of salvation, he complies with these opinions; and in the confident belief that he has reached an acceptable state, indulges a hope of pardon in Christ. The pleasures produced by this hope, being so new and delightful, confirm him in his confidence; and he rejoices in his happy prospects, determining to obey Christ, in order that he may endure to the end and be saved.

*E.*, while searching for the way of salvation, considers that Christ loves and is favorably disposed toward him, while he hates and condemns his *sins;* and this encourages him to resolve to obey him, in order to secure the blessings of his favor. Or perhaps he considers that Christ is the way, the truth, and the life; that he has become so for him; and that he should believe and enjoy it. These thoughts produce a secret pleasure in the goodness of Christ in first loving him thus, and in providing for his salvation; which being perceived, he becomes confident of already loving Christ in return, and hopes in his pardoning mercy. In order to perseverance, he resolves to obey Christ, and to devote himself to the promotion of the greatest possible happiness of his fellow-creatures, in the expectation that he will thereby most effectually advance his own.

*F.* adopts exalted views of the dignity of human nature, and believes that by its due cultivation his eternal salvation can be secured. Rejecting the main doctrines of the evangelical faith, and setting aside those scriptures which condemn his views, he cultivates elevated sentiments of the majesty, power, and benevolence of God; dwells upon the duties of natural benevolence, patriotism, and philanthropy; and insists upon due honesty and morality. As he endeavors to make himself sincere on these points, he acquires some confidence that he will hereafter escape the miseries which he is hardly conscious of deserving.

*G.* is a believer in the Scriptures, but considers that the work of grace in the soul is quite gradual; and, in laboring to secure a good hope of his eternal safety and peace, relies upon the peculiar means with which he thinks himself favored, especially in the authorized administration of them by persons whom he regards as the direct successors of the apostles. He endeavors to exercise sorrow for past sins; receives baptism at such supposed authorized hands, wherein he believes that he obtains the influences of the Spirit to enable him to work out his salvation, to secure the remission of sins, the favor of God, and everlasting life, and that consequently *some* spiritually regenerating grace is conveyed, and some saving effects are produced by that ordinance. Or, perhaps he receives it as a spiritually regenerating ordinance. But whatever may be his views relative to the spiritual effects of such baptism, he becomes thereby encouraged to hope more strongly in Christ for pardon and acceptance; and this produces more or less pleasure according to his degree of interest in his own eternal welfare, which is received as evidence of the new heart. In order more effectually to promote which, he purposes to obey the Lord, trust in Christ for safety and peace, and observe the authority and rites of his church. Accordingly, at the proper time, he receives confirmation at the hands of his diocesan, publicly assuming his previous engagements made in baptism, partakes of the eucharist, and grows in his attachment to his church, which very much determines, in his view, his right to an interest in Christ.

*H.* has been educated in the belief of the Roman sect. He believes in a purgatory after death, and in an eternal perdition; and his chief desire is to alleviate and shorten the pains of the former, to escape the latter, and to secure his eternal peace. In order to this, he implicitly receives whatever the priests choose to teach, and embraces a system of outward forms and ceremonies. He receives baptism and confirmation; confesses to the priest, and does penance; attends mass; trusts partly to his own supposed merits, partly to those of the Virgin Mary and the so-called saints, and partly on Christ, for acceptance; and he makes his relation to Christ dependant on his relation to his church, and measures the degree of his piety by his attachment to such church. His is peculiarly a religion of fear; for fear is the inducement to his observances, fear destroys almost all the comfort he might take in his delusion, and fear closes the scene at death.

*I.* is a believer in the necessity of spiritual regeneration. When under deep distress and fear in reflecting upon his lost state, and with a view to secure an evidence and hope of future safety and peace, he weeps profusely; this, he is encouraged to think, is an evidence of his penitence, and he looks for a development of *the power* of the Spirit in his heart as a witness of his being born again, and of his title to a pardon. He is comforted by believing that he is seeking Jesus sorrowing. If he goes forward to the altar for prayers, he examines whether he does not feel *a little* different; or he is encouraged by others to *say* that he does, in the expectation that it will produce new feelings or evidences; and if he discovers any calmness or other unusual state of mind, he instantly concludes that it is the desired witness, and hopes and rejoices in Christ. Perhaps he resorts to the Bible, as to a lottery, to decide upon his prospects; and if he opens upon some comforting passage—such as "thy faith hath saved thee, go in peace,"—he receives it as a divine message to himself, and rejoices in hope—the pleasures of which confirm his belief in his pardon and acceptance. Perhaps, in his nervous excitement, he thinks that he can see Christ hanging in person on the cross, covered with blood shed for *him*, or that he hears comforting words from his lips, which are received as tokens of his acceptance, and he rejoices accordingly. Perhaps he sees, in imagination, the rainbow of promise stretching over the heavens, or lights glowing with great beauty, or an ocean of blood prepared to wash away his sins; or hears angelic beings assuring him of pardon, and welcoming him to heaven. By such supposed evidences his anxiety is dispelled, and a hope of salvation is infused in his soul, and he trusts in Christ for future safety and peace; purposing a strict obedience to him, in order to make his salvation sure.

*I.* I thank you for these delineations of the secret workings of the human mind. They will prove useful.

*P.* I have now finished the inquiries and observations which I wished to make on this part of our subject; and we will proceed to the topic which was suggested as important to be next examined.

## CHAPTER II.

### ELEMENTS OF MORAL CHARACTER IN GENERAL.

*Pastor.* WE will now proceed to an examination of those fundamental principles of the Christian religion which are necessary to our understanding what Christ would have us become; and in doing so, while we are free to employ our reasoning powers, we must hold our conclusions in strict subordination to revelation, and must implicitly defer to God as the only authoritative expositor of his own will and principles. Should a young man for whom you felt a profound regard ask your advice, as he was about to launch out upon the busy sea of life, whether he ought always, and under all trials to which it might expose him, to maintain a strict integrity of character in his intercourse with mankind, what would be your counsel?

*Inquirer.* Always to preserve an upright character. No reputable person, it seems to me, would hesitate what to advise, or what course of conduct to pursue in this respect. Apart from every consideration of policy, there is an intrinsic propriety in uprightness, which the most depraved must reverence, and which those who have lost prize too late, as the dissolute do the health which they have destroyed. You surely do not suppose me capable of advising him to become unprincipled and debased under any possible circumstances?

*P.* No; and you have only expressed the views of every upright mind. You would advise on the principle that, although trials and injuries are painful, and therefore undesirable, uprightness is more *estimable;* and that the latter should never be sacrificed to the former?

*I.* I should; for whoever sacrifices his integrity at the call of interest or pleasure, can neither escape the censure of the good, nor find an adequate excuse in his own bosom.

*P.* In common with every upright being, our Creator entertains the same general views. He regards happiness as of great natural value, but he places a far superior moral estimate upon upright principles; and, in his regards, the moral preponderates over the natural. Wherefore he requires of his creatures the possession of a holy moral character, as indispensable to his approbation and love. "Be ye holy, for I am holy, saith the Lord." —1 Pet. 1:16. Those who become so, he will approve, love, and bless.—John 13:1; Dan. 9:23; Ps. 125:4; Prov. 11:20; Rom. 14:17, 18. Those who do not, he will disapprove, dislike, and punish.—Heb. 12:14; Deut. 25:16; Rom. 2:8. The creature's happiness, however valuable to himself, will never be preserved by God in the eternal state at the expense of holiness.. "Know ye not that the *unrighteous* shall not inherit the kingdom of God?"—1 Cor. 6:9.

*I.* No one, it seems to me, can justly censure, but must approve of him, for acting on such principles.

*P.* In order clearly to understand what is meant by holy character, we will first examine the nature and incidents of moral character in general. There are two kinds of character—namely, natural and moral. *Natural* character consists in one's natural temperament, or in the peculiar dispositions, traits, or qualities impressed upon him by nature; such as the amiability of one, and the energy of another. *Moral* character consists in the right or wrong use one makes of himself; in the impress which one receives from the right or wrong—that is to say, *moral* principles, which habitually govern his feelings and conduct. In other words, it consists in those habitual traits and qualities which one derives from the right or wrong principles which he adopts, loves, and pursues; as we say that one is of an honest moral character who is always governed by strict integrity in his dealings with others, and that another is of a dishonest moral character who is not.

*I.* The distinction is very obvious.

*P.* Virtue, or morality in an inferior sense, is involved in a moral character which proceeds from recognizing and acting upon the rights and claims of our fellow-creatures; while virtue, in its superior aspect, is involved in that which proceeds from recognizing and *cordially* acting upon the rights and claims of God over us; and, in this sense, it is synonymous with holiness.

*I.* What is the difference between character, reputation, and happiness?

*P.* Reputation is the opinion, good or bad, which the public entertain of our character. Character is what we *are;* reputation is what others *think we are.* Character is our own, and is to be preserved, when good, at all hazards; but our reputation is at the mercy of the world, and is often unjustifiably sacrificed by it. Happiness is an emotion, a feeling on satisfaction, on the accomplishment of some desire; and pain is an emotion of dissatisfaction when some desire is disappointed. Character is the impress of some moral principle or rule of action; while happiness is a pleasing sensation, which may result sometimes, but not necessarily or invariably, from a holy character, and sometimes, in this world, in spite of an unholy one. Character, reputation, and happiness are, as you can perceive, essentially different things.

*I.* No doubt. We always commend one for his supposed upright character; but never for his being happy, nor for his good reputation, except as we perceive he deserves it; and that desert constitutes his character.

*P.* Yes. By a law of our moral constitution, we always approve or disapprove of others according to their perceived moral character; and, except when personal considerations intervene, it is in view of such character that we like or dislike them. The Scriptures represent God as acting on the same principle.—Job 1:8; Ps. 146:8.

*I.* How is our moral character to be determined?

*P.* By the character of our motives, or objects of action; that is, by that of the ideas or considerations which influence our desires, purposes, affections, and conduct, or by that of the end which we contemplate therein.

*I.* Will you please enlighten my mind further on this point?

*P.* We always have some reason for acting, and some object which attracts us to make an effort for its attainment. An idea is a thought or conception of something, and is usually the representative in the mind of some outward object or thing. The idea *moves* us to act in the given case; and when it does so, it is called *a motive,*

*I.* A thought, then, only becomes a motive when it has sufficient influence to induce us to act under it.

*P.* An idea is called an *external* motive, because it is derived from something exterior of the mind, through the action of the intellect. Thus, the thought of some long-absent friend might induce you to visit him. This thought would be external, because it refers to something exterior from the mind itself; and it would be a motive, because it moves you to make the visit.

*I.* I can easily understand it.

*P.* In one class of cases, the thought first excites a *desire* in the mind for itself, or the thing it represents. This is called an *internal motive*, because it is a feeling originating in the mind itself, and because, by its means or power, the idea moves one to act. Thus, the idea of your friend would first excite a desire to see him, under which you would make the visit; this desire would *move* you to act, and would be an internal motive.

*I.* Such is my uniform experience.

*P.* But this desire exerts a moving influence, by inducing one to *resolve* to do whatever is necessary to accomplish its object; and such resolution is by a volition, or mandatory act of the will. Thus, the desire to see your friend would induce you to resolve to visit him; which would be a *volition* on that subject. In its turn, the resolution produces all the external conduct deemed necessary to accomplish the object; such as, in the case supposed, your immediate departure for the residence of your friend.

*I.* Yes, this is natural.

*P.* The *hope of succeeding*, gives all their motive impulse to the desires, over the will and conduct; for, as you can readily perceive, if you had no hope of finding your friend, do what you could, you would neither resolve to go to his residence, nor put forth any external means therefor; while the expectation of seeing him, if you should make the necessary efforts, would be the stimulus to your resolution and exertions.

*I.* Such, I now see, is the correct principle.

*P.* The pleasure which one takes is derived, as I have said, from the gratification of some desire, or from the anticipation of succeeding in its accomplishment. Thus, you might not only derive much pleasure from an interview with that friend, but the expectation of seeing him might make you happy in anticipation.

*I.* Yes; and all our other feelings are, as I can now perceive, produced by some thought originally presented to the mind; so that, if we ceased to think, we should cease to feel and act.

*P.* You are right. The mind is always governed by that thought which is calculated to exert the most power at the moment—that is, by the strongest motive present. Now, every thought has some intrinsic motive power. And it has also some moral character of its own, either good or bad; it bears the moral impression of the external object, if any, of which it is the representative. Thus, in the case supposed, those friendly thoughts are potential; and also possess an amiable characteristic, which rises in our estimation when it is compared with that brutality which incapacitates some from exercising them.

*I.* No doubt all our ideas have some moral character.

*P.* Whenever an idea or object *moves* the mind to action, its moral character becomes impressed upon the desires, purposes, and other feelings which it excites.

Thus, the amiability of friendship and its thoughts would be stamped upon your desires, and purposes, and conduct, and hopes, and pleasures, in reference to your friend; and all would pronounce your character to be amiable. And these feelings would exist in moral harmony; that is to say, the desire would not be unamiable, and yet the resolution to visit him be amiable; but all would necessarily partake of a common amiable character. The moral quality of the idea or object is not impressed upon the mind as a signet produces its likeness upon the wax; but is imparted to the agent by his own voluntary adoption of it as a motive influence, or principle of action. It thereby becomes his own, a real moral unity with himself; he and his principles become one in morals, one in approveableness, or the contrary; so that, if his motive is right, *he* is right, and if that is wrong, he is wrong also.

*I.* What is the most usual rule by which our moral character is determined?

*P.* As we shall see hereafter, the Holy Spirit, in the Scriptures, most usually presents, for that purpose, the ultimate object which one has in view; by which is meant the most extreme or final end, or that to which all the rest is directed; and we will conform to this example. You will observe that I have purposely avoided all those technical expressions which are not necessary to a proper understanding of this subject, and which would tend only to confuse the uninitiated in the mysteries of speculative mental philosophy.

*I.* Will you have the goodness to illustrate the principle just laid down?

*P.* I will; and in doing so will also elucidate some

other points. Let us suppose that *K.* harbored the idea of plundering the vaults of a bank in the metropolis, and that we saw him actually commence his journey there with that view. His object would be palpably wrong; and the question is, what estimate would you form of his moral character in that transaction, and why?

*I.* I should have no hesitation in pronouncing it wrong, and in censuring him as unprincipled and vicious, and as deserving of punishment; and the reason would be, that the object he had in view was vicious.

*P.* That object would impress its vicious character upon all his thoughts, desires, plans, purposes, and other feelings excited in view of it; and you would disapprove of them, and of him for them, and would dislike him on their account?

*I.* Certainly. Every virtuous person would feel so. His character would be blameworthy, and no one could avoid censuring him on account of it.

*P.* Suppose *K.* was so hopeful of succeeding in his object as to feel much elated, and to take great pleasure in every thing that he judged would conduce to its accomplishment?

*I.* I should entertain no better opinion of him; for his hope and its pleasures would not change his vicious character, but would rather confirm it, and make it more decided. They would be equally vicious and hateful, since they were produced by a desire for, and terminated upon such a vicious object.

*P.* Such is the principle on which our Creator also judges, as can be seen in the declaration in Romans 1:32: "Who, knowing the judgment of God, that they which commit such things are worthy of death, not only do the same, but *have pleasure in those that do them.*" Their pleasure in other transgressors, on account of their conduct, seems to be considered the chief and culminating point of iniquity in their own characters. In order to hold *K.* thus responsible to censure, he must have acted voluntarily in selecting his object, and in laying and pursuing his plans for it; he must have been at liberty to weigh the considerations for and against it, and to have chosen or to have refused them. If he had been coerced, so as to have acted against his will, he would not exhibit his own character therein, but that of the person who had compelled him to such conduct. So that he could form that character for himself only, by freely yielding to the vicious considerations

*I.* True; but suppose his will was already so perverse on the general subject of honesty, as to yield to such considerations without resistance, being induced to choose them of course?

*P.* This would not excuse him, but would be an evidence of a previous radical perversion in his principles. As he was intended by his natural constitution to be a free moral agent, and as God did not make dishonesty any part of either his natural or moral constitution, it follows that his devotion to it was of his own creation, and that he is responsible for all the consequences.

*I.* But suppose he had become so perverse as to have lost all his recuperative moral power—that is, his ability of himself to resist successfully—would not this inability excuse him, at least until some sufficient external aid should be afforded him?

*P.* No; having brought it upon himself, he cannot depose the responsibility of any of the consequences upon others, or excuse himself for any deficiency it may produce. The more profound his inability, the more wilfully and habitually perverse he must have acted, and the more censurable he would be. His consequent dependence upon exterior aid would evince, not his misfortune, but his criminality of disposition; and the measure of it would exhibit the exact extent of his perversion and criminality, so that if his dependence was entire, they would be complete. He could make no claim to such aid as a right, but would remain bound to reform without it; since a crime can never, in good morals, absolve one from the obligations of a previous duty. If he never received such aid, he would be left to meet his deserts without any just cause of complaint; and if he did obtain it, it would be an act of undeserved kindness, for which he could not be too thankful.

*I.* I see no good objection to these principles.

*P.* Suppose that *L.* should entertain the idea of rendering assistance to a family residing in the same place, who were peculiarly deserving of sympathy; and, with that view, should commence a journey there in company with *K.* His object being benevolent, we should esteem his character as benevolent in the transaction; and we should approve, and like him, on account of such object. If he should become doubtful and distressed under a fear of failure, so as almost to despond of success, but should, notwithstanding, persevere, our estimate of his character would remain unchanged; indeed, his discouragement and sadness, proceeding from the apprehension of having his benevolent desires disappointed, would make him more estimable, because they would evince the sincerity and strength of those feelings, while his decision and perseverance under difficulties, would show a commendable stability in well doing.

*I.* I coincide perfectly in these views.

*P.* If *K.* and *L.* should be mistaken, the one for the other, by their fellow-passengers, and the vicious reputation of the one should be attached by them to the other, it could in no way affect his true character. An agreement between them to exchange characters could not effect a substitution, because each must have acquired his own; and although one could lose his good character by violating his principles, and the other could acquire a good one by reformation, yet neither could impart his own to another, or receive a transfer of his in return.

*I.* My views accord with yours.

*P.* There is an important difference in the principles by which the character of a *person* who acts is tested, and those by which the character of his *external actions* is determined, to which I invite your attention. It will affect, in some degree, the whole course of our future investigations. Let me inquire, how do you account for the fact that wicked men often perform good actions?

*I.* They suppose that such actions are indicative of good feelings, and that they are themselves good.

*P.* No doubt men of evil moral character may be prompted to good actions by benevolent or other *natural* feelings, for seldom can any be found entirely divested of those humane impulses which all derive from nature; but this refers to traits of natural character only, while my question respects moral character exclusively. It is said that some pirates captured a vessel loaded with provisions for the starving population of Madeira; and that, on learning its destination, they released the vessel and crew, and sent them on their way. This was a good action, prompted by some remaining humanity; but it does not prove that the pirates were *morally* good men, that is, possessed of integrity and good moral character.

*I.* I perceive the difference. It is clear that the character of a person is determined by that of his motives or object; and I have supposed that his external *actions* also would be right or wrong according to the character of his motives, being decided by the same standard.

*P.* Then, if one does evil, in order that good may come—if he perpetrates a bad action from the motive of effecting some good end—the action will cease to be evil; and not only so, but it will become good; since, on this ground, the motive must make it right. The end, then, will sanctify the means, whatever they are. But this is pure Jesuitism, and is denounced in the Scriptures: "And not rather, (as we be slanderously reported, and as some affirm that we say,) Let us do evil that good may come? whose damnation is just."—Rom. 3:8. According to revelation, therefore, the end does not sanctify evil means, the motive of the agent does not relieve the depravity of the bad action, nor decide its character at all.

*I.* Will you please explain what principle does decide it?

*P.* Let me remark, preliminarily, that I refer now exclusively to *outward* actions, and not to our resolutions or intentions. The character of our intentions is, as we have seen, always decided by our motives or objects; and that of our emotions by our motives, desires and intentions indifferently, since these are always uniform in character, and our emotions rise spontaneously. When a person performs some outward action, it evinces an *intention* to do it; but it does not conclusively show the *moral character* of that intention. It is true that we usually suppose men will act consistently, and so are disposed to infer a good motive for a good action, and a bad motive for a bad one; whereas all know that a good action may be done from a bad intention, and a bad one from a good. Should a debtor pay an honest debt at maturity, we would infer an upright and honest motive and intention. But he might be thus punctual with a view of establishing his credit, and thereby of eventually defrauding his creditor out of an immense amount of money; in which case the inference founded on the supposed consistency between his conduct and motives would be erroneous, and the action, though right in itself, would be seen to proceed from an evil intention. There is such a consistency usually in the motives and conduct of wicked men, that it is a safe rule, "Ye shall know them by their fruits" (Matt. 7:16); but the hypocrite may, and usually does, violate that consistency by imitating the just in their conduct, but from sinister intentions. There is also usually a consistency between the motives and conduct of upright men; but the just may be, and often are left, through ignorance, to perpetrate some of the bad actions of the wicked.—Prov. 24:16.

*I.* I perceive my mistake. What is the true rule?

*P.* The character of our external actions depends exclusively upon their being in fulfillment or in violation of some law which is authoritative over us, or of some obligation which we are under to others. In determining the character of the *agent*, we refer, as has been said, to that of the motive or intention which produced his outward conduct; but in determining that of such *conduct* we ask, was its legitimate tendency (whether so designed by him, or not,) to fulfill a law or obligation resting upon him? If it was, we pronounce the action good; if it was not, we pronounce it evil.

*I.* On these principles, if a deserving mendicant should come into my house, and ask alms, to give him pecuniary aid would be a good action, because it is in fulfillment of my obligations to him as a fellow-creature; and my family might approve of me in it, by inferring a benevolent motive. But if my sole object was to get rid of him as speedily as possible, my own character, in the transaction, would not be commendable, but rather censurable? This is self-evidently correct. But does the character of an action produce no reflex impression on that of the agent?

*P.* I will answer by an illustration, which will enable us to see this important distinction more clearly; when we will leave the subject. Suppose that *M.* has a neighbor who is reduced to poverty by a protracted illness; and that he should, with many professions of kindness, loan him a considerable sum of money to meet the wants of his family,—to be rēpaid at some future and more prosperous day. We should be disposed to attribute benevolent motives to *M.*, and would commend his character in the transaction. We would also approve of his conduct, as being obviously proper toward a suffering fellow-creature. But suppose we are credibly informed that he had no such motives, and that, notwithstanding his plausible professions, his real objects in that transaction were to get the poor man and his family in his power by involving him in debt, to exact exhorbitant interest for his money, to enslave him and them to his own vile passions, and the like. Our estimate of his character would now change to disapprobation, with feelings of detestation; and if he should attempt to justify himself on the ground that his pecuniary loan to the poor man was a good deed, we should admit that, viewed by itself, that action was good, inasmuch as it was in fulfillment of his obligations, but that it did not relieve his personal character from condemnation. On the contrary, we would insist that he deserved increased censure and abhorrence for designedly covering his evil purposes under a good action, that is, for adding hypocrisy to his depravity.

*I.* I am satisfied. But still, if a person intending to do right, happens to perform an action which is injurious to others, he is not to be blamed?

*P.* Not for any criminal intention; but he may be censurable for want of consideration, or for that ignorance, in consequence of which, the injurious act occurred. In the case of *M.*, what counsel would you give?

*I.* I should say, in the language of Scripture, "these ought ye to have done, and not to leave the other undone."—Luke 11 : 42. He ought to have relieved his suffering neighbor, but should have done it with pure motives. Then he would have been commended and loved; but now he could only be censured and despised for the same action.

*P.* To observe, in our actions, the laws of the divine and human governments, and to fulfil all our domestic, social, and civil obligations, are things which ought to be done; while to do them with proper motives, and, as respects God. with those of the holy heart, are the things which are not to be left undone. In concluding this part of our subject, I will only remark that there are many varieties in general character. One, for example, is of an ambitious character, because of his habitual aspirations after power, honor, office, or fame; and another is of a good moral character, who is habitual in his endeavors to fulfill his duties to mankind. We are now prepared to enter upon the subject of a holy personal character.

## CHAPTER III.

### ELEMENTS OF HOLY CHARACTER

*Pastor*. A HOLY CHARACTER is the essential element in regeneration, conversion, submission to God, obedience, repentance, faith, the new heart, and every other Christian duty; and it confers upon each all the moral value which belongs to it. By its power, whoever enters upon either of these duties becomes measurably assimilated to the character of Christ, and enters upon that spiritual progress which will, through grace, terminate in a perfect conformity to his moral image in the heavenly state.—Prov. 4:18.

*Inquirer*. In that view, those requirements are both reasonable and indispensable.

*P*. As an infinitely just being, God must have some good and justifiable reason why he assumes the government over his intelligent creatures; and as a wise ruler, he must contemplate some adequate end to be accomplished by his administration. By ascertaining what these are, we shall discover the principles which are to be adopted in order to the possession of a holy character.

*I*. I shall be glad to investigate them.

*P*. Why has God the legal and supreme right to control you and your actions?

*I*. Because he is the Lord.

*P*. That is correct; and that reason is sufficient for

every unsophisticated mind. But the exigencies of our subject make it necessary for us to inquire why this fact confers such a right upon him?

*I.* The reason exists in my mind as a simple apprehension, but I am unable clearly to express it in words. Will you please to explain it?

*P.* Is that watch, which you hold in your hand, your own property?

*I.* It is, by purchase from the maker.

*P.* Having worked up his raw materials into that watch, he became its exclusive owner, under God; and by its due transfer to you, you have succeeded to all his rights. As its legal owner, you have every right of property in it, such as the right to possess, enjoy and control it; and this is exclusive of all others, except God, (who, as the owner of the original materials, has a property which underlays yours,) and you may exercise it without the permission or interference of the rest of mankind. This legal right of property is recognised and guarded by God himself.—Ex. 20:15. 17. It confers on you no authority over other persons, their property or other rights; but within the limits of your other personal claims, you may use the watch as you see fit, and all just laws would sustain you in it. Thus, if I should seize upon the watch, and convert it to my own use, you would justly complain of the act as an infringement upon your exclusive rights, and would insist upon its immediate restoration.

*I.* Certainly I should. My ownership would be a sufficient title against all the world, and would authorize me to possess and use the watch as I pleased.

*P.* God, as the original maker of all the material universe, has the ultimate and more absolute right therein. Creatorship is necessarily the primary source of all ownership; and this authorizes him to confer those subordinate rights of property on mankind which they now enjoy. As such original owner, the natural and legal right of property which God possesses over his creation, is of the most perfect kind. He created the Sun, for example, and caused its light and warmth to be shed forth upon the waiting earth; and who can doubt his perfect right to do with it as he will? Who has the privilege of questioning his authority, or the mode in which he may exercise it, or the purposes which he may choose to accomplish by means of it? Who can do any thing to make his rights of property in that orb more perfect? Or who can in the least impair them? No one. He may do as he will with his own (Matt. 20:25); and if you will allow the supposition, if the Sun could resist and should refuse to do his will, it would have no right to do so, and he would be justified in annihilating it, and in creating another in its place.

*I.* Common reason teaches us that the rights of property derived from creation, are perfect in God. No one, I suppose, pretends by argument or otherwise to increase or diminish them.

*P.* In the Scriptures, God explicitly puts forth such claims. I will cite only a few passages in proof of this, for a few will be as conclusive as a multitude; and I will adopt the same course on all the other subjects which may arise hereafter. God is declared (as in the first chapter of Genesis) to be the sole *creator* of the world of matter. "Thus saith the Lord God, he that created the heavens, and stretched them out; he that spread forth the earth, and that which cometh out of it."—Is. 42:5 and 45:12. God also claims the *ownership* of all material things, for the reason that he had founded, or began and built them. "The earth is the Lord's, and the fullness thereof—for he hath founded it upon the seas, and established it upon the floods."—Ps. 24:1, 2. "The heavens are thine, the earth also is thine; as for the world, and the fullness thereof, thou hast founded them: the north and the south, thou hast created them."—Ps. 89:11, 12. God also claims all the *rights of property* over material things, on the ground that he is their owner. "If I were hungry, I would not tell thee: for the world is mine, and the fullness thereof."—Ps. 50:12.

*I.* The Scriptures are very clear on these points.

*P.* For the same reason, God has a perfect natural and legal right to control his moral creatures. He created us, body and soul, and thereby became our owner. As such owner, all the legal rights of property attached to him; and he has the same privilege to possess, and govern his moral and intelligent, that he has his natural, creation. All the considerations that apply to the one, attach with equal force to the other; all his rights are the same, only in respect to his moral property he has, by the exigencies and circumstances of their creation, restricted the mode in which he will direct and enforce the observance of them. The basis remains unchanged, and indeed is unchangeable; for God cannot claim rights which his creation, or the preservation of his creatures, (which is equivalent to their continued creation,) did not confer upon him.

*I.* Of course, whatever his creation, whether it is

material or moral, the ground of his right to control must be the same. The thing created can make no difference in that respect.

*P.* The Scriptures are very explicit on these points also. They represent God as the sole creator of all the human race. "I have made the earth and created man upon it."—Is. 45:12. "The souls which I have made."—Is. 57:16; Gen. 1:27. He consequently claims the ownership of all mankind. "Behold all souls are mine."—Ez. 18:4; John 1:11. He claims to exercise, on that ground, the rights of property over the race, even to punishing those who infringe upon his laws. "As the soul of the father, so the soul of the son is mine: the soul that sinneth, it shall die."—Ez. 18:4. "Remember now thy Creator in the days of thy youth." —Eccl. 12:1; 1 Cor. 6:20. The Scriptures declare that his authority over moral beings is supreme and peremptory. "And he doeth according to his will in the army of heaven and among the inhabitants of the earth; and none can stay his hand, or say unto him, What doest thou?"—Dan. 4:35. Although God is always influenced by wise and good reasons in his government of his moral creatures, (Ez. 14:23; Gen. 18:25) yet no one who is ignorant of them has a right to resist his authority on that account, or to interpose any question as to his mode of exercising it; it is enough for those who are bound by the obligations of a creature to a creator, to know that "he worketh all things after the counsel of his own will."—Eph. 1:11; Rom. 9:20, 21.

*I.* The word of God is very full indeed on the point. Although he sometimes condescends to give a reason why he commands one thing rather than another, yet the reason why he may command at all must ever remain the same—namely, his proprietary rights over us.

*P.* Yes; his authority does not depend on the soundness of his views, or on the wisdom of his administration, although he is both sound and wise; but upon his creative rights, which alone authorize him to exercise his natural and moral qualifications imperatively in respect to us, whether we will or no.

*I.* The principle seems to be indisputable.

*P.* The Scriptures present the Deity as a tri-une God; and the Father, the Son, and the Holy Ghost, as the three distinct, co-equal, and co-eternal persons in the one substance of the Godhead. It was God the Son who made and upholds all these worlds; who appeared to Moses as the I AM; who, as the great JEHOVAH, gave the law on Sinai; who inspired the ancient prophets; and who is now invested with the government of the world.—Col. 1:16; Heb. 1:2, 3; Ex. 3:14, and John 8:24. 58; Heb. 11:25, 26; 1 Pet. 1:10, 11; Matt. 28:18. While on earth he claimed and exercised the same authority.—Matt. 7:29. By whatever name he is designated, our devotions will partake of idolatry unless we elevate him to the supreme rank as the Almighty ruler, and worship him as the true God.—1 John 5:20. In that character I shall always speak of him. Names and titles among the Jews, as with all primitive nations, were significant of some trait or characteristic attached to their owners. Thus, the term God (derived from the Icelandic Godi) has, both in the original and in our language, the signification of a magistrate or ruler. The title Lord, given to Christ in the New Testament, is usually a translation of the Greek name *Kurios*, which signifies a lord—that is, a possessor, owner, master. "Truth Lord; [*Kurie*] yet the dogs eat of the crumbs which fall from their master's [*kurion*] table."—Matt. 15: 27. The English term landlord, which signifies the owner of land who has tenants under him, will aid us to understand its meaning. "Ye call me master [*didaskalos*, master in the sense of an authoritative teacher] and Lord, [*Kurios*, lord in the sense of an authoritative owner and possessor] and ye say well; for so I am."—John 13:13. The angels announced to the shepherds, "Christ the Lord," the owner and ruler of the world.—Luke 2:11. Christ rebuked those who admitted that he was their Lord, owner and master, and who yet did not obey him as such.—Luke 6:46. And the apostle, in his address at Athens, gave his creative rights as the ground upon which he had supreme authority over all: "God that made the world, and all things therein, seeing that he is Lord [*Kurios*, ruler by virtue of such ownership] of heaven and earth,—commandeth all men, every where, to repent."—Acts 17:24. 30.

*I.* I fear that I have sometimes entertained less exalted views of Christ, but will be more cautious hereafter. You have satisfactorily explained my meaning in the reply, that Christ has a right to control us because he is the Lord.

*P.* You will observe that rights and duties are always reciprocal; and that as God has a creative right to control us, we are under obligations, on our part, to yield to his rule for that reason; and that, in good morals, our obligations can be fulfilled as only we obey upon that principle.

*I.* Certainly; for to observe the things he has commanded, for the reason, for example, that we think it will prove more lucrative than to refuse, can be no fulfillment of an obligation to *him*. But does not our position savour of bondage?

*P.* Not in the least. The essence of bondage consists in a compulsory and involuntary service. The proprietary rights of God may exist; and yet, if he makes no use of coercion either in the inception or continuance of our service, this allegation will not lie against that relation. Especially will it be free from it, if the creature renders a service in all respects free and voluntary in recognition of his legal obligations to him. Such is the service which God requires, and such only will he accept. He will use no physical compulsion, or any thing tantamount to it, in reference to his creatures; but each must render his service "of his own voluntary will."—Lev. 1:3. Still, as is just, God will not depose his rights over him, but will leave him to act at his own peril. In his relations to his moral creatures, he combines the tenderness, without the weakness, of a parent with the authority of a master: "A son honoreth his father, and a servant his master; if then I be a father, where is mine honor? and if I be a master, where is my fear? saith the Lord of hosts."—Mal. 1:6.*

* We ordinarily use the terms *free* and *voluntary* as synonymous; but there are cases in which there exists a decided and important difference between them. For example, a person gives alms to a poor man, who exposes his wants and miseries. This action is at the same time both voluntary and free;—voluntary, because done by a consent of his will, and free, because such consent was not extorted, but was rendered for reasons sufficient, and freely chosen without constraint by him. But suppose a man who travels alone and unarmed, falls into the hands of robbers, and that these miscreants menace him with

*I.* You have convinced me that God does possess a legal authority, one that rises naturally from his relation to his creatures, which all just laws would sustain, by which we are bound even previous to our consent, and for the violation of which he may inflict punishment; and that it entirely avoids the objection which I have just raised. But has not his moral character some bearing on this subject?

*P.* Yes. It is in view of his excellent character that we should love him, for it is infinitely worthy of our highest affections. Besides, it is so just, and so eminently qualifies him to counsel his creatures, that it must elicit the confidence of every one who will carefully examine it. But you will observe that there is a radical difference in the grounds assumed, and in the influence exerted by one who advises, and one who commands. The former relies upon the supposed reasonableness or policy of his counsel, and its influence as reasonable and politic upon the person, leaving him at his option whether to adopt it or no; whereas one who commands, assumes some legal right to do so, and does not leave it optional with the inferior to obey or disobey, but insists upon

instant death unless he gives them all he has. The surrender which this traveller makes of his money in order to save his life is indeed a voluntary action, because done by a consent of his will, but it is not a free one; it is not done from such reasons as he approves and freely concurs with; but his consent is constrained by the fear of death or the hope of preserving his life in that miserable exigency, by the sacrifice. Hence the act is void of liberty. Being so void of freedom, the mind refuses to be bound by its consent; and on being released from the power of these men, the traveller would feel authorized to reclaim his money; and he would be justified in good morals in so doing.—See BURL. on Nat. Law, p. 19. Philem. 14.

obedience as a *duty*. God, in his condescending goodness, often advises and counsels his moral creatures; but when he *commands*, it is peremptory, as thus: I created you; I sustain you in being;—obey, or my hand will be withdrawn!

*I.* My conscience intuitively responds that I ought to obey him, and that I must. However lovely God is, in his justice for example, I can readily perceive that it will be impossible to love him until we have become reconciled to his sovereignty. What are some of the moral characteristics of God?

*P.* Benevolence, or sympathy toward his creatures, is a natural trait of the divine character; but it is made the occasion of exhibiting his *moral* character by his invariably subjecting its gratification to the decision of rectitude, or of right principles in the given case Therefore, compassionate as God is in view of their condition and prospects, even to the sacrifice of his only Son for a dying world, he will never indulge it by delivering men in opposition to the demands of rectitude. A holy character is indispensable to man's acceptance, notwithstanding that the sympathies of Christ were excited in his behalf, even to tears.—Luke 19:41.

The mercy of God is his act of setting aside a punishment justly impending. It is an exercise of grace or undeserved favor; but is subordinated to the same principle of rectitude, which will be satisfied only with the penitence of the sinner, and the justification of God by means of the atonement of Christ. "The Lord passed by before him, and proclaimed, The Lord, the Lord God, merciful and gracious, long-suffering, and abundant in goodness and truth;—*and that will by no means clear the guilty*."—Ex. 34:6, 7. Many mistake his mere compassion for mercy, and receive the expressions of his benevolent pity for a present willingness to exercise mercy. This encourages them to continue in sin, under a hope of impunity from such compassion whenever they shall attempt to retrieve their position;—a delusive experiment, which has ruined its myriads.

The justice of God implies his purpose to render to all beings their rights, according to an equitable and righteous scale. In a more particular and usual sense, it intends the punitive dealings of God toward incorrigible offenders against his government and laws. This attribute is also made the occasion of exhibiting his moral character, inasmuch as he is governed by rectitude in its exercise. Justice yields to the calls of mercy only when rectitude will allow, however strong may be the promptings of mere compassion; and in the contest, the moral predominates over the natural, and God is seen to be holy in the sustentation of his justice, without impairing his goodness. In his compassion, God pities the sinner; his language is, "How shall I give thee up, Ephraim? how shall I deliver thee, Israel? how shall I make thee as Admah? how shall I set thee as Zeboim?" But in his holiness he disapproves and dislikes him for his character and conduct; "thou hatest all workers of iniquity."—Ps. 5:5. And in his dread justice he declares, "The wicked shall be turned into hell, and all the nations that forget God."—Ps. 9:17. There are various other holy traits in the divine character, the consideration of which must be postponed for the present.

*I.* Will you have the goodness to explain what ultimate end God proposes to accomplish by means of the administration of his government over moral creatures?

*P.* I will; premising that, on account of the depravity of their natures, mankind are incompetent to decide that principle by their mere reason. If they follow the dictates of their *hearts*, their premises will be false; their reasonings from such premises may be sound, and their conclusions therefrom correct; but these will be as false to *the truth* as the premises themselves. We can rely with entire safety only on the declarations of God himself in the Scriptures; and he must surely be considered the most competent, and the best entitled to decide authoritatively on the point.

*I.* Certainly, his exposition of his own principles of action must be implicitly received by us.

*P.* The ultimate end which God designs to accomplish, is the promulgation and extension of his own glory. The Scriptures are so full upon this point, that to select proofs is not difficult. The Old Testament abounds with declarations to that effect: "Bring my sons from far, and my daughters from the ends of the earth, even every one that is called by my name; for I have created him for my glory."—Is. 43:6, 7. "The Lord hath made all things for himself."—Prov. 16:4; Ps. 72:19; Mal. 2:2; Is. 63:12, and 48:11; Jer. 13:11. The New Testament is equally explicit. "Who hath called us unto his eternal glory."—1 Pet. 5:10. It was the ultimate end at which our Lord Jesus Christ aimed in every action: "I have glorified thee on the earth, I have finished the work which thou gavest me to do; and now, O Father, glorify thou me with thine own self, with the glory which I had with thee before the world was."—

John 17:4, 5. "Father glorify thy name! Then came there a voice from heaven, saying, I have both glorified it, and will glorify it again."—John 12:28. It was the end which the apostles kept strictly in view: "Pray for us, that the word of the Lord may have free course and be glorified."—2 Thess. 3:1, and 1:12; Phil. 4:20. It was the chief thing in the hearts of the people of God. "And the shepherds returned, glorifying and praising God."—Luke 2:20. "And immediately he received his sight, and followed him, glorifying God; and all the people, when they saw it, gave praise unto God."—Luke 18:43. "And they glorified God in me."—Gal. 1:24. The spirits in heaven are engrossed in the same object. "And they sing the song of Moses the servant of God, and the song of the Lamb, saying, Great and marvellous are thy works, Lord God Almighty; just and true are thy ways, thou King of saints: Who shall not fear thee, O Lord, and glorify thy name? for thou only art holy."—Rev. 15:3, 4. For the glory of God did lighten the city, and the Lamb is the light thereof."—Rev. 21:23; Luke 2:13, 14.

*I.* No possible proof could be more conclusive.

*P.* For the promotion of his glory, God, in the administration of his government, has promulgated various laws or authoritative rules of conduct, which are to be our guides in life. Superadded to these, is the requirement to make his glory the chief end in all our services. "Whether therefore ye eat, or drink, or whatsoever ye do, do all to the glory of God."—1 Cor. 10:31. "And whatsoever ye do, do it heartily as to the Lord, and not unto men."—Col. 3:23. "By whom we rejoice in hope of the glory of God."—Rom. 5:2.

*I.* Our duty is plainly taught in the Scriptures. What is intended by the glory of God?

*P.* The development of his character; or the exhibition, in all their approvableness and loveliness, of his natural and moral attributes. In the work of creation of the material universe, God developed many of his natural attributes in great power and beauty. He exhibited such depth of knowledge, such profundity of wisdom and forethought, and such a degree of physical power in forming and establishing the multitudes of systems which now roll in the expanse of infinite space, that, in the view, "the morning stars sang together, and all the sons of God shouted for joy."—Job 38:7. In his creation of man, and in his wise and holy government over him, he displays his vast knowledge, his wisdom, his power, truth, holiness, faithfulness, goodness, forbearance, grace, mercy, justice, and the like, in such brilliant forms, that they encircle his throne as a halo of heavenly light. These exhibitions constitute that moral glory, which his creatures are to exemplify in their principles and conduct, and are to extend to the knowledge and love of mankind, so far as they have ability. These traits are now seen "as through a glass, darkly," because of the moral obscuration of the mind of the beholder, produced by sin within and around him.

*I.* What is intended by the "*beauty* of holiness," of which so much is spoken in the Scriptures?

*P.* It intends the moral excellence of the divine character, the moral luster which envelops the glory of God. It is the splendor of that moral beauty, into a perception and love of which the soul is ushered on its regeneration by the Holy Spirit: "Thy people shall be willing in the day of thy power, in the *beauties* of holiness *more than* the womb of the morning."—Ps. 110:3. Watch the early morning, as it unfolds its loveliness to the eye that is cultivated to appreciate natural beauty. "First appears the dull light, then the gray streak, then the brighter blushing tinge, until at last the orb which gives us day emerges from the abyss of space, and pours its golden flood through the slowly scattering mists. The whole prospect is covered with brightness and glory! The lands smile, the waters sparkle, the dew-drops reflect their mimic spangles, the green foliage waves gently beneath the refreshing breezes of the morning, and the birds carol with delight. Men arise, and go forth and rejoice! for it is day, and the sun has gone out on the errand of its Creator to diffuse light, and life, and gladness." The beauties of holiness as infinitely transcend those of the opening morning, as does moral beauty in its own nature exceed the natural. The brightness, the splendor, the peerless magnificence which, emanating from the high principles, exalted character, and matchless goodness of Jehovah, exhibit him HOLY, JUST, and GOOD, cast their own beauty around the children of the light, and entrance their hearts as they are changed into the same image, progressing from glory to glory. The expressions of delight and praise which we are accustomed to hear from the new convert to Christ, spring from his perception and love of the divine majesty, excellence, and beauty; but his untutored tongue can find no language adequately to portray his deep emotions. The veteran saint, he who has well learned the language of the spiritual Canaan, is to be heard exclaiming, "O worship the

Lord in the beauty of holiness!"—Ps. 96:9. "Let the beauty of the Lord our God be upon us."—Ps. 90:17. "One thing have I desired of the Lord,—to behold the beauty of the Lord, and to inquire in his temple."—Ps. 27:4. And when this desire is granted, we hear its results in the overflowing soul: "As the hart panteth after the water-brooks, so panteth my soul after thee, O God!"—Ps. 42:1. And when at last the soul is ushered into the presence-chamber of its Father and its God, and casts its crown before him there, its full-toned praise is poured forth amid ten thousand voices, "Holy, holy, holy, Lord God Almighty, the whole earth is full of thy glory!" And what is more approvable than perfect rectitude? What can be more estimable than a perfectly upright character? What more beautiful and lovely than the union of such excellence and goodness in a Parent and a Sovereign?

*I.* I can conceive of nothing superior; and can imagine no end of active existence which is more worthy of man, or more honorable to God.

*P.* If God ultimately designed his own personal gratification, he would be liable to unmitigated censure. But so far from this being the fact, it forms no part of his considerations. It is his moral, and not his natural self, that he loves and pursues. He loves his glory, not because it is *his own*, but because it is intrinsically excellent and lovely, and is so worthy of his regard; and doubtless were there a being more glorious than himself, he would love him with a superior ardor; but this would be impossible. For the same reason, he loves every one who partakes, however faintly, of his own moral image; and it is such a moral likeness to himself that he requires his creatures to attain in their degree, and into which regeneration is intended to introduce them. —Rom. 8 : 29.

*I.* And by such means, regeneration produces a moral union between himself and his creatures?

*P.* Yes. And to this end, amongst others, he requires our hearts, because the heart is the moral man. "With the heart man believeth unto righteousness."—Rom. 10: 10. "My son, give me thy heart."—Prov. 23 : 26. "For in Jesus Christ neither circumcision availeth any thing, nor uncircumcision, but faith which worketh by love."—Gal. 5 : 6. "Make you a new heart and a new spirit, for why will ye die?"—Ez. 18 : 31. Unless it is our purpose of heart to glorify God in our actions, he cannot accept of them, or of us in them, as being done *unto him.* And besides, it is obviously indispensable that the beneficiaries of his bounties should exercise right affections in return, in order to his approbation and regard. And further, the new heart is indispensable, because without it no one would be capable of entering into the holy occupations, or of enjoying the peculiar blessedness, of heaven. It is not an unnecessary command, therefore, "Thou shalt love the Lord thy God with all thy heart."—Matt. 22 : 37. Under the impulses of such a love, the believer will be steadily fruitful in good works; and thus the love of the glory of God will be seen to be the most unfailing and permanently useful motive influence which is known to man. In requiring us to love himself, he necessarily requires us to love him preferably to any and all other objects; because his glory is intrinsically superior and more attractive, and, if loved at all, it must be in preference to all other things.

*I.* Will you now please to state precisely what constitutes a holy character?

*P.* The holy character of God springs, if that expression may be allowed, from his devotion to his own glory as his ultimate object. You will remember that we ascertained that the character of a person or agent was determined by that of his ultimate object; and this principle applies as well to God, as to other moral beings. The holiness of his glory, combined with his devotion to its promotion, by means of his universal creation and of the administration of his legal creative rights over his moral creatures, renders his character holy; for the moral image of the object is reflected upon and transferred to his own heart. God is *perfectly* holy, because his glory is perfect, and because he loves it with the most profound devotion, and pursues it with an unwavering purpose. He is *infinitely* holy, because he ever has been thus devoted to, and ever will thus love and pursue it. And he is *immutably* holy, because his purpose will never know of a change. The holy character of angels and glorified saints in heaven arises from the same supreme devotion to the divine glory; and their superiority in degree over saints on earth results from the greater depth of their devotion to it, and the unwavering influence of it upon their feelings and conduct there. In like manner, the holy character of men is determined by their superior devotion to the same object; and their imperfections of heart and life arise from its influences being temporarily supplanted or suspended.

*I.* I can now understand it clearly.

*P.* And you can also see what God would have us

become. Such a devotion to his glory is the Christian religion. It is that which Christ, who had no sins to avoid and no pardon to hope for, possessed in its perfection; and who is set forth as our example, that we should be followers of him. And who can devise a nobler? The soul that enters into it, possesses God himself, being made a joint heir with Christ.—Rom. 8:17. He is adopted, justified, directed upon a process of sanctification, and at last glorified with Christ in his heavenly kingdom.—Rom. 8:30. There he will enter into all its holy blessedness. Delivered from every sin and sorrow, his soul will rejoice in God, the infinitely glorious one, who, as an unfailing fountain, will ever afford a supply of spiritual food, so that it will never languish. Exalted to a conformity, in kind, to the image of his Creator, pardoned through the unmerited grace of Christ, blessed with every thing the most unbounded desires of his holy heart can grasp, and an infinite existence before him in which to enjoy them, surely he will find that "in his presence is fullness of joy, and at his right hand there are pleasures for evermore."—Ps. 16:11.

*I.* This explains the answer given by the Westminster divines to the question, What is the chief end of man?

*P.* Yes. As they truly observe, the ultimate end of man is to glorify God; and from a heart bent on glorifying him, proceeds his capacity to enjoy him for ever. Having now ascertained what God would have us become, we will proceed to examine what he would have us avoid.

## CHAPTER IV.

### ELEMENTS OF UNHOLY CHARACTER.

*Pastor.* THE Scriptures, in forms almost innumerable, allege that "all have sinned, and come short of the glory of God" (Rom. 3:23); that all are originally deficient in that holy character which springs from a supreme devotion to the divine glory. We will now inquire into the cause of such a sinful state. You are aware that in your ordinary conduct you act freely; and that you always have some reason for acting, or some object to attain in whatever you do. These, as we have seen, are essential characteristics of every moral agent.

*Inquirer.* I well know that there is always some reason which influences my conduct; for if there were none, I should never act at all.

*P.* For the sake of greater perspicuity, let us now recur to the earlier period of your life, before you had indulged that hope in Christ which we have examined. You are well aware that you then committed many sinful acts, although you may not, at the time, have paused to examine their character; which, however, cannot affect their sinfulness. In these actions, you was governed by some reason or object: Can you inform me what influenced you to do them?

*I.* I suppose my sinful desires and inclinations prompted me to such conduct.

*P.* No doubt. Persons under your then circumstances, always act from the impulse of some desire; and when passion moves them, it is by the desire included in it. But what rendered your desires *sinful?*

*I.* I have not given the subject sufficient examination to answer decidedly. Will you explain the reason?

*P.* Was it not a desire to please yourself, in some form, that then induced you to do things which you knew, or might have known, to be wrong?

*I.* Yes; it was to gratify myself. There were many things I never should have done, merely to gratify other persons.

*P.* When you thought one course would give you more pleasure than another, you were accustomed to select that; and when any proposed course seemed onerous or unpleasant, you would desist from it on that account?

*I.* Certainly; every body acts in that way.

*P.* Let me illustrate this principle. Suppose that this is the Sabbath, and that we observe *N.* passing along with his gun and dogs, in pursuit of game. I remonstrate against his disregard of the divine authority by violating the Lord's day; and he assures me it had not occurred to him that he was disobeying God, and that he had no seriously-formed intention to do so. But, I reply, you are doing it nevertheless, and are guilty in his sight. Why are you out to-day, knowing it to be the Sabbath? He answers, I felt a desire to go out, and went to gratify my inclinations. But, I rejoin, you had some reason why you desired it—some object which you wished to accomplish by it? Yes, he replies, to shoot some game. But, I ask, why desire to shoot some game?

For the sport of it, he replies. And you desire the diversion of hunting because it promotes your pleasure and happiness; so that it is your love of pleasure or happiness which makes you disobey God by violating the day which he has commanded us to remember to keep holy? Yes, he replies, that is my reason; for if I was confident of finding no pleasure in it, I should at once rētrace my steps homeward. This illustration sufficiently explains the principle that it is the desire to please one's self, and to promote his own supposed interests or happiness, that influences a person to disobey God.

*I.* I see the principle clearly.

*P.* And do you not see also that, in your own case, whenever you did wrong at that period of life, it was from a desire to gratify yourself, and to promote your own pleasure and happiness by means of it?

*I.* Yes, that was the reason. If there was no pleasure in sin, no one would commit it; but I did not always succeed.

*P.* Your disappointment does not affect the principle. You *expected* to succeed at the time, else you would not have done the thing. The capability of taking pleasure is constitutional, and is therefore a natural good when properly exercised. But the evil in the supposed case of *N.* was that he desired happiness too much; in other words, that he *preferred* it to the authority and glory of God. It was his preference of his own pleasure that induced him to disobey, in order to its gratification; whereas, had he preferred the authority and glory of God, it would have led him to observe the Sabbath, and to restrain all those desires which conflicted with it.

It is clear that all the works of God are created suitable to the happiness of man; and in this the Creator exhibits his great goodness. But the happiness he designed was to be held in subordination to himself, and to be taken in the discharge of our duties, and in the contemplation and promotion of his glory. By preferring himself and his happiness to his Creator and his glory, the sinner rejects him, overlooks his duties, incapacitates himself to take such holy enjoyment, and perverts the holy design of God into an occasion of moral evil.

*I.* I perceive and admit the correctness of this view.

*P.* A desire is a feeling of the mind which is directed to the attainment of some object; while a preference is a desire for one object *more than* for another. A person may have a desire for two things; but if he so desires one of them as to choose it rather than the other, he evinces a preference of it to that other. And there may be two things, for the first of which he has no desire, while he indulges one for the second; his desire for the second stands alone and independent of the other, and it will be necessarily exercised as a preference to it. A preference does not necessarily imply a vehement or ardent state of the desires or emotions; but simply that, whether mild or fervent, the desire is strongest and most influential for the preferred object. In the case of *N.*, as in your own previous to indulging that hope, there was no desire for the authority and glory of God. The desire for his own interest, gain, pleasure, or whatever else would confer happiness, was alone and independent of God, and consequently existed as a preference to God.

*I.* Yes; I perceive such would be the fact.

*P.* And when *you* did wrong, the desire for your own

interest, gain, advantage, or pleasure, (for they are all the same in principle, since they are desired for the sake of your own ulterior gratification or happiness,) existed independently, and consequently as a preference to the authority and glory of God, and influenced you as such.

*I.* Yes; for I had not been converted, and of course had no proper regard for him. Besides, I am conscious of that deficiency.

*P.* When you exercised anger or any other passion, for example, it was done to gratify the passion, or yourself by its indulgence?

*I.* Yes; and therefore I found it so difficult to check my passions. When I foresaw trouble from indulging them, restraint was more easy. But I have sometimes acted to please others?

*P.* But it was ultimately to advance some interest of your own, or to please yourself. You did it to gratify some private feeling toward them, or to avoid ridicule or censure, or to promote something for yourself by their means.

*I.* You are correct. I had myself in view in some form, though I did not always pause to consider that fact.

*P.* Because the desire to please yourself, and to promote your own supposed interests had become such an *habitual* influence, that it moved you almost without reflection. And such was the case on all subjects, whether secular or religious.

*I.* True; and that accounts for my failure to analyze my motives.

*P.* Reflection will deepen the conviction that, in your unregenerate days, the desires for your own happiness, to be promoted by forwarding your personal interests, gain, advantage, or enjoyments, uniformly influenced your conduct; and that your own gratification or happiness, in some form, was invariably the ultimate end which you had in view in all your actions.

*I.* It is very obvious to me now.

*P.* SELFISHNESS consists in this *preference* of our own happiness, or interests, or whatever else will contribute to our pleasure. Selfishness, says Dr. Owen, is the making a man's self his own center, beginning, and end, in all he does. Every person, says Dr. Payson, has some object which he loves supremely; and, in every unrenewed mind, that object is self. And the apostle says, "All seek *their own.*"—Phil. 2 : 21. Self, as you are aware, is loved for its interests and happiness.

*I.* It is not to be denied that self-interest is the governing principle among mankind.

*P.* This selfishness, or preference of one's own interest, pleasure or happiness, is the cause of all the evil passions that exist, and of all the injurious conduct that is perpetrated in the world. Look abroad upon society, and you will see its developments in horrible realities. Why do we find some indulging in pride, worldly show and extravagance, in arrogance, intolerance, and in seeking the praise of men? It is simply to gratify their love of their own selves. Why do we hear of so many plunging into licentiousness, debauchery, intemperance;—indulging vicious thoughts, profane language, and violating every command of God which interferes with their pleasures? It is to gratify this preference for their own enjoyments. Whence those malignant envyings and other passions that rage in the bosoms of many? They are produced by injuries, real or supposed, to their own interests; or emanate from the ill-will of a soul exclusively bent on itself. I might enumerate the evils and wrongs which curse the earth, and trace them all, without exception, to man's selfishness as their source.

*I.* Selfishness, then, is the parent-principle of all the wrong doing on earth.

*P.* And it is, consequently, the source of all the misery which exists among mankind. The selfishness of our first parents plunged them, and their posterity after them, into wretchedness, as well as sin; and now the pains of disease and death come upon all. Man has become the greatest enemy of man. The tears and groans of the afflicted, caused by their own selfish indulgences, or by the inhumanity of other's selfishness, fill the earth; and well is it for us, that a veil is now spread over them—a veil which is to be removed, when God comes forth to judge the world in righteousness.

*I.* You no doubt attribute it to the right cause.

*P.* And selfishness is the antagonist principle in the human heart against God. Self, or God, are the only ultimate objects which moral beings ever pursue; and the preference of one's self is as really the elevation of himself into an idol, as would be the exaltation of Baal. There may be many objects of desire, but there can be only one object of ultimate *preference;* the pursuit of it will be exclusive of all others; and it will make all others subordinate, and, if possible, subservient to it. Thus, as we have seen in the case of *N.*, a preference of his own pleasure or happiness led him to disregard the authority and overlook the glory of God, in his feelings and conduct; and the same principle governed you not only, but controls every unconverted person in his intentions and actions toward him. Why are mankind, as a general thing, so careless of the ever-present eye of God, and of his rights over them, and of their continued transgressions of his holy law, and even of his denunciations of wrath? It is simply because they are engrossed in themselves, their pursuits, and their pleasures. Why are they so unanimously disinclined to observe the laws of the divine government, to exercise the humble graces of piety, and to govern their daily conduct by the rules of Christianity? It is because they cannot find therein that pleasure which they so much prefer. Why do all disrelish the holiness of God? Because it is an antagonist principle to their own selfishness. Why do all dislike, and some hate with the deepest intensity, the punitive justice of God? Simply and only because they perceive that it bodes destruction to those pleasures and that love of self in which they chiefly delight. I might enlarge, but your own reflections will abundantly supply examples of the truth of my position.*

*I.* I can see its truth with the utmost clearness. Why does selfishness appear to mankind to be so harmless?

*P.* Because it is pleasurable, and they love it. Besides, it is so habitual with them, as to have lost its aspect of sin; and as they really care nothing about God, they have no heart-principle by which to decide its criminality. The error is aided by the fact that selfishness,

* "The absence of positive good principles, leaving the common natural principles of self-love, natural appetite, &c., (which were in man in innocence,) leaving them, I say, to themselves, without the government of superior principles, will certainly be followed with the corruption of the whole heart."—EDWARDS on Original Sin.—Part IV. Chap. ii.

under the dictates of interest or policy, can induce men to perform commendable actions, and can influence them to cultivate amiable feelings, gentle manners, and make loud professions of right principle. It has been aptly remarked, that men seem to imagine that selfishness loses most of its guilt by losing all its grossness; whereas they would frown upon it when clothed in malevolence. It is neither wise nor honest to give the semblance of purity to the substance of corruption; it is to steal the robe of righteousness to cover the deformity of sin. It is fitting that what is foul within, should be foul without also.*

*I.* What do the Scriptures teach on these points?

*P.* The Scriptures every where characterize sinners as being selfish. Thus, the apostle describes them as "lovers of their own selves," and as "lovers of pleasures *more than* lovers of God."—2 Tim. 3 : 2. 4. Pleasure, as I said, is loved for the element of happiness involved in it; and the ways or pursuits of pleasure, for the happiness they promise to confer. The same apostle rebukes

* "He whose religion has selfishness for its basis, 'does good to mankind and obeys,' or rather fancies he obeys, 'the will of God,' not because he desires the good of mankind, or because it is right to obey the divine will, but solely to avoid future punishment and obtain 'everlasting happiness.' Hence, if this world were his only state of existence, he would trample on the rights of others, and sacrifice their interest, whenever they happened to interfere with his own. And though he may *appear* to make some sacrifice to the wishes, or interests, or wants of others, yet it is in no degree for their sake, but wholly for his own; for, unless he hoped to gain by it, sooner or later, he would not deny himself the smallest gratification for the sake of saving others from the greatest evils, or securing to them the most important benefits."—PARK. Mor. Phi. Chap. ii. p. 27.

such selfishness, and enjoins on men "not henceforth to live *unto themselves;*" (2 Cor. 5 : 15) implying that our intellects and sensibilities were to be used aright; that the latter are not to control us. The desire of property, for example, was not designed to lead us to rob or defraud, but was given to be controlled by us. We find the sacred writers often using the words *sarx* and *soma*, [meaning literally the *body*, or *flesh*,] to indicate substantially the same idea of selfishness. When used in a metaphorical sense, they intend those feelings of the mind, and corresponding actions of the body, which are produced by a preference of one's own gratification or happiness. These they denominate the *works of the flesh.* "Walk in the Spirit, and ye shall not fulfill the lusts of the flesh," the desires for personal gratifications by means of the body.—Gal. 5:16. "Now the works of the flesh are manifest, which are these: adultery, lasciviousness, idolatry, witchcraft, hatred, variance, emulations, wrath, strifes, envyings, murders, drunkenness, and such like."—Gal. 5:19—21. "So, then, they that are in the flesh [under the domination of their desires of pleasures] cannot please God."—Rom. 8:8, and 13; Jude 23; John 6:63.

*I.* I thank you for this explanation.

*P.* Happiness in the position of a preference, or thing loved and pursued more than God, is selfish; and such pursuit of it is also selfish, for its own character is transferred to him who is devoted to it, and also to all his desires, purposes, affections, hopes, pleasures, and conduct. This is the unregenerate state. Its moral opposite is the regenerate state, or that where the authority and glory of God are preferred, and where new desires, purposes, and affections exist and terminate on God; whereby his holy character becomes impressed on the soul, in some degree.

*I.* Will you state the precise points of opposition in which the sinner places himself against God?

*P.* There are three principal points of diversity, the combined results of which produce an entire hostility of heart, and an unrelieved departure from duty, against God. The first is the sinner's claim to a right to control himself, in opposition to the proprietary right of God to govern him. This claim is seldom put forth in words, but is invariably asserted in practice. He *tacitly* assumes the ownership of himself, and an exemption from all control but his own; and uniformly evinces it in his conduct. How soon his anger is aroused, if this claim is interfered with? And how profoundly would he contemn a fellow-being who should endeavor to dominate over him? The claim is, without reflection or argument, extended to God; for in his exclusion of others, his independent spirit makes no exceptions. They "despise government; presumptuous are they, and *self-willed.*"—2 Pet. 2 : 10. They declare "Our lips are *our own:* Who is *Lord* over us?"—Ps. 12 : 4. The creative right of God being such an antagonist principle, it can exert no motive influence over the mind of the sinner while in his selfish pursuits; and on this account many try to discard it, and to substitute in its place some consideration which is adapted to their selfish desires, and which will leave this claim to self-control unaffected in practice. Among other devices, nothing is more common than to select the compassion or benevolence of God, mistaking it for his trait of mercy; and to combine with it his wisdom and power, excluding his justice. From thence they *infer* that he will do sinners the greatest good they can desire; and then propose to serve him on that account. By such a process, the sinner's unregenerate desires are gratified, and his hostile principle is retained, while he *seems* to be enlisted for God! The same is seen in his always demanding some reason, other than God's creative right, why he should obey. But God expressly disallows this claim: "Ye are *not* your own."—1 Cor. 6:19.

*I.* I confess that I formerly acted upon this same implied claim of self-ownership, and consequent self-control; but it was done unconsciously. Still, I am aware that my doing it so habitually as not to be alive to the fact, and my neglect to discern the deep hostile principle toward the Creator involved in it, does not absolve me from censure.

*P.* The second point, is the sinner's elevation of his own interests or happiness, as a more desirable end to be accomplished, in disregard or opposition to the glory of God. By making himself the end of his desires and purposes, he excludes all others from that position of course, and God with them. The Scriptures designate this as the pursuit of "*his own* pleasures." Thus, the drunkard pursues his own pleasures in the inebriating cup; the gambler, in spoiling his victim; the sensualist, in the ruin of innocence. Said Henry Martyn, "men frequently admire me, and I am pleased; but I abhor the pleasure." It was the pleasure of gratified pride, unvirtuous and criminal; as indeed all pleasure must be which is taken in opposition to God, in transgression of duty to others, or in fostering and gratifying the evil desires or passions of the heart. Bent thus on his own pleasures, it was to be expected that the sinner would endeavor to substitute them for those holy pleasures which flow from a superior devotion to the divine glory; and that in his inquiries and efforts he should seek to obliterate the latter, as unknown to his own consciousness—an argument which only proves that he was never regenerated—and to take up with the pleasures of a hope of his own ultimate happiness, with its attending exercises, instead. But the Creator firmly enjoins upon him to turn away from his "own pleasure," and to honor *him;* and when he takes delight, to take it in holiness and in the Lord.—Is. 58:13. He reproachfully asks his people, "when ye fasted and mourned, [mortified your enjoyments] did ye at all fast UNTO ME? And when ye did eat and when ye did drink, [when you took enjoyment] did not ye eat *for yourselves*, and drink *for yourselves?*"—Zech. 7:5. And he expresses his purposes toward the devotee of pleasure: "Therefore hear now this, thou that art given to pleasures—therefore shall evil come upon thee; thou shalt not know from whence it riseth: and mischief shall fall upon thee; thou shalt not be able to put it off; and desolation shall come upon thee suddenly, which thou shalt not know." —Is. 47:8. 11.

*I.* I can clearly perceive that the seducing nature of pleasure, has very much blinded me to its evil character when improperly enjoyed, and especially when placed in antagonism to the divine glory.

*P.* The third point, is the sinner's unvaried perversion of the means of grace to the promotion of his own ends, in opposition to the command of God that they should be employed to the promotion of his glory ultimately. The Scriptures condemn this course under the appellation of "his own ways," because, whatever they may be, whether intrinsically proper or improper, they are chosen and employed to promote his own pleasurable ends. "They defiled the land by *their own way.*"—Ez. 36:17. "We have turned every one to *his own way.*"—Is. 53:6. It was to be expected, therefore, that sinners should direct all their powers, and endeavor to subordinate the gospel and all its duties and requirements to the promotion of their own ends, rather than those of God. Indeed, as they have no desire for the aims of God, they can desire and appreciate them only as means to promote their own; and hence they uniformly pervert them to that purpose. They thus habitually "yield their members as *instruments* of unrighteousness *unto sin.*"—Rom. 6:13. Whereas God forbids this whole course of procedure: "Not doing *thine own* ways" (Is. 58:13); and he not only directs, "yield yourselves *unto God*" as your great superior and end, but enjoins, "and your members as *instruments* of righteousness *unto God,*" unto the promotion of his glory.—Rom. 6:13.

*I.* I begin to perceive why my religious efforts were for so long a time unavailing. I sought, by means of them, my own ends rather than the glory of God; that is, I secretly endeavored to sustain myself in my own principles and to succeed in my own plans, by means of instrumentalities which God designed only for his own holy purposes.

*P.* That was so. You will observe that the Scriptures do not authorize the unconverted person to pursue his own happiness ultimately, even though he makes use of means not censurable in themselves, the promotion of the public welfare, for example. No course, however innocent in itself considered, can properly be employed as means to conduce to such an end; for the end itself is forbidden as unholy and antagonistic to God. The command is, not that the sinner should decline to promote his own ends by improper means; but that he shall not use any means whatever to promote his selfish aims. It is "that they which live should *not* henceforth live *unto themselves*, but unto Christ."—2 Cor. 5:15. Thus, while the promotion of the public welfare, when properly pursued, is a correct procedure, it will be perverted to an occasion of moral evil, if used as a means to the sinner's personal aims; and it will be made an occasion of moral good, if used as subordinate to God, and if made subservient to his glory as the ultimate end. There is no moral worth in that happiness which the sinner desires, in view of which he can act, but it is wholly immoral; and it is forfeited by his sins; either of which considerations is sufficient to justify God in forbidding his pursuit of it in any degree. His desires for it cannot be moderated in a moral sense, except by acquiring a superior regard to the divine glory; for until then, whether they are vehement or mild, his own advantage or happiness will be preferred. In the sinner, self-love can never be a morally good influence; it may, indeed, prompt him to consider and act for his own ultimate good more carefully than would his mere passions, and in that view it might seem to be a good impulse (Ps. 49:18); but it is suited only to forward the interests of self, and is therefore a selfish influence, in whatever form it may appear.

It *never*, in the sinner's heart, prompts to the love of the glory of God; but in that of the Christian it does, and therefore becomes a morally good influence in his case. Nor does it ever influence the sinner to pursue what is, really, his best good; for, however he may disguise the fact, it necessarily terminates upon his selfish happiness. He can know nothing of the best good—namely, that of loving the glory of God and of enjoying the light of his countenance (Ps. 4 : 6)—until, by conversion, he has experienced it; and then only can self-love guide him to that which is such greatest good. The Fathers were right, therefore, in using, in respect to the sinner, the term self-love as synonymous with selfishness; and in regarding its influences, as purely selfish motives.

*I.* The Scriptures declare that we are "by nature the children of wrath, even as others."—Eph. 2 : 3. What are we to understand by the doctrine of the total moral depravity of the natural heart?

*P.* That it is exclusively selfish, and therefore unholy. It does not imply that all men indulge in the grossest passions, or in the worst possible courses of external conduct; nor even that their outward conduct is always censurable, considered apart from the principles which control the agents; for, as we have seen, wicked men may perform many right actions. But it does imply that the sinner's principles are unholy, that his affections are estranged from God, that his passions are liable to malevolence, and that his entire conduct is an infraction of his obligations toward God. "The carnal mind [the purpose, desire, will of the *flesh*, that is, the predominant desire and purpose of self-gratification, or selfishness] is enmity [the cause or source of hostility, or discord] against God; for it is not subject [not subordinate] to the law of God, neither indeed can be," since it is an antagonist principle.—Rom. 8:7. It must be destroyed as such a principle. "For I know that in me (that is, in my flesh) [in my selfish heart and affections] dwelleth no good thing."—Rom. 7:18. The reasons of its hostility to God we have already seen. It is self-evident that God cannot approve, but must wholly and entirely disapprove of such hostility to every thing that is holy in himself; and that, disapproving the selfish heart, he can approve or accept of nothing that proceeds from it, or under its influence; for as it is the criminal cause of all sin, all its streams must partake of the moral pollution of their source, and be stamped with its depravity. This selfish state of the natural heart is *depraved*, because being so in hostility to the highest virtue and moral excellence, it is the seat and the occasion of all moral vitiosity and corruption. It is a *moral* depravity, both because it consists in the perversion of the will, and because it is the free act of the sinner, being pursued from considerations which he freely chooses;—in which view, his conscience always imputes the blame to himself. And it is *total* moral depravity, because such depraved considerations invariably govern all his feelings and all his conduct, however amiable or unamiable they may be, or may appear to mankind.

*I.* We are too apt to attach depravity only to grossly wicked external conduct, or to the baser and malignant passions; but regarded in respect to our principles, and the feelings they tend to produce against God, the doctrine is sustained by the universal history of our race.

As our practices always flow from our principles, the latter must decide the whole question.

*P.* Let us now notice some of the results of the relative positions of God and sinners. The first is, that they are in the most decided opposition that is possible to moral beings, that of principle, feeling, and pursuits. And it is impossible that the sinner can be reconciled to God, except by going over to his principles; for his own, God will never abandon. Another is that, as God most cordially approves of his own principles and character as the height of moral excellence, he must disapprove of the sinner, with his opposing principles and character, as the extreme of moral deformity; and this estimation can undergo no change while the sinner retains his hostile position. Another is that, as God is always governed in his feelings by his moral sentiments, he most cordially dislikes the sinner on account of his principles and character. He compassionates his condition and prospects; but he has displacency toward him at the same time for his character and conduct. "Thou hatest all workers of iniquity," (Ps. 5:5,) not the iniquity only, but the workers of it, the persons for their iniquities;—not with a revengeful or malignant hatred, but with a virtuous indignation, a holy anger (Ps. 7:11), because directed by holiness against sin and the sinner. If we would measure the intensity of this abhorrence, we must be able to comprehend the depth of his love to his own glory, which the sinner would, were his principles legitimately pursued, certainly destroy; the degree of his interest in the holy good of his obedient creatures in heaven and on earth, all of which the sinner would demolish; and the extent of misery which the sinner by his conduct *compels* him, as a just governor, to inflict on the incorrigible, and from which all his sympathies revolt. Could we clearly comprehend the force of such considerations, we should not only perceive the necessity laid upon God to administer rigid justice, but also the full deserts of the sinner himself; and we would cease to wonder at the terrible exhibition which the Scriptures make of the wrath of God: "And my fury, it upheld me."—Is. 63 : 5. And another result is, that God will certainly punish the incorrigible sinner with "everlasting destruction from the presence of the Lord, and from the glory of his power."—2 Thess. 1 : 9. The sinner disobeys God, insults and dishonors him, hates him when he dares permit his feelings to flow forth, and sometimes abhors him.—Zech. 11 : 8. Horrid as was the prayer of that abandoned one, "O that I were stronger than God, or that there were some more powerful God than he, that he might be dragged from his throne, and prostrated beneath our feet!" it lies concealed in the folds of the sinner's heart; and eternity will echo with the vain expression of it, even if circumstances should never excite such an idea in this life. God is reduced to the necessity of punishment; the sentence has already gone forth, and impends over every sinner, and is delayed in its execution only by a forbearance that is as wonderful as it is kind (Eccl. 8 : 11); but "their foot shall slide in due time."—Deut. 32 : 35.

*I.* Terrible as these truths are, God is holy, just, and good. Could we suppose him to feel and purpose differently—could we believe that he would abandon his own holy principles and character, in favor of the sinner's—that he could bring himself to approve instead of disapproving him, to take complacency instead of displacency in him, to love instead of abhorring him, and to reward instead of punishing him for his principles, feelings, and conduct—we could not forbear a virtuous disapproval and indignation toward God himself, and a regret that such a being ever created or upheld and governed the world. But the mere supposition seems blasphemous. No doubt the sinner must go over to God, or be damned. O, how I dread an error on that point of duty, since a mistake there must be so fatal!

*P.* True; and therefore let no consideration on earth prevent you from now pursuing a patient examination of it; and if you have made any mistakes, ascertain them promptly, in order that you may correct them, and be ready when the Master calls.

*I.* With the divine aid, I will devote my whole attention, candidly and honestly, to that subject; and will implicitly follow your advice.

*P.* Let us proceed. The time when, or the place where a person expects to secure some desired object, cannot in the least affect his moral character in the pursuit of it, for that depends exclusively upon the character of his motive, or of the object sought. Thus, if you should desire to promote some personal interest of your own, it would be a selfish desire; if you should, under its promptings, set about some act whereby you hoped to secure such personal interest immediately, it would be a selfish action; and if you expected to obtain the happiness to-morrow, or next year, or after the lapse of five hundred years, the act would still remain selfish, for the object would be the same, and the time of securing it would be immaterial to its character.

*I.* These principles are evidently true.

*P.* But five hundred years hence you will be in the eternal state of existence; so that if you should act for the ultimate promotion of your personal happiness in eternity, it would be as selfish as though you had expected to reap it in time.

*I.* Certainly; a difference in the periods contemplated cannot affect the character of such an action.

*P.* God acts for his own glory, and is therefore holy. Sometimes he acts with a view of advancing it on earth, and is holy in so doing; and sometimes he acts with a view of promoting it in the eternal state, and he is equally holy in that. The Lord Jesus Christ glorified his Father on the earth, and aimed to glorify him in eternity (John 17:4, 5); and in either case was holy. The same is true of Christians on earth. And the same principle applies to sinners, in respect to their character. To act for their own happiness in time as their chief object, stamps them selfish; and to do so for eternity is equally selfish, on the same principle that to act for the glory of God to be accomplished in the eternal state was a holy act in Christ. The difference in the character of the objects, can make no difference in the principle.

*I.* Not the slightest.

*P.* This world is, so to speak, a mere parenthesis in existence, between a preceding and an ensuing eternity; and is soon to be absorbed in an unceasing state of duration. The soul approaches death with its habitual selfish desires for happiness strengthened by the appalling exigency of its position; in the process of death the same impressions remain; and when the soul escapes from the body, (which is the death of the body) it rises with the same desires, and reaches forth with inconceivable intensity to grasp its happiness; and disappointment only serves to stamp its selfish character indelibly. On this ground, he that is filthy here, will be filthy there, still and for ever.—Rev. 22:11.

*I.* I perceive that death can no more affect the character of one's desires, than would our starting upon a journey to some foreign land.

*P.* Admitting the selfish soul to heaven would no more adapt him to the enjoyment of its holy blessedness, than would the admission of one stone-blind into a brilliantly-illuminated apartment capacitate him to perceive and enjoy the surrounding splendor. Mr. Parkhurst, in his *Moral Philosophy*, (chapter ii. page 29,) remarks: "After all, there is no danger that such happiness as is enjoyed in heaven, will ever be, to any sinner, the object of supreme desire. The human mind is so constituted that no one can have a conception of any thing which is different in kind from all that he has experienced. The pleasures of religion are, like their source, different in kind from all others. Of course those who have never tasted these pleasures, cannot have any conception of them; and that which they cannot conceive, cannot be to them an object of either supreme or subordinate desire. Therefore the future happiness which such imagine and desire, differs not in kind from what they enjoy on earth; so that they cannot be shielded from the imputation of selfishness, by alleging the purity and celestial nature of the object of their pursuit. As to those who have enjoyed a foretaste of the real happiness of heaven, they love God supremely, and their neighbor as themselves; and of course regard their own happiness, even in eternity, as a subordinate object."

*I.* His position is on the principle that the desire of pleasure by the gambler, for example, would undergo no change in its detestable character, by means of his hoping for and pursuing the enjoyment of it in the company of the moral and virtuous, and at some distant day? The excellence of the anticipated company, and the postponement of its enjoyment, could not make that pure which is intrinsically evil.

*P.* You are right. We have seen that one may be amiable in his feelings, that is, may have a good *natural* disposition or character, and may be correct in his external deportment, and so may be accomplishing good actions; but that, as his personal *moral* character is determined by his motives or objects, unless these are morally approvable, *he* cannot be morally approved and accepted in such feelings and conduct. Thus, "the plowing of the wicked [however necessary and right in respect to his own necessities] is *sin*," is the occasion of his sinning against God, inasmuch as the object of every wicked man therein is selfish, and the divine glory is consequently thrown out of view.—Prov. 21:4. Mankind, looking merely at the person's industry, and the benefits of it to himself, his family, and the community, would *approve;* but God, looking at the involved antagonism to his superior rights, must disapprove of him in such conduct. Hence, what is highly esteemed among men, may be abomination in the sight of God.—Luke 16:15.

*I.* I see the distinction very clearly.

*P.* To apply it more particularly: One may live irreproachably moral as respects mankind; he may be amiable in his disposition, kind to the poor, generous toward religious and benevolent institutions, honest in all his dealings, benevolent, patriotic, and philanthropic in his impulses—may respect the wisdom, power, and other natural attributes of God—may be pleased with his compassion and benefactions—may be a strict observer of the Sabbath, of his family duties, and indeed of all the external requirements both of the law and gospel —and every observer would pronounce his actions to be good; but if he is selfish, if he is deficient in a holy motive, if he does not act from a supreme regard to the glory of God, *his moral character* therein cannot be approved, nor he be accepted by *God.* He "passes over judgment and the *love of God,*" and it may be said of him, as in the case before noticed, "these things ought ye to have done, and not to leave *the other* undone."—Luke 11:42. "Though I bestow all my goods to feed the poor, and though I give my body to be burned, and have not charity, [love to God and his glory] it profiteth me nothing."—1 Cor. 13:3.

*I.* Certainly; I can readily perceive that no one can be *holy* in such feelings and conduct unless they are prompted by a preference of the glory of God; and it is evident that no one can be accepted unless his character is holy therein. "For not he that commendeth himself is approved, but whom the Lord commendeth." —2 Cor. 10:18.

*P.* In closing this part of our inquiry, let me request your particular attention to a point which is indispensable to a correct understanding of subjects which will arise hereafter. It relates to the radical difference between acting from principle, or a love of right as it is seen to exist in our relations with others, and from a perception of and desire for any course as the proper or *right way* to effect some ulterior object.

*I.* Will you please illustrate the difference?

*P.* Suppose we should see *O.* advancing, while ruminating upon various plans of acquiring money, to which he is most inordinately attached. At the same time we perceive that the house of *P.* is taking fire; and we call out to *O.* and request him to give the alarm, and hasten with us to extinguish the gathering flames. *O.* utterly refuses, alleging that he feels no interest in the matter, since the preservation of the house can afford him no pecuniary gain; and he then passes onward. Now, it is evident that, in the supposed case, *O.* is not only destitute of the ordinary sympathies of humanity, which might prompt others to render that assistance, but he is also destitute of love to the rights of his neighbor over him; rights which he can perceive and would admit to exist, and which he would be the first to insist upon, were he in a like situation with *P.* We should have no hesitation in pronouncing him unprincipled; nor in referring to his absorption in his own pecuniary interests as the cause of his insensibility.

*I.* I should have no doubt on the subject.

*P.* But suppose further, that in consequence of our favorable representations of the wealth and generosity of *P.*, he should imbibe the idea that he would, in all probability, secure a large pecuniary recompense, provided he should render him prompt assistance. Stimulated by the love of gain, and with a view to acquire it by that means, *O.* loudly gives the alarm, and hastens toward the scene of the conflagration. His character would obviously be perfectly selfish in the transaction; for whatever he might know or admit concerning the rights of *P.* as a fellow-creature, it is evident that he would be *moved* to assist him solely by his desire for money, and his hope of acquiring it by those means; that is, he would adopt those means solely with a view to promote his pecuniary interests?

*I.* Certainly; it would be an unprincipled act. He would be governed by personal considerations exclusively; and if he had as clear a *perception* of the rights of his neighbor as a fallen angel could have, it would not relieve his selfishness, but would rather increase its deformity, inasmuch as he would then be acting in conscious dereliction of a known virtuous principle.

*P.* Suppose we should warn *O.* that *P.* would never reward him, if he should become acquainted with his motives and his previous gross refusal to aid him, and that we intended to apprise him of the whole affair. In consequence of this check upon his selfish prospects, *O.* pauses in his course, determined to leave *P.* and his burning house to their fate, since he could gain nothing by his efforts. This would be natural.

*I.* Certainly; if his motive is destroyed, if his object is seen to be beyond his reach, he will stop of course.

*P.* But suppose a new plan should occur to him. He thinks that if *P.* is so particular about people's motives and character, he can secure the reward by accommodating him in those respects. After casting about for that precise course which he judges will best promote his purposes, he settles his plan; and, with a view to please *P.*, and make him favorably disposed to reward him, and from a perception, as he supposes, that to please him will thus be the *right way* to secure the reward, he determines to assist him; and he accordingly hastens toward the scene. Now, it would be obvious that he would be as unprincipled as ever. He *knew* that his neighbor had rights over him, but he had no more love nor did he act from any more regard for them than before. On the contrary, he used the word *right* in the sense of *proper* or suitable for his object, as he judged. He preferred his own interests, and desired to use those means as the supposed *feasible way* of promoting them; so that his desire to do right, as he might erroneously call it, by so pleasing *P.*, was as selfish as his desire for the money to be acquired by those means, and for the same reason.

*I.* Undoubtedly; it would be a mere effort to secure his own ends. In his eagerness, he would overlook the radical difference, and would confound a desire to act in a right or proper way to acquire the money, with a love of the rights or just claims of his neighbor, who stands in the relation of a fellow-creature.

*P.* True; and suppose we should convince *O.* of it. Again he would be brought to a stand. But suppose, as a last resort to succeed in obtaining the money from *P.*, he determines effectually to please him by acting from *a love of his rights* in the case, that is, from honest principle. With this view, he admits that he ought to regard his rights in the matter of saving his property from destruction, and ostensibly determines to help him on that principle. He now thinks he has succeeded in securing the reward—that he has taken a course that will certainly please *P.*, and make him favorable in that respect. Feelings of pleasure, proportioned to his previous anxieties, now arise in his mind, which become an evidence that his feelings have undergone a change on the subject; and looking upon *P.* as sure to be willing to reward him, he feels pleased with him for his anticipated friendship, regrets his late unkind feelings toward him, is gratified even with the conflagration, since its occurrence affords such an opportunity to make money, and is pleased also with his fellow-laborers at the fire, because they act as a foil, enabling him to exhibit his own superior dexterity and alacrity and desert of a reward. The hope of success produces so much pleasure, that he becomes entirely confident that he has now struck upon the right way. Now, no uninterested spectator, who understood all the circumstances, could fail of perceiving that all his supposed regard for the rights of *P.* on their own account, and all his professed action upon principle, was a mere mistake, a delusion produced by his inordinate love of his own pecuniary interests. His desires were the same, as before, for the money; his ultimate object in that transaction was the same as before, the money; and all his means, whatever they might be in themselves considered, were adopted for the sole ultimate purpose of securing the money, and *his character* was selfish in their employment. His determination to act from right principle was futile, because it was itself produced by a pre-determination to use it to a more ulterior purpose, to prostitute it to his own ends; and therefore, while in name and appearance he was acting from a love to the rights of *P.*, in reality and in fact he had no such feeling, but was subordinating the principle to the love of his own interests as the supposed *right way* to effect them.

*I.* It is clear that he was endeavoring to render virtue subservient to the ends of selfishness. Of course he had no more right principle than before.

*P.* And you will observe that his supposed change of mind consisted merely in having his anxieties relieved, and his love of money gratified, by the hope that he had at last found the feasible way to succeed; that this hope conferred all the pleasure he felt in *P.* as his friend in the matter; that it produced his regret on reflecting upon his past unkind feelings, and contrasting them with his present views of the supposed kindness of *P.;* and, in fine, his satisfaction with his fellow-laborers, the fire, and every thing besides which seemed to aid him in the affair. His change was not to a love of rectitude in the case, and was therefore no more to be depended upon than his previous efforts for the same object. His hope of securing the money was selfish; his pleasure, produced in view of the acquisition of it, by means of such supposed change and efforts, was also selfish; and all the gratitude to *P.* and gratification in his co-laborers which resulted from his hope, and all his subsequent efforts, and all his other feelings of fear or joy, were equally selfish.

*I.* Yes. It is perfectly evident that all his supposed changes, pleasures, hopes, and labors were in view of his securing his pecuniary interests ultimately; and that as that object was selfish, its character was transferred to all those exercises and efforts. But it seems to me it would be difficult to convince *O.* of his delusion, until after he has finished his labor at the fire, and, on making application to *P.* for a reward, he should be actually refused.

*P.* Not so very difficult, unless he was prēdetermined to be foolish, as well as vicious. His mind would be open to a perception of the real facts, and, if he would, to a conviction of his error; and as he began to waver, and found that with his doubt of success his pleasurable evidences began to take wing, the work of correction would become more easy. And just so soon as he should clearly see that, notwithstanding all his simulated efforts, his motives were as objectionable as before, and that consequently *P.* would not reward him, he would lose the hope and pleasure he had just enjoyed, and might reprove himself for his folly; and perhaps, if he should declare his real sentiments, he would blame *P.* for refusing to reward him after so many sincere efforts on his part, and might wish that his house might be consumed;—for there is no limit to the extremes to which disappointed selfishness will resort

*I.* I thank you for this explanation of the difference between acting on virtuous principle, and endeavoring to subordinate it to selfish ends. They are moral opposites, but are often mistaken one for another.

*P.* We have now finished all I wished to present preparatory to an examination of the moral character of your early religious experiences. In pursuance of our original plan, we have investigated your early exercises, have ascertained the principles upon which God would have us act, and have developed those which he would have us avoid. We will next proceed, after noticing a few preliminary points, to compare your experiences with each of these opposing classes of principles; and as the result, you will be enabled to decide with perfect certainty upon the moral character of your own. If any error should be perceived, you will then be in a position to proceed to rectify it; whereas, if it should remain undetected, and if it be fundamental, you can never correct it, but must encounter every resulting evil consequence.

*I.* I have long sought precisely such information, and shall prize it beyond every other.

## CHAPTER V.

### MORAL CHARACTER OF THE EXERCISES BEFORE ANALYZED.

*Pastor.* A FEW years since, the British mail-steamer Tweed was totally wrecked in the Caribbean Sea, and several of the passengers and crew were drowned. The wife of one of the crew, residing at Southampton, the mother of six children, on being abruptly told by a neighbor that the Tweed was lost, and that all hands had perished, fell down dead. What rendered the circumstance more affecting was, that the husband arrived safely at Southampton a short time after, being one of the persons whose lives were providentially saved.—I have given this narration, for the purpose of refreshing your mind upon two or three principles of much importance. The first is, that one may be very sincere in his belief, and yet be mistaken in point of fact; as was the case with that poor woman.

*Inquirer.* And as is of very ordinary occurrence. Our believing a thing ever so firmly, cannot make it true; else it must have been a fact that her husband was drowned, since she was so fully persuaded of it.

*P.* The next is, that our feelings are the natural result of our belief; and that they will be pleasant or painful according as it is adapted to produce one or the other. Thus, the belief that her husband was lost, naturally produced feelings of great anguish in the mind of his affectionate wife; and the shock was so sudden as entirely to unsettle her nervous system, and destroy her life. Had she not believed the report, such results would not have occurred.

*I.* And had her husband been lost, but had she believed that he was among the saved, it would have produced pleasure, because of her evidently strong affection for him.

*P.* Yes. The next is, that such feelings, whether pleasurable or painful, are no evidence whatever that the thing believed is true; but are evidence only that we *believe* it to be true. Thus, the painful feelings of that woman were no proof that her husband was lost; but they were incontestible evidence that she sincerely believed he was.

*I.* Yes; and had he been drowned, and had she believed him to be safe, the happy feelings produced by it would not have proved that he had been saved, but only that she thought he had.

*P.* The next is, that as our belief produces pleasant or unpleasant feelings according to the state of our hearts and the nature of the thing believed, a correction of it when erroneous will necessarily dispel the feelings so produced, and will introduce such others as the corrected belief is calculated to excite. Thus, had that woman survived the painful shock, the return of her husband alive and well would have corrected her belief, would have dispelled her anguish, and would have produced feelings of surprise and joy.

*I.* Yes; and the contrary results would have occurred had she supposed him to have been safe, but discovered afterwards that he was lost; the happy feelings of the one, would have given place to the distress of the other.

*P.* The next is, that hope will produce much the same feelings as the full belief. Thus, had she, as you have supposed, had some reason to think that he was among the saved, the hope that he was alive would have sustained her spirits; and, if strong, it would have dispelled her anxieties, and filled her bosom with pleasurable feelings and anticipations. It would answer most of the purposes of a firm belief, until she should be undeceived; but on discovering the death of her husband, her hope would be dispelled, and its pleasures and anticipations would cease.

*I.* Certainly. Hope is merely the representative, in our minds, of success in our desires and plans; and when we become aware of a failure therein, it will cease of course with all its pleasures, and leave us to disappointment and trouble.

*P.* Consequently *a hope* of having succeeded is no evidence whatever that we have been successful; but, like belief, is evidence merely that we think we have been.

*I.* I perceive the principle. A hope of enjoying a thing, while it produces all the pleasures of anticipation, forms not the least valid proof that we shall eventually acquire it.

*P.* We will now recur to the views and exercises which you so constantly entertained previous to the indulgence of your hope in Christ, and while you were confessedly impenitent and unconverted. You will please confine your attention to that period, for a few moments. As we have seen in your own case, and as is true of every other member of our race, except Christ in his human nature, who knew no sin, (2 Cor. 5:21) you were then perfectly selfish at heart. You recollect that you had loved and pursued the world for the interest and pleasure it afforded yourself, under the predominant, or superior and controlling, desire of your own happiness.

*I.* Certainly. And I can perceive now that it was selfish.

*P.* And you looked upon religion as designed for your own eternal happiness; whereas, like every thing besides, it is intended ultimately to promote the glory of God. In that respect, also, your views were selfish.

*I.* Yes, in common with all other sinners.

*P.* And when, in early life, and before you indulged that hope, you sought religion, as you termed it, it was with an ultimate view to secure your deliverance from punishment, and your happiness in the future state. It was the desire of this which influenced you to pray, to read the Bible, and to do all those things which you thought would aid you. This also induced the wish to love God, to please him, and have him love you in return; and it made you seek for a hope of pardon, and for an evidence of a hope in some new feelings or change of heart, as you called it. Your ultimate aim in all was your own future safety and happiness; it was for this you not only desired these things, but for it you used every means of which you was possessed.

*I.* I see it very plainly.

*P.* Of course, being unconverted, and totally depraved in heart, you had no love to the glory of God.

*I.* No. My conscience always condemned me for sin.

9*

*P.* And as you became convicted of your sins from time to time, it produced desires for a hope as a means of relief; so that the stronger these convictions became, the more earnest were your corresponding endeavors after pardon and acceptance, and consequently the more selfish you grew in their pursuit?

*I.* Yes; I was not aware of it at the time, but I can now perceive it most clearly.

*P.* And in this entirely selfish state of heart you entered upon the convictions and efforts which resulted in that hope in Christ about which we have said so much; that is, you began them from a supreme desire to promote your own safety and peace, and you continued them, at least for a while, with the same view.

*I.* Yes. All sinners must be selfish on the start, or when they commence a serious examination of their prospects and a determined use of the means to secure their salvation.

*P.* Undoubtedly they will all be selfish then. Let us, if you please, now confine our attention for a few moments to the period of those convictions immediately preceding the hope we have spoken of. You remember that you then encouraged reflections on your state and prospects, and resorted to various means to deepen your feelings, and to acquire sorrow, love, and other right affections before God, in order to comply with the terms of acceptance so far as you understood them. These efforts and feelings were all selfish of course, since you sought them from a desire for, and with an ultimate view to, your own safety and peace.

*I.* I now see they were.

*P.* Your insensibility to the love of God alarmed you

in reference to your success, and your fears that it might prove the last offer of sovereign grace increased that alarm, and made you willing to renounce every thing that hindered your salvation; these were all selfish, being produced by an apprehended disappointment in your object.

*I.* Yes, I see it. Indeed, starting with such selfish desires, every thing I did or felt under them must have been selfish. Of course all sinners are selfish during their convictions, and up to the period of their conversion; which consists, I suppose, in the feelings and actions of the new heart.

*P.* Sinners always remain supremely selfish until they are converted—as you truly suppose.

*I.* Still, I thought at the time that there was something good about my feelings, which encouraged me to hope in ultimately succeeding.

*P.* That was because they were so ardent; but there can be nothing morally approvable in the feelings and efforts produced by selfish desires, however decided they may be; they must necessarily be morally disapprovable. Consequently, yours formed no valid ground of encouragement.

*I.* But I hoped they were such feelings as the Spirit gives.

*P.* Conviction of sin consists in a remembrance of our guilty conduct, which produces entire self-condemnation therefor. The Holy Spirit in conviction reproves the world "of sin, of righteousness, and of judgment" (John 16:8); and by his censures thro' the conscience of the sinner, convinces him of his criminality and desert of the everlasting displeasure of God. These condemnations of conscience produce remorse, and thus incidentally arouse the anxieties for present relief and alarms in view of the future, of the selfish heart. These anxieties and alarms are not the gift of the Spirit, but are the mere excitements of a heart alive solely to its own interests, and are consequently selfish. It is like the law of God, which, when perceived by the selfish mind, frequently so disturbs his selfishness as to produce all manner of evil desires and inimical feelings, which it would not do in a holy one; evincing that the source and fault is in the selfish heart, while the law itself is not responsible for such feelings, but remains holy, just, and good.—Rom. 7:8, 12. The Holy Spirit, in reproving the sinner, recalls to his memory, sometimes like a sudden flash, the evils of his past life, and makes his conscience pass judgment of condemnation and death upon him. At this point the selfish heart puts forth its desires and efforts, perhaps amid much regret and weeping, for its own deliverance, but not for the more ultimate glory of God; for which feeling the Spirit is not at all responsible, but remains holy in his censures. Whatever encouragement the sinner may be disposed to take to himself from such selfish feelings, these reproofs are rather an evidence of the disapprobation of God. The sinner is already condemned, and is awaiting the execution of his sentence of eternal death; and this charging his fault to his face is calculated to excite a sense of guilt, and to lead him to justify God in his punishment. It may be aptly compared to the censure of a condemned criminal by an earthly judge, who is about to pass sentence upon him. He enumerates his offences in order to make him feel the justice of his punishment; and he may also desire, as does the Spirit with the sinner, to stir him up to eventual repentance; but the offender's alarms, anxieties, entreaties, tears, and efforts to escape the impending punishment, do not lessen the judge's aversion, nor suspend the sentence, nor delay its execution. So far from the Spirit's being mollified by such feelings, it will be found that the multitudes who have gone from under the gospel to the perdition of ungodly men, have mostly been often reproved and convicted of sin by him while here, as an earnest of their guilt, of the divine displeasure, and of their impending fate.

*I.* It must have been my deceitful heart, which inclined me to look upon conviction of sin as such an indication of the divine favor.

*P.* The passages which speak of a good work being begun in the heart, as in Phillipians 1:6, refer to regeneration. The sinner's feelings under conviction are any thing but morally good exercises; for the unconverted and depraved heart cannot put forth any thing commendable in the sight of God.

*I.* I am satisfied on this point; and that all the encouragement I derived from my convictions was groundless.

*P.* In the process of conviction, you came up to the resolution to obey the Lord, with increasedly stronger desires to secure an evidence, either immediate or gradual, of your acceptance, pardon, and future peace. And the others to whom these truths apply, arrived at the point where they ostensibly turned to the Lord, with the same desires.

*I.* Of course, as my desires were selfish at the commencement and during the continuance of my feelings under conviction, they were equally so at its termination; and I well know that the termination of conviction is not the commencement of conversion. Besides, I am conscious that such was the fact. But I must observe that I have placed little or no confidence in that resolution; and that my dependence has been more on the new feelings which I enjoyed soon afterwards.

*P.* However that may be, let us examine your exercises in the precise order in which they occurred. You had in vain tried every other way to secure a pardon and acceptance; and that course, as we saw, seemed to be your last resort.

*I.* It did.

*P.* Your desires to take the right course for pleasing God and securing your safety and peace were still strong; you were inclined to think that that step might prove to be the feasible way to succeed; and under the hope that, perhaps, you might be accepted and delivered, you resolved to serve the Lord in the best way you could. This, as we saw at first, was the position you took; and this resolution was entirely selfish. It proceeded from desires to secure your own future happiness; it was entered upon with that aim, and it was valued only as a means to that end.

*I.* True; but I desired to do right also.

*P.* You *knew*, as always before, that God had rights over you, but you had no new desires for them; while you took that course as the supposed *right way* to accomplish your existing desires. It was like *O.* in the last illustration, who knew that his neighbor *P.* had a right to his aid and services, but who resolved to render them because he desired the money, and thought it would be the right way to get it, which he mistook for a love to his just claims. Had you seriously doubted whether that procedure would secure your welfare, you would not have entered upon it, as we saw at first. You wished to find and take that way, for the same reason that you desired future happiness, and the mere knowledge of the rights of God did not affect your action.

*I.* I am convinced I acted under such desire, and that there was no principle in it. What should I have done?

*P.* Had you given your heart to God, with a love to him and his glory superior to those desires for yourself, it would have been the required duty. Instead of which, you resolved solely from a love for, and with a view to promote your own safety and peace. You was "a lover of pleasure *more than* a lover of God," for you then had no love whatever to his glory.

*I.* I see that the resolution was perfectly selfish; and that my distrust of it was well founded. It is clear that it was not conversion. I am glad to know it in time; for however painful it is to discover such a mistake, it is all-important to me to get right; and that I am determined upon, at all events, if it is practicable.

*P.* That is well said. The truth, however unpleasant at the moment, can never injure us, if we faithfully pursue it.

*I.* I felt satisfied, however, with being on the side of Christ.

*P.* But, as you can now see, in order to ascertain whether you were really on his side, it is absolutely necessary to determine the reason *why* you took that seeming position.

*I.* True; but I did not think of that at the time. I wished to please God.

*P.* In order that you might secure his favor, and thereby your own pardon from punishment and future peace; which was purely selfish. The Christian has a higher and nobler object in his desires to please him, namely, to glorify him in his heart and life.

*I.* I see my desire to please God was selfish. But my conclusion was to serve him, come what might.

*P.* So you *said;* but you anticipated that his favor with your safety and peace would come, and you *acted* in view of that; which is pure selfishness.

*I.* It was just so. Still, I did not hope to succeed in securing my safety and peace by my own strength or merits; but confided in Christ alone for pardon and eternal happiness.

*P.* It is proper, and a duty, to confide in Christ for proper things; but it is as improper to depend on his aid for improper things, as in that of any other being, and far more so. You trusted in him for assistance toward your selfish ends, by means of his pardoning favor and atoning merits; and this was perfectly selfish and wicked. It would no doubt be wicked to rely upon his aid to help you violate every human and divine law, and to commit all conceivable enormities; but in confiding in him to aid you in such selfish objects, you, *in principle,* contemplate that very thing; for selfishness is the parent-principle and producing cause of all sin and evil, and he would have upheld it, in your case, by countenancing your selfish plans, and would thereby have also settled the principle that it was to be upheld in all others. This would involve his renunciation of its opposite, the glory of God; it would be an abandonment of his own holy character, which results from his supreme devotion to that glory; and it would be an assumption of a selfish and unholy character. It would destroy the work of the atonement, and bring sin and ruin on the universe; for Christ is God. You ignorantly sought to make Christ "a minister of sin." Where, however, the heart is supremely fixed on God and his glory, and the desires of the soul are bent on its advancement in preference to every thing beside, and where the soul pants to be delivered from unholiness of heart and life, and to enter into the presence-chamber of God, that it may enjoy, praise, and ever promote that glory, (Rom. 5 : 2) then to trust in Christ for remission of sins, and for aid in such noble objects, is right, because it is honorable to him; and it is also a high privilege and duty of the believer. Christ in return will accept the trust, will execute it faithfully, and will glorify his Father in presenting that soul "faultless before the presence of his glory."—Jude 24. But how different is this from your dishonorable reliance on him for your selfish purposes!

*I.* I am ashamed and confounded at my selfish presumption. I entirely overlooked the moral character of the thing for which I confided in him, supposing that the mere act of trusting was sufficient. I am convinced that all such trust in the aid of Christ is unauthorized until after we are truly devoted to those objects which are according to his will. But since the pursuit of the sinner's own happiness ultimately is so obviously selfish, and at discord with the divine glory, I am surprised that the apostle should urge us to work it out, even with fear and trembling.—Phil. 2:12.

*P.* He only seems to you to do so, in consequence of your confounding your own selfish happiness, with holiness and the glory of God and its enjoyment; and from your erroneously supposing that he meant, by the term salvation, the same thing that you and all other sinners did. The direction to work out their salvation with fear and trembling, was not given to unconverted men, and therefore did not at all refer to their effecting their selfish happiness by their labors and exertions; but it was addressed to *the saints* at Philippi, and to those who, he declares, had *always obeyed* since their conversion. We must be careful on this point; for, as you might give many encouragements to a child which you would not to an enemy, and which that enemy would not be authorized to apply *in the same sense* to himself, so Christ gives many directions to his children and friends, with which his enemies have nothing to do. And this is one of them; for the *salvation* which he commands his obedient people to work out, is one which prēsupposes them to be regenerated, and is only another name for holiness and its blessings; and so far from implying the pursuit of selfish happiness, it intends just the contrary. The Scriptures denominate it "the salvation of God" (Luke 3:6; Is. 52:10); and it consists in that holy character and course of conduct, as well as in that holy blessedness, which results from a supreme devotion to the glory of God; and which none can appreciate or enjoy until, by regeneration, they acquire a new heart, or one which is supremely bent upon God, and new desires and affections which can take their delight in his glory. "Whoso offereth praise, glorifieth me; and to him that ordereth his conversation aright, will I show the salvation of God."—Ps. 50: 23. The devotion of the selfish heart to its own purposes is unholy; but where self turns to God, seeks his glory, and rejoices in his loveliness and goodness, it is a holy act; and the resulting happiness, partaking of the character of its source, is virtuous and holy. As God will destroy the happiness of him who retains an unholy character, because it is unholy; so he will preserve the happiness of him who is of a holy character, because it is holy. It was the holy joy of glorifying his Father, and of possessing the glory which he had with him before the world was, that induced our Lord to endure the cross.—John 17: 4, 5; Heb. 12: 2. It was the same holy enjoyment in glorifying God that formed the recompense to which the pious Moses looked in his trials and afflictions with the people of God.—Heb. 11: 24—26. And such is the holy salvation which all *believers* should seek, (for sinners cannot until they become converted,) and which they shall surely find: "Receiving the end of your faith, [the result and issue of your love and faithfulness] even the salvation of your souls."—1 Pet. 1: 9.

*I.* On reflection, it is evident that as God and sinners have adverse objects in view, the enjoyment which each contemplates from their promotion must be as different in character as are their sources. And yet I can see how liable sinners are to be deceived upon this point, since they know of only their own objects, and desire only the happiness flowing from the love of them.

How can they know the difference, except as they are taught from the word of God?

*P.* They cannot (1 Cor. 2:14); and it is impossible even to conjecture the wide-spread ruin which has followed their being encouraged to pursue their own selfish happinesss, under the idea that it was the very "salvation of God" which is presented to believers.

*I.* I also trusted in the imputation of Christ's righteousness to deliver my soul from the divine wrath.

*P.* Hereafter we will notice the subject of imputation more at large; for the present it will be sufficient to remark that merely believing that the merits of Christ were imputed to you, did not make it any more a fact, than your believing any other thing would make that true; and your feeling pleased and satisfied in consequence of such belief, was no valid evidence that they were imputed, but only that you believed they were.

*I.* True; for we feel as we believe, and our feelings can be only evidence of the sincerity of our belief, and not of the real truth of the thing believed.

*P.* And Christ never imputes holiness, or the new heart, where it does not exist in fact; and his atoning merits are applied only to those who are regenerated, and never to those who are unregenerate—whatever they may believe.

*I.* There can be no doubt of the truth of these positions.

*P.* But you were selfish in your procedure, as we have seen; in that ostensible turning to the Lord, your own happiness, and not the glory of God, was ultimately in view, and occupied your desires. Consequently, your belief in the imputation was an error, for the same reason, precisely, that your trust in Christ was unauthorized; and your subsequent satisfaction and other feelings under that belief, were invalid as evidences, and were unacceptable to God.

*I.* I perceive my mistake in appropriating the blessing before I had complied with the prērequisite moral change. Of course my feelings in consequence all go for nothing. Still, in forming that resolution to serve the Lord, I endeavored to be sincere.

*P.* No doubt you believed that you were taking the right way to obtain and act from such feelings as would secure your safety and peace. But you will observe that such feelings, however sincere, profound, or satisfactory, could only be selfish, since your own ends were ultimately in view.

*I.* You are correct; that endeavor did not affect the selfishness of the act. I am now perfectly convinced that I was entirely selfish in that resolution. Heretofore I have given it up, at times, as an experiment, because I was in doubt only; but now I am convinced of its invalidity, and renounce it for ever.

*P.* I cannot too much commend the determination with which you act upon truth; persevere, my friend, in this most honorable course, and you will eventually bless the grace which enabled you to do so. It will be expedient now to explain, as briefly as possible, the moral characteristics involved in the various other experiences detailed in the first chapter. I wish you, in our progress, to give attention to this examination, because there are some general principles involved in it important for you to understand.

*I.* I will give my attention to it, as you desire.

*P.* I remark of the person represented by *A.* that the encouragement derived from his convictions and desires for his own salvation was deceptive and invalid; that having his own future safety and peace ultimately in view, his efforts to deepen his feelings and to obtain love to Christ were purely selfish; that his acknowledgment of his self-ruin and inability to secure salvation in his own strength, was the admission of mere facts which could produce no change of heart; that his efforts to cleanse his heart, to relinquish outward sins, to engage in suitable duties, and to imitate the example of others who had been successful, were all selfish, inasmuch as he was prompted by the same desires with which he began, and as his own future happiness was his ultimate aim; and that his resort to meetings for prayer, and presenting himself as an inquirer for the direction and prayers of Christians, were equally selfish, since they were done with the same selfish view. The encouragement derived therefrom was deceptive; and his resolution to give himself up to God was as selfish as that we have just been considering, since it was done as a means of ensuring his acceptance under the desire to secure his own future safety and peace. His view, from beginning to end, was the preservation of himself from deserved punishment, by means of these things; and he consequently remained prēdisposed to his own welfare ultimately, rather than to the glory of God in a real preference of it.

*I.* The selfishness of his preliminary proceedings and of his subsequent seeming dedication to God, is perfectly evident; so much so, that it appears to me no one who has examined their grounds, can honestly mistake it.

*P.* I remark of the person represented by *B.* that his estimate of the world was selfish; that his view of future pleasures was selfish; and that his determination to forsake the former for the latter, was a mere exchange of the pursuit of worldly selfish pleasures, for supposed eternal selfish happiness. His ostensibly giving up all for Christ, was a mere plan to secure such pleasures by his means, and was consequently selfish and dishonorable to him.

*I.* This course is so palpably wrong, that it seems strange any one is deceived by it.

*P.* I remark of the person represented by *D.* that in all he received and did, he was governed by a prē-disposition to secure his own future welfare, which was made his ultimate aim. Consequently, whatever stress he might lay upon the intellectual belief of the gospel, or on his peculiar mode of baptism, or in receiving remission of sins and the Holy Spirit with a pure heart and good conscience, *he* was perfectly selfish in the use of them, and his character remained unchanged in the process. It is unnecessary to disprove the sufficiency of his historical belief in the gospel, or of the supposed efficacy of his baptism, or of the fancied holy results; for they were so obviously used to forward his selfish ends that, even if they were usually as intrinsically efficacious as he supposed them to be, they failed to produce a change of heart in his case, or a love to the divine glory superior to his desires for his own future welfare. Selfishness, only, was baptized and encouraged in the process.

*I.* His self-deception is as clear to me as the light.

*P.* You can see one serious error into which the person represented by *E.* fell—namely, his mistaking the love of pity or compassion of Christ, which never disposes him to pardon the sinner, for his complacency or love to his moral character, which always does so dispose him. He *first* loved those who are now Christians, not with complacency, but with compassion; and under it he made the atonement whereby they were privileged to repent, and devote themselves to the love and glory of God; as it is said, "we [are permitted to] love him, because he first loved us," compassionated our condition and made provision therefor.—1 John 4: 10. 19. It must have been so, else Christ took complecency in their unholy character and conduct, and thereby became unholy himself. Mistaking thus the feelings and purposes of Christ, *E.* resolved to obey him with a view to secure his own happiness by means of his supposed favor and willingness to pardon him; the perfect selfishness of which is too evident for comment.

*I.* The selfish heart, I have no doubt, in its deceitfulness, involves multitudes in the sad consequences of a misconstruction of that text.

*P.* You cannot fail, we think, to perceive that the sole object of him represented by *F.* from the beginning in rejecting the orthodox doctrines, and in dwelling upon the natural characteristics of benevolence, patriotism and philanthropy, and in insisting upon due morality, and in forming his purposes relative to his conduct in life, was the promotion of his own happiness by insuring more comfort of mind in this life, and by securing his own welfare beyond the grave.

Indeed, his whole aim was so obviously to effect these objects that, in order to show his selfish character, it is unnecessary to pause and disprove his sentiments, or show that, with his views of doctrine and duty, he can never be made free, or that the evangelical doctrines can alone, under God, liberate him.

*I.* Whatever his *professions* of good principles, his *heart* is evidently fixed supremely on himself, and not on the glory of God.

*P.* The person represented by *G.* is accustomed to regard the means of grace as designed to secure his ultimate safety and happiness; and he accordingly enters upon and prosecutes them throughout with such a pre-purpose, which of necessity makes all his impulses, subordinate purposes, and actions, selfish. Thus he endeavors to excite sorrow for his past sins, as one means of succeeding in that object, and seeks for pardon with the same view, which leaves his moral character the same as before, entirely selfish, whatever may be the feelings he has aroused. Whether he is favored with a peculiar ministry and church privileges or not, he makes a selfish use of them, and they can do him no real good. Thus, he receives baptism as one means of succeeding in his purpose, and is therefore selfish in it; and whether he *believes* that he thereby obtains the influences of the Spirit to enable him to work out his salvation, to secure the remission of sins, the favor of God, and everlasting life, with *some* spiritual benefit, or that in baptism he receives spiritual regeneration itself, it makes no essential difference; for, as has been seen, his belief of receiving those things does not actually confer them, however hopeful or happy he may feel under it. It is to him a conscious fact—the most conclusive of all evidence—that he prized that ordinance as a means of his own salvation, and that he used it with a deep-seated aim to promote his own future safety and happiness—an end so well established as hardly to come under his own review at the time as a thing to be questioned. His purposes of obedience to Christ, his reliance on him for salvation, his devotion to the authority and rites of his church, his receiving the ordinance of confirmation, (whether scriptural or not) his partaking of the eucharist, his attachment to the church, and, in fine, all his feelings and proceedings, grow out of a predominant desire to secure his own future happiness, and are taken in pursuance of such a purpose; and he is therefore unmitigatedly selfish in them all.

*I.* How very apt sinners are to pervert every means of grace to their own purposes, rather than to use them, as they were designed, for the promotion of the divine glory in a superior love to that! After long indulgence in that course, it must become difficult to convince and tear the deluded heart from its perversions. May God help them!

*P.* Or they perish. I remark of the person represented by *H.* that the whole design of the papal scheme is to forward the selfish interests of the creature, at the expense of the glory of the Creator; that its purgatory to be shortened by his observances, its perdition to be avoided by a blind submission to the authority and ordinances of his church, his own happiness to be secured by baptism, confession and penance, the mass, and those other miscalled sacraments, are the incentives, means, and objects which engross his heart. His scheme knows of no new heart in its true spiritual sense; and it is unadapted to promote it, but is directly adapted to exclude it by fostering selfishness as a principle. Hence, we can account for the amazing wickedness that is an element of the system, and which always has and always will prevail in his sect, selfishness being rampant over priests and people. The very few of his church who, in past ages, have truly loved God, have done so after rejecting its fatal errors. They have always been suspected and persecuted, even to death, because their holy light evinced too strongly the darkness and depravity of its popes, and priests, and people. In order to his conversion, the whole system must be rejected by him in favor of Christ as the sole Head of Regeneration by the Holy Ghost, and of Justification only through Faith.

*I.* This also explains the radical defect of the Greek, Armenian, and other Eastern churches. They all make their own or selfish happiness, rather than the glory of God, the aim of their systems; they adapt their invented, or gospel-perverted means, to the vain endeavor to accomplish that end; and the vicious deportment and selfish and sensual desires and passions of the natural heart which they allow, are *practically* deemed not inconsistent with their final pardon and happiness. And I can now perceive that the same fundamental error belongs to Judaism, and that the Jews are so much averse to Christianity for that reason.

*P.* Yes. All the forms of a vitiated Christianity, as well as Mormonism, Paganism, and Mohammedanism, have the selfish happiness of the creature for their ultimate object, and are prized by their devotees solely on that account; while they vary in the means proposed to effect it, some making use of those more vicious and injurious than others. But the evangelical doctrines of Christianity are alone adapted by God to produce a superior regard to his glory in the human heart, and a holy and commendable course of conduct in the life; and hence, when they are substantially rejected, holiness is made impossible. This fact makes it peculiarly imperative on evangelical Protestants to propagate the pure gospel among all the nations.

*I.* If they do not, who is left to do that work?

*P.* Let us now return. As any one who should apply the foregoing facts to himself in accordance with a perceived propriety, would no doubt become convinced of the selfishness of his first resolutions or other steps, we will next proceed to develop the character of your feelings and other exercises which ensued. The relief and composure which you immediately enjoyed were produced by the cessation of your mental struggles, and by the hope that you had found the right way to be accepted. This composure, in its turn, encouraged you to think that you had already succeeded, in some degree, in obtaining the evidence of your acceptance, and you felt happy in the thought. This being a new and pleasurable feeling, was soon received as the change desired; when you hoped in Christ for pardon, and was much pleased with him for his supposed mercy. In the first place, all these feelings arose naturally under the circumstances, and were not therefore such special gifts of the Spirit as you supposed.

*I.* I see my mistake.

*P.* In the next place they were selfish, being produced by the idea of succeeding in your selfish happiness; and the stronger your confidence of success, the deeper they became.

*I.* That is true.

*P.* In the next place, your belief and feelings, whether selfish or not, were no valid evidence that you had taken the right way to escape perdition. For we have seen that our belief of a thing does not make it a fact; and that the feelings produced by such belief, or by a hope of the thing, are evidence only that we believe or hope in it, but not that such belief or hope is well founded.

*I.* I see the correctness of the application.

*P.* Whence, the fact that such new and pleasurable feelings occurred is no evidence that your heart was really changed. On the contrary, as these were produced by the hope of having succeeded in your own safety and peace ultimately, they were conclusive evidence that your heart remained unchanged in respect to loving God more than your own ends.

*I.* They were so indeed. My feelings were new merely because I had never before believed myself safe from perdition; and I felt happy of course.

*P.* The ground of your hoping in Christ for remission of sins and their punishment being thus unauthorized, that hope, however joyful, was unauthorized also. Indeed, you can perceive that it was purely selfish, your own safety and peace being the ultimate object which you desired to obtain, and for which you hoped.

*I.* I perceive that my hope was selfish.

*P.* And all the pleasures which sprung from it, and which constituted the bulk of your subsequent exercises, were as selfish as their source.

*I.* Yes, that follows of course.

*P.* And the renewed resolutions which you formed to serve Christ the remainder of your days were prompted by the desire to preserve your future safety and happiness by persevering in the use of the supposed means; and were consequently purely selfish. The pleasure you took in contemplating such service was equally selfish, since it was caused by anticipated success in the same end; while your natural feelings only gave strength to the selfish purpose. Both sprung from a desire to preserve Christ's favor and your salvation, and from the satisfaction such a prospect produced.

*I.* I am convinced that I was altogether selfish in my resolutions and feelings up to the point of hoping and taking pleasure in Christ; and as I was selfish in that very hope and pleasure also, I fear you will find little about my exercises afterwards that was right. Truly, "the heart is deceitful above all things."

*P.* It is now necessary to present some further details in order to understand those whose first steps have not been before characterized; and I have to request your particular attention to them.

*I.* I shall be pleased to render it.

*P.* I would remark of the person represented by *C.* that the belief that he was one of the elect, or that Christ died for him in a particular sense, or that he was able and willing to save him, was no evidence whatever that such was the real truth; that the relief and pleasant feelings that resulted were evidence only that he believed such to be the fact, but none whatever that such was the fact; and that such belief and the feelings it produced were purely selfish, since he had his own pardon and safety ultimately in view. The hope in Christ, proceeding from such a foundation, and so terminating upon his own welfare as the most desirable object, was also selfish, as were the pleasures resulting from it. His after resolutions to obey God, however pleasurably and willingly made, were entirely selfish also, since they were prompted by selfish desires, and were designed to preserve his happy prospects of pardon and deliverance by perpetuating the favor of Christ through the discharge of known duties. In no one of his exercises was there involved any preference of the glory of God to his own purposes and objects; and consequently there was no true regeneration by the Holy Spirit.

*I.* I used to think that the very essence of religion was to obtain a hope of pardon from punishment, and of peace beyond the grave; and hence sought for a sense of pardon, without regard to its source or character; and I perceive that *C.* has fallen into the same error. Selfishness delights in such a religion, of course, and must be expected to cling to it until its nature is exposed. I used to think also that the faith required in the Scriptures consisted in receiving as true whatever might be favorable to us, that Christ was willing to save us, for example; and that the less evidence one had, the more commendable he was in believing

*P.* Rather, the more foolish he became. The declaration of God in the Scriptures is a most valid ground of our belief, and to receive and heartily observe his communications will truly honor him; but he can be only dishonored by such assumptions as you describe. Had God declared specifically that *C.* was one of the elect, he would have been authorized to believe it, and would have honored God in so doing if his heart had gone over to him; but there was no such declaration; he could know whether he was of the elect only by being born again (John 3 : 3); and his simply *believing* he was one of them, was an act of folly, a caricature of true faith. Our minds should always be open to a conviction of ascertained truth, but closed against error.

*I.* It is very evident that believing a thing without valid evidence, and then receiving the spurious feelings or pleasures it produces as proof of its truthfulness, cannot be acceptable to a rational Sovereign.

*P.* You can perceive the selfish origin and character of the exercises of another class of persons represented by *E.*, both of which may have heretofore been concealed from view. In the period of their convictions and anxieties for deliverance, the thought that Christ is the way, the truth, and the life—that he has become so for them, and that he is consequently willing to forgive, them—produces a sudden emotion of pleasure at the prospect of salvation; and this being new, is received as "the love of Christ shed abroad in their hearts." The belief of his favor, as seen in this supposed evidence from above, produces great joy, and sometimes ecstatic delight, which is taken for the new heart itself, and then hope in Christ is confirmed; and in order to insure their future happiness, the purpose is formed to obey Christ, and perhaps to promote the greatest degree of happiness amongst mankind also. The belief of Christ's willingness to forgive was false, because *E.* was then merely in a convicted, and not in a converted state. The pleasure resulting from such belief was selfish, as we have seen, being in view of his supposed safety and peace, and toward Christ on that account; and being natural, was not the special gift of the Spirit. The mistake of this new selfish pleasure for the new heart in no wise affected its moral character; and the hope founded thereon was necessarily of the same selfish aspect. The purpose to obey Christ, and thereby insure his selfish prospects, was evidently selfish; and however proper the promotion of the happiness of mankind might be under certain aspects, yet his character remained selfish in the purpose, inasmuch as it was adopted as a means to further his own ends. And his subsequent pleasures therein necessarily partook of the same character as their source.

*I.* I have often wondered what some meant by the allegation that they *knew* that Christ first loved them. I now see they mistook these deep feelings of selfish pleasure, exercised by *themselves*, for affections which *Christ* exercised toward them! What a singular delusion! And it appears strange to me now that any should receive such feelings as an evidence of pardon; but it has not seemed so heretofore.

*P.* Of much the same description is the reader represented by *I.*, although he acquires what he calls the love of Christ in some additional ways. His profuse weeping over his danger, and vain efforts to secure his future safety and peace, acts perfectly selfish, are taken by him to be true penitence. This mistake produces some hope that Christ may accept him, which is also clearly selfish, since his own welfare is the object ultimately; and this hope soon ripens into greater pleasure, which is received as the desired change. This error, in its turn, produces a confirmed hope of success through Christ; an act so evidently selfish that proof can make it no clearer. Another of this class is made to scrutinize his mind for evidences, and to make efforts to produce them himself; and any perceived calmness, or momentary insensibility, is received as such. The sudden joy produced by the belief of his success, is mistaken for the additional witness of the Spirit, and he hopes and rejoices in Christ; in all which he is as profoundly selfish as it is possible for his object, his own future happiness, to make him. Another, by an unauthorized resort to the Bible for comforting passages *to apply to himself*, thinks that God reveals to him his pardoning kindness by some of them, and under this error, rejoices; which rejoicing becomes the ground of an equally selfish hope and pleasure in Christ. Another, suffering under a nervous affection from his intense excitement, imagines those sights and sounds before described, which he mistakes for special communications from an exalted and intelligent God. This mistake produces joys; and they, in their turn, lead to a hope and its pleasures—selfish, because self is the source, and selfish happiness the aim of the whole; for while he loudly cries, Glory to God! he means only to express his joy at escaping hell and going to heaven. The unholy joys produced in any of these ways, he calls conversion, or getting religion.

*I.* The multitudes who fall away after indulging such exercises, ought to convince them, it seems to me, that this selfishness is the radical defect which keeps them unconverted; for I suppose it is the predominance of selfishness yearning anew for worldly happiness, after being satiated with that of a hope of the future, that induces them to return to sin and the world—or rather to indulge in them again; for, in heart, they never left either. Such a hope should be abandoned, I now see, even though it is all the religion they have.

*P.* Your stricture is undoubtedly justified by the facts. And, finally, whether the particular means employed by the person have been detailed or not, and whatever may have been his confidence in them as scriptural, or his pleasure in them as valid, if his ultimate aim was to secure his own future happiness, and if the prospect of success originated his encouragement and pleasures, it is apparent that his moral character therein was selfish. Laying aside less material matters, let us develop the *leading principle* involved in his own case, and with its aid decide his character. If that was a preference of his own future welfare to the glory of God, he must pronounce against himself while it can be made available to his own rectification; for if he does not, let us be assured, whatever encouragement he may now receive from erroneous opinions, the ignorant counsels of others, his own religious habits, or the deceitful promptings of his own heart, that God will pronounce against him in that day when no remedy can be found.

*I.* My chief reliance has been on the feelings I had after indulging a hope in Christ. I have to acknowledge that all that preceded was one tissue of selfishness; but you will remember that, for a season at least, I took much pleasure in Christ, and in various religious duties. How do you characterize these?

*P.* We will proceed, as briefly as perspicuity will admit, to examine your subsequent exercises in detail; and also those of the persons just mentioned. And first, in respect to the character of your feelings toward God. As we saw at first, while you continued to approve of the holiness and justice of the Father, your love was exclusively directed toward Christ in view of his goodness in dying for you, in preserving you so long while sinning against him, for his grace in pardoning you, as you hoped, in loving and befriending you in so many ways, in permitting you to enjoy so much happiness here, and in opening such happy prospects of heaven, and the like. These feelings were produced by your hope, as we have seen; and that being selfish, all these fruits of it were selfish also.

*I.* That is a necessary consequence.

*P.* You were pleased with Christ because you thought that he would gratify your desires for your own ultimate welfare; on the same principle that *O.* was pleased with *P.* when he thought he would confer the reward which he so much desired for aiding him about his house. He had no superior love for the rights of *P.* in the matter, as you had none to the holiness of God, and to that justice which you often feared might slay you, as we have seen. And if it needed confirmation, you can find it in the fact, that when you afterwards doubted your title to a hope, you recoiled from being in the hands and at the entire disposal of the Father, in apprehension of his holy justice; whereas, had you truly loved him for that trait, it would have been otherwise; for, there is no fear in love.—1 John 4:18.

*I.* I perceive that your view is correct; I was not pleased with the Father out of Christ.

*P.* Your feelings toward Christ were exclusively those of gratitude in view of his past kindness, and his supposed present merciful intentions toward you. You took pleasure in him as a benefactor simply, as one who had indicated a design to do you good; and this naturally excited pleasant feelings toward him in return, just as the gift of a large fortune by some relative would excite gratitude toward him.

*I.* Certainly my feelings were those of gratitude, and Christ deserved them as I supposed; but it never occurred to me that gratitude could be wrong.

*P.* There are two kinds of gratitude—namely, selfish and holy. Gratitude is always produced by some perceived benefit on the part of the benefactor; and in this respect both kinds have a common cause of excitement. But they differ in respect to the moral aspects of the benefit, and the moral qualities of the benefactor which elicits the regard. Selfish gratitude is excited simply in view of the advantage of the benefit to the receiver, and fixes upon the supposed favorable views and feelings of the benefactor toward his own desires and ends. Hence it is a mere expansion of selfishness, a pleasure and satisfaction of the selfish heart; and it will cease just so soon as the benefits are withheld, or he becomes convinced the benefactor does not possess, or intend to act upon, such supposed favorable intentions. This spurious and selfish gratitude, Mr. Parkhurst observes, (*Mor. Phil.* p. 113,) is what our Saviour had in view when he said, "If ye love them that love you, what thank [in the original, what approvableness or acceptableness of disposition] have ye? for sinners [*amartoloi*, the depraved and detestable] also love those that love them;" or whom they think love them. "And if ye do good to them that do good to you, what thank have ye? for sinners also do even the same."—Luke 6:32, 33. It is difficult for the selfish mind at once to condemn the principle, because it knows practically of none better; but the same may be said of every other selfish exercise. In the case of Job, however, there is given a practical illustration of its character. God had pronounced him a man of upright principles, and one who truly loved him and his glory. This commendation excited the envy and malice of Satan; and he forthwith charged Job with being selfish in his gratitude. He asked, "Doth Job fear God for nought?" and proceeded to show what temporal benefits God had bestowed upon him, and alleged that these were the sole reasons of his love; and that, if God would remove them, his gratitude would cease with them, and he would show that he cared nothing for him in respect to his intrinsic worth, by cursing him to his face. It was tacitly admitted by both, that if such was the cause, his gratitude was unapprovable; and the trial was permitted. In the result, Job still blessed the Lord, showing that his love had a higher object than mere benefits received, and the supposed friendship of the giver. But Satan renewed the charge, alleging that Job's love was produced by his anticipation of the divine favor for the future; and that if God would, by threatening his life, remove such expectations, he would curse him to his face. But while the trial proved the selfishness of Job's wife, it showed that Job himself loved God for reasons besides those of his anticipated friendship and blessings.—Job 1:7—22, and 2:1—10.

*I.* That was, indeed, an unanswerable proof of the moral disapprovableness of selfish gratitude. But, it seems to me that Satan, in the inconsistency of malevolence, now encourages men to have confidence in the very principle which he then so positively denounced; and that he induces many to embrace that same religion of selfishness, the deformity of which he exposed in the case of Job's wife.

*P.* That is just what might be expected of the prince of evil; and deplorable must be the fate of those who fall into his snares, especially when they ply themselves with arguments to remain insnared. Holy gratitude can only exist in a regenerated heart; for although it is excited by a view of benefits, it contemplates also the fact that they are virtuous, right, holy; and a selfish benefit, however pleasing to remaining corruption, would be received in a pure heart with disapprobation, and could excite no pleasure toward the giver. Holy gratitude also terminates upon the excellent moral character exhibited by the benefactor in his actions, producing a complacent regard toward him, which would remain, were the sentiment of friendship obliterated. Hence, as in the case of angelic beings who witness the blessings of God toward the children of men, the sentiment will rise nearly, and sometimes quite, as high when they are conferred upon others, as when upon one's self. In the one case, Christ is loved for his *favors merely;* in the other, for the holy character exhibited in them, as well as for the kindness which prompted them. Or rather, in the one case, he is loved solely because he appears to *love me;* in the other, because, while exhibiting his condescension and kindness, he is seen to do so in moral harmony with holiness and the divine glory.

*I.* I am now convinced that my gratitude was selfish and spurious; but, believing that pleasure in Christ was enough, I never thought of searching into the reasons why I indulged it. I supposed that the self-deceived were destitute of all feeling toward him; and I concluded that I was not hypocritical, because I had become so sensitive to his favor.

*P.* The self-deceived frequently have more of feeling and vehement joys than real Christians; for they rejoice in the supposed gratification of selfishness, which is a most powerful influence, and have none of those views of themselves and their sins, which sober and humble the Christian's heart. But you were not hypocritical, since you were not influenced by a deliberate intention to appear to be what you were not; you *thought* you were doing right, although it was the way of death.—Prov. 16:25. But, if you would avoid that detestable and dangerous, because God-provoking, character, be careful to ascertain and follow the exact truth to the extent of your ability.

*I.* Christ aiding, I shall do so

*P.* Next, as respects your feelings and purposes toward sin. As your exercises toward God were selfish, it is evident that those which referred to what was in opposition to him, must have been selfish also; and that, indeed, they could not have been otherwise. Thus, your pleasure in his kindness, real or anticipated, naturally produced regret at the *unkindness* of your wrong conduct in return; just as *O.*, in the case supposed, felt regret in the remembrance of his harsh feelings toward *P.* under his disappointment, when he came to think that he would favor him with the pecuniary reward;—a feeling equally selfish in you both. The displeasure you felt at your past conduct proceeded from this, and from seeing that it militated against your eternal interests; and it partook of the same character. And your determination to avoid sin thereafter was also selfish, being prompted by the desire to retain your evidences, and by the wish to avoid displeasing God in order to preserve your future happiness inviolate, and was aided by those selfish feelings in view of the ingratitude of your conduct.

*I.* I perceive the influence of the selfish principle.

*P.* The Christian is alive to the base ingratitude of his conduct, and feels deep regret in view of it; but his heart being fixed upon a new moral object in the glory of God, his feelings and purposes toward sin necessarily partake of the same new character. Thus, his chief sorrow in view of his past evil conduct, arises from its moral deformity, as being so dishonorable to his risen Lord; and he regrets disobedience when seen in others, for the same reason. He hates sin, because it is the moral opposite to that which he supremely loves, the authority and glory of God; and his aversion being a matter of principle, he will abhor it, whether he is to be punished for it or not, or whether committed by others or by himself. This feeling David expressed toward sinners: "Do I not hate them, O Lord, that hate thee? I hate them with perfect hatred" (Ps. 139: 21, 22); if he loved God and his glory, he could not

12

avoid disliking, in the same proportion, his opponents and the dishonor they cast upon him. The Christian dislikes himself also on account of his selfishness and sins; and it is the perceived vileness of his past conduct which destroys all self-complacency, and not unfrequently dispels his hope in Christ. But, like Gideon, though "faint, yet pursuing," he still loves God, mourns over his guilt and moral deformity, and renews his efforts to avoid sin, in order that he may, in some degree at least, glorify his Creator. The self-detestation and abhorrence expressed by Job have many counterparts among humble and devoted believers; but are feelings which, as we have seen, you never exercised.

*I.* I am convinced that all my feelings and resolutions in respect to sin, were then entirely selfish.

*P.* Next, in respect to your feelings toward Christians. These must, in their moral character, have been a counterpart of those you indulged toward God; for you could have no better feelings toward his people, than toward himself. Consequently, you can perceive that, while you *approved* of the rigid principles and conduct of some, your sympathies and pleasure were excited toward others for exclusively personal considerations; such as their naturally amiable dispositions, engaging manners, supposed congeniality of feeling and pursuits, their friendship and beneficial example, their attachment to your supposed heavenly friend, their encouragement of your hopes, their pleasant society, and the like. So that, when you became doubtful of your hope, you lost much of your gratification in them. But, while the Christian is not insensible to such personal considerations, he loves his fellow-disciples for the same reason that he loves God; which is the only cause why it is a test of his character. And his love to them is in precise proportion to the degree in which they reflect Christ's moral image; and where that is not seen, or supposed to exist, he cannot love them as disciples. But yours, as you can now perceive, was of a different character.

*I.* Yes; my regard for Christians, I am now aware, was personal, and therefore selfish. Indeed, I soon lost whatever peculiar satisfaction I had taken in them.

*P.* Next, as respects your feelings and conduct toward sinners. It is evident you could have no feelings for others of a character different from those you entertained toward yourself; and that what you esteemed and desired as most valuable for yourself, you would esteem and wish as such for others. Accordingly, your desire for your own safety and happiness, made you sympathize with their lost condition, and desire their deliverance with the same ultimate view. This sympathy, however amiable in a natural sense, was made selfish by the selfish nature of the designed benefit; and your desire for their future happiness, being independent of any love to the glory of God to be promoted thereby, was as antagonistic to it as was that for your own. Your disapprobation of their ingratitude arose from the same causes as that of your own, and was of the same character. And your efforts for their deliverance, being prompted partly by such selfish sympathy, and partly in order to preserve your hope by engaging in commanded duties, were unqualifiedly selfish. The Christian sympathizes deeply in the present state and terrible prospects of the sinner; and in his compassion earnestly desires his deliverance. But he has a superior principle, one which he would not have violated could every sinner in the universe be delivered from punishment at its expense; it is to have that done which, under the circumstances, the glory of God shall dictate. He knows that the mercy and grace of Christ would shine forth more resplendently, should the sinner repent; and therefore he indulges both his sympathy for him, and his love to Christ, in seeking his repentance; and he knows that without repentance it would be the contrary, and therefore he does not seek his salvation at the expense of that. He desires for him only the "salvation of God," which, as we have seen, intends his regeneration of heart, his deliverance from the love and practice of sin, and his possession of a love to and blessedness in God. And when he contemplates a failure in his repenting, and that the divine glory, in that case, demands his punishment, he yields him up with a sigh of compassion over his fate, but in a superior accord with the righteous will of God, as being holy, just and good.

*I.* My short-lived sympathy and efforts for sinners were so palpably selfish, that I wonder now that my own reflections did not show me the principle. Indeed, I had misgivings all along as to the validity of my position, but I endeavored to silence my fears rather than to scrutinize their grounds.

*P.* Your pleasure in social and secret prayer, was derived from its gratifying your desires and hope; and as these were selfish, so was that pleasure of course. As we have seen, your religious comforts and enjoyments were greatest when your hope was strongest; and when it became weak, your pleasure in duty proportionably declined; and at those times when you had almost abandoned or forgotten it, you took no pleasure in duties, except as they served to revive your hope. Prayer gratified your selfish desire for those evidences and aids necessary to sustain your expectations of future happiness; and it was pleasurable, and perhaps sometimes even delightful, as a means of indulging your joy in the supposed mercy of Christ, at those times when your belief in your eternal safety was entirely confident. When your hope languished and your pleasure with it, prayer was very much neglected, except as mere habit influenced you, or your fears drove you to it, or as you resorted to it to allay the remorse of a condemning conscience. But, while the Christian loves to express and enjoy his *holy* gratitude in prayer, he enjoys the duty principally because he can then indulge his love for the honor and glory of God by holding communion with him, can fit himself the better for his duties, gain needed grace and strength from the Spirit, and express his desires for the glory of God in the conversion of the world. It is not unusual for him entirely to lose sight of himself in contemplating the moral excellencies of God, and to become wholly engrossed in his praise and love. God, rather than his own personal safety, is the source of his pleasure; so that, when destitute of a comforting hope of pardon, he can find, in prayer, consolation and peace in God himself.

*I.* You have convinced me perfectly of my selfishness in these respects.

*P.* Actuated by the same desires in reading the Scriptures, you perverted that duty also to selfishness. Thus, as we have seen, apart from the general information which you wished to derive from the Bible as from every other book you perused, your design was to make your future happiness secure by ascertaining and pursuing its injunctions; and also to sustain your present hope and fortify your evidences, by selecting and applying the promises to yourself. Your own ends prompted you throughout. The Christian takes pleasure in the promises also; but his main object in studying the Word of God is to ascertain how to glorify him in the manner he himself has designated; and he finds an excellence and beauty in the Scriptures, so attractive in themselves because they reflect the character and make known the will of that Being whom he loves so supremely, that it is his chief comfort to resort to them in his saddest hours, when his hope perhaps has fled. In your case, they gave no comfort, except as their perusal at first encouraged your hopes, or afterwards temporarily allayed your fears and the pains of a guilty conscience.

*I.* I see my selfishness therein clearly.

*P.* Your process of self-examination was equally selfish, because the promotion of a hope of your own happiness, and the acquisition of evidences of its security through Christ, was your ultimate aim. Hence your enjoyment in it vacillated with your success or failure; and finally the duty was abandoned when you lost your hope, no superior object being left, in your mind, to accomplish by it. The Christian is desirous to know his true position before God, and applies his holy evidences to ascertain it; but he has also a far higher object—one which he desires and seeks independently of the question of his own prospects—namely, whether he is properly glorifying God in his heart and life, or whether he is making such progress as will honor God before the world.

*I.* I perceive the difference. I examined myself only to prove my hope or create new evidences.

*P.* It was a duty to aid in all religious and benevolent objects, as it was also your duty to pray, "lifting up holy hands" (1 Tim. 2:8); but you perverted it by acting under your selfish desires and with merely personal views. You not only, in many of your benefactions, wished to be reputed benevolent, and also to gratify your natural and personal sympathies, but you considered that such aid to the cause of benevolence was indispensable, at least to some extent, in order to please Christ in the use of your substance, and so perpetuate your future happy prospects. Alms-giving is often considered as *almost* religion itself; but you will observe that the Centurion (Acts 10:1—4) was accepted in his prayers and alms, not on account of any merit in him, or them, to propitiate Christ, but solely because they were an indication or *memorial* of his sincere preference of God and his glory,—a preference which you had not. The Christian feels ashamed when any such motive as yours creep into his heart, and he abhors it; he aids the spread of the gospel with his benefactions from a love to the Lord and in obedience to his command, as well as from a sympathy with his race; and hence the two mites of the poor but humble widow, being all her living, were more acceptable as a memorial of her love to God, than was the abundance of the selfish and rich.—Mark 12:42—44.

*I.* Of course, acts proceeding from such selfish considerations were not acceptable to God.

*P.* Had you, in pursuance of the hasty advice of friends, made a public profession of religion by uniting with the visible church, it would have been a selfish proceeding; and instead of relieving your troubles, it might have greatly increased them. Your object would have been merely to fortify your hope and to render sure your future selfish happiness, by means of pleasing Christ in the discharge of that duty. That step consequently would not have effected any change in your moral character before God, however happy it might have made you for a season. It would have been evidence only that you sincerely believed yourself to be a Christian, or else that you wanted to become what you supposed would be one; which very sincerity would only have made the grasp of error and delusion the more powerful, since sincerity never makes us really what we think we are, while it hinders the discovery of our mistake. By such a profession you would have been placed under influences which would have stimulated your efforts more earnestly perhaps, and these would have quieted your fears, and made you a more easy prey to selfishness and destruction; but it could not have kept you from backsliding in heart, or rather from relapsing into open selfishness, for you never had any holy principle to recede from. That secret reluctance you spoke of to unite with the church, was probably the dissuasions of a reproving conscience, excited by the serious nature of the contemplated duty. Thousands have been hurried into the visible church, or have hastily gone there of their own minds, who had no better qualifications than yourself; and when there, have pressed on in their selfish hopes, and pleasures, and duties, mistaking themselves for Christ's children; and not a few have so commingled their selfish ideas, and principles, and practices with those of true believers, that religion in its purity, beauty, and holy and energetic impulses, has become very much impaired in many of the churches.

*I.* I see that I would have been selfish in making such a public profession of piety. But would it not have been easier to have truly repented, had I used the means of uniting with the church?

*P.* No. There would have existed increased impediments in your own heart, and you would have been liable to false advice under the mistaken idea that you was a Christian, which you have now escaped—even had God in his mercy led you to be willing to discern and acknowledge that mistake at all. Still, I have known many in the visible church, who were self-deceived, who discovered their error, and gladly fled from it to the Rock of ages, and found shelter and support under his shadow. O, how have they rejoiced in God over their deliverance from sin into his love!

*I.* And well they might. Were I in the church, and had I any serious reason to doubt my own piety, not an hour should be lost from testing my feelings and conduct by the clear light of truth; and if my doubt should prove well founded, I would instantly reject my hope, and seek the true ways of Christ. I can conceive of no more unpleasant position than to have entered the church, sincerely believing that I was in the right discharge of a duty, and then to find reasons for apprehending that I was mistaken. Knowing that I was not willful in it, in respect to a knowledge of being wrong, or in respect to thinking I might not eventually become right, no consideration on earth should withhold me;—especially as it would be a private matter between God and my own heart.

*P.* Such was the commendable resolution taken by a lady who had mistaken conviction for conversion, and had united with the church. She became doubtful at first of her piety from hearing Christians describe their holy exercises; and at last she was convinced. She applied to her Pastor and Elders for advice; but they refused to treat her as deceived, since she had enjoyed a hope and had been correct in her deportment. Under their instructions, she tried to feel and live better; but the Spirit happily tore away her refuges, and she renounced her hope. Persisting in her own conviction of her true state, after a time the Lord delivered her from spiritual bondage; and she rejoiced, as a new-born soul, in the hope of the glory of God. But for her decision, she would probably have been lost.

*I.* In such a case, caviling or delay must be ruinous.

*P.* Let me here remark that in those particulars in which the exercises of the Christian, as before given, seem to have agreed with yours, you will observe that his were not selfish, although they contemplated the gratification of his natural desires; for they were held subordinate to God, and subservient to his glory; and the happiness taken in them was not independent of God, but under the acknowledged and loved supervision of his authority. This deposition of his happiness from the position of a *preference* to God, removed the stamp of selfishness from it; and the subordination of it in his heart to the purposes of the divine glory, made that an occasion of holiness which before was only an instrument of sin.

*I.* I see the difference.

*P.* To return. In respect to yourself and those whose exercises have been now examined, you can discern the selfish principle pervading and producing whatever other feelings and conduct was entered upon, and which I have not particularized, provided you will be candid with yourself and ingenuous in regard to the truth. As your hopes and pleasures became familiar, the desires for your future happiness were in a great degree satisfied, and they consequently failed to impel you as powerfully as before to keep up your evidences. Sin entered in, exciting your fears and arousing your conscience, until religion and its duties lost most of their enjoyments; and as your hope failed you gradually turned to the world for that gratification which you had so much ceased to find in religion. Here was no backsliding, but a mere modification of the action of your selfish heart; it again sought its chief end, happiness, in the pursuits of the world, instead of in the hope of future safety and peace; and its moral character was precisely the same. And it would have been the same, had you persevered in external duties, and only partially turned to the world; for your own future enjoyments or temporal interests would have swayed you in each.

*I.* Yes; I see the principle involved in my relapse, and it was mere selfishness. Self-love, as I now perceive, has often led me to mistake my right theories for my principles of action.

*P.* Without going into an unnecessary minuteness of detail, you will remember that, in every extremity, the recurrence to your early new and happy feelings always partially revived your hope, so that in every subsequent effort hitherto you have been influenced by your desires to secure your own future happiness; that your efforts to go anew to Christ, to do your first works over again, and other endeavors, have all been made with a view to regain your former supposed evidences of safety and peace, or to acquire new and more lively ones if possible, so as to revive your hope; that your feelings have been pleasurably excited or have been disappointed, as you have from time to time thought you had succeeded in these efforts. In fine, you can now perceive that they have all been similar in kind to those which we have so minutely examined, and were therefore selfish.

*I.* Yes; it has been as you describe. I was aware of this similarity from the first but did not then perceive their entire selfishness.

*P.* And you are supremely selfish in heart at this very moment; for, as we have seen, your present strongest desire is to secure your own future happiness. You wish to accomplish it in a supposed proper way of course, since it can be had in no other; but, as has been abundantly shown, the desire to secure it in such way is purely selfish, your own happiness being the ultimate object.

*I.* I see it all now.

*P.* Probably your deportment has been correct; but your heart has been altogether wrong. "This people draweth nigh unto me with their mouth, and honoreth me with their lips, but their heart is far from me."—

Matt. 15:8. Selfishness, as we have seen, is capable of producing a correct deportment when it will best answer its purposes; but it is powerless to effect a reform of the heart. Says the pious Payson, "The manner in which people generally obtain a false hope is this: they first come to believe that God is reconciled to *them*, and then are reconciled to *him* on that account. The Christian is reconciled, because he is pleased with the whole character of God; but the other, because he hopes God is pleased with him." My friend, I am aware that you must now feel an increased desire to secure your eternal welfare, as much so perhaps as when you were under those convictions which terminated in attaining that hope we have so minutely considered. Now, suppose the intervening years, with all their resolutions, hopes, pleasures, anxieties and religious efforts, were effaced from your memory and from fact, would you not be conscious that your present desires for your future happiness are the same in every respect with those you possessed when under conviction? and would you even dream of making them the basis of a hope?

*I.* Obviously they are the same, though they may not be so strong and impulsive. You afford me no encouragement; perhaps I do not deserve any.

*P.* However grateful to my sympathies, to encourage would ruin you by falsehood—an act which no candid person would wish to have done.

*I.* But I possess no *feelings* of enmity against God?

*P.* No; the hostility lies deeper than that, in the antagonistic selfishness of the bent of your heart. If you should be so unhappy as to fall under the divine justice, hostile feelings will be the last things you would find absent.

*I.* I am convinced that my whole course has been entirely opposed to God and his glory.

*P.* Before we close this part of our subject, allow me to illustrate your series of exercises and their selfish character by a supposed case. *R.*, while possessing a strong natural love of life, suddenly falls into the water, and the imminent danger of death arouses his desires for life with great power. These would not indicate any new heart; they would be the decided exercise of his old one, or former love of life.

*I.* Certainly.

*P.* In like manner you originally possessed a desire of happiness, which you had permitted to become predominant; and when you began to realize your exposure to eternal perdition, the desire to do something to effect a deliverance was strongly excited. This feeling indicated, not a new heart, but the strength of your old one, or the former love of happiness.

*I.* I see it was so.

*P.* Suppose that a person should seize *R.* while in the act of drowning, and drag him into a boat. When he came to realize his deliverance and safety, he would rejoice in it with great delight. His feelings would be *new* because he had never before been placed in circumstances to elicit them, and they would be *happy* because his love of life was gratified; but they would be no evidence of a change of heart, being merely the excitements and enjoyments of his old one.

*I.* Yes; it is perfectly clear.

*P.* So, under your first resolutions, you hoped that

Christ had drawn you safely into the ark of salvation; and the belief of it produced enjoyments which were new, because you had not before possessed such a hope, and happy, because your desires of deliverance from punishment were hopefully gratified. But these were obviously only the pleasures of the old heart—not the affections of a new one.

*I.* I wonder how I fell into the mistake of thinking they were evidences of a *change* of heart!

*P.* When *R.* should discover who was his deliverer, he would naturally feel grateful to him for his kindness, whether he was a moral man or not; and he would regret any previous injury he had done him, whether he was justified in the injurious act or not. These would be the natural workings of his old heart, in view of the great benefit he had received; they would constitute no new heart, or new affections in respect to their moral character.

*I.* I perceive they would not.

*P.* And precisely such was your gratitude to Christ for his supposed kindness in delivering you, and such were your regrets in view of the unkindness of your conduct to him in return for his goodness. They were irrespective of his moral character, and the natural results of your views of his friendship and expectation of his mercies, and partook not at all of a new heart.

*I.* I am convinced.

*P. R.* would naturally love those in the boat who sympathized with and encouraged him, as you liked Christians who did the same for you. He would, from the fresh impressions of his own recent danger, more earnestly desire the deliverance of other drowning persons, as you felt in regard to other lost sinners. If his safety seemed to require it, *R.* would seize an oar and labor to reach the shore, and even take pleasure in it on account of its contributing to his own escape, just as you took pleasure in pious duties (which had always before been distasteful) because they appeared necessary if you would reach the eternal shores with safety. In none of these things would a new heart appear, but only the natural feelings and fruits of the old one. And after *R.* should gain the shore, the excitement would soon subside, and with it all his pleasures and other feelings; just as did yours, after becoming accustomed to your hope, or on losing it.

*I.* Sir, you have said enough. I am convinced of my entire selfishness, and am only amazed that I was ever so blind as to be mistaken. May God forgive all those who aided me in that delusion!—for if my Christian friends had possessed sufficient knowledge to enlighten me, and had summoned decision enough to attempt it, I might long ago have been undeceived.

*P.* The more closely you scrutinize your past exercises, the more vividly will you be impressed with the fact that you started merely from a feeling of concern for yourself, and not for God; that you have ever since followed its leadings and impulses exclusively; so that while you thought you was on the Lord's side, you were altogether on your own.

*I.* I confess I was always afraid to scan my motives; and I now see that it was my selfish heart which prompted me to object to its being done by others. May God forgive me!

*P.* It follows that your hope, being entirely selfish, is perfectly invalid.

*I.* Yes; it is good for nothing. I am not experimenting with the truth now.

*P.* It further follows that you was mistaken in thinking yourself to be a Christian.

*I.* Yes; of course I am not a Christian.

*P.* Instead of being approved and accepted of God as one who possesses a holy character, he now disapproves and rejects you as unholy and entirely depraved in heart.

*I.* It is so; and he is just in his condemnation.

*P.* Should you die in your present selfish state of heart, God could not love, accept, or reward you in heaven. It is morally impossible for him to love what he disapproves, to accept what he cannot love complacently, or to reward where he neither approves nor loves. Were he to do so, (and I say it reverently,) the moral sentiments of all upright beings would condemn him; and he would become the reproach of the just and the scorn of the wicked. You can never enter heaven with your present unholy heart. "Know ye not that the unrighteous shall not inherit the kingdom of God?" —1 Cor. 6 : 9.

*I.* I have not the least expectation of being received into the favor of God, or of enjoying everlasting life, in my present state of heart.

*P.* And painful as the truth is, candor compels me to remind you that, should you die in your present state, you must be irretrievably lost. God is under a moral necessity to punish the incorrigible sinner. If you will remember, all your principles have been antagonistic to God, and the nucleus of all moral evil; your feelings and affections have all been estranged from him, and placed upon yourself; and when you have seemed to entertain regard for him, it was merely as one who would, as you supposed, pander to your unholiness, so that the stronger the expressions of such regard were, the more you dishonored him. Not unfrequently, perhaps, your mind has risen in hostility to him, especially in his sovereignty; you have indulged your evil passions as suited your own pleasure; in innumerable instances you have violated your obligations to him by disobeying his holy laws; and such of them as it was your policy to observe, were made the occasion of insults, since by rejecting him, their Maker, as your supreme motive, you treated him as unworthy to be regarded therein. Whether you have acted from reflection and deliberate purpose to disobey and dishonor God or not, does not affect your criminality, except in respect to the degree of its willfulness. You are an immortal being, destined to an endless existence; you have violated obligations infinite as that existence, as exalted as the majesty of Jehovah; and God is left no alternative but the exercise of a strict and rigid justice—a severity of vengeance—to punish you according to your deserts, while he shall make you an example of his power and wrath, and useful in perpetuating his eternal authority over others in the ages to come.—Rom. 9:22. "When they shall say, Peace and safety! then sudden destruction cometh upon them."—1 Thes. 5:3.

*I.* I deserve it all.

*P.* Should you die in your present state, your spirit would first fly away, and return to God who gave it.—Ps. 90:10; Eccl. 12:7. Then you would behold Jesus Christ your judge, in his glory; for it is he who will judge the world in righteousness.—Rom. 2:16.

There exists no difference of feeling or purpose toward the ungodly among the several Persons of the Trinity. "Woe unto the wicked, it shall be ill with him!" (Is. 3: 11), is their common feeling and determination. As you approach his bar, were it possible for Christ to weep there, his tear of compassion would fall upon you, while his dread voice, nerved by a righteous justice, would pronounce your doom: "Depart from me, ye cursed, into everlasting fire, prepared for the devil and his angels."—Matt. 25:41. And if there is a more bitter ingredient than any other in that terrible doom, it will be in the thought that you are self-ruined in defiance of even the death of the Son of God in the flesh?

*I.* I thank God for being delivered from my delusion and forewarned in time.

*P.* Were you compelled to hold fast to a blazing firebrand with your naked hands, the pain would produce an instinctive opposition to him who coerced it, whether he was justified in doing so or not; and with the increasing pain, your hostility would increase, and burn, and blaze to the height of your power. It would not be under your control in the least, and could suffer no alleviation or abatement so long as the painful cause existed. While you thus revolted against the inflicter of the pain, and while its infliction was continued, you could not love him; no pause in your hatred could then occur of which you could take advantage to excite love to him; while, on the contrary, instinctive hatred would reign in spite of yourself.

*I.* Certainly the natural love of happiness would produce an instinctive and unconquerable animosity against its destroyer.

*P.* On the same principle, when the divine wrath falls in agony on the lost soul for his unholy character, heart, and conduct, the intensity of his misery will produce a kind of instinctive hostility toward God, the inflicter. He will be totally unable to love him while under the pain and its resulting hostility; and while the punishment continued, not a moment could be found in which the soul could become released from its animosity so as to exercise love; and as long as the punishment is maintained, the hostility must continue, and with increasing intensity. But, that must be perpetuated so long as the reason for its original infliction remains—namely, the unholiness of heart and conduct of the sinner; and that reason will remain good as long as he continues a sinner; and as no change can possibly, under such circumstances, be effected in that respect, his punishment must endure for ever? Thus, you perceive, that reason itself indicates the principle that punishment, once inflicted, must be endless; as well as the ground which makes it a natural necessity, so to speak, when the soul has become once lost.—Rev. 19 : 3. It was not the least of the tokens of divine goodness, to reveal beforehand the certain and irreparable doom of the incorrigible sinner.

*I.* No one can fail to perceive, it seems to me, that there can be no radical change of affections toward one who punishes, while self-love is smarting and suffering under its torments; and that consistency evidently requires its continued infliction while the cause remains which originally produced it. It is indeed a mercy to forewarn us on this point.

*P.* Allow me now to invite your attention, with the

hope that it will be wholly given, to an important fact relating to your present position. You will understand that I do not now speak of what the Holy Spirit is able to accomplish, but merely of what you yourself, in your present moral position, cannot avoid. It is this: Every resolution you may now form to secure an interest in Christ, will necessarily be selfish. It is important for you to discern this fact clearly, in order to our future progress; and I will therefore endeavor to show its truth by proposing a few questions for you to answer. It is necessary that you should arouse your mind to action, if you would practically understand this fact; and I therefore wish you, if you please, to answer my questions aloud.

*I.* No doubt you have a good reason for the request, and my answers shall be made audibly.

*P.* You know you ought to serve the Lord: Will you endeavor to obey him hereafter?

*I.* (*aloud.*) Yes.

*P.* Why? Was it not because you desired to secure his favor, and thereby your own future safety and happiness?

*I.* It was, of course.

*P.* Consequently, you was selfish in that resolution. The same selfish desire for your own future happiness which has always heretofore influenced your efforts, produced this resolution.

*I.* I perceive it was so; having no other desires, it must necessarily have been a selfish influence.

*P.* Again; you are aware that you ought to leave yourself unreservedly in the hands of a sovereign God: Will you now let his will be done with you?

*I.* (*aloud.*) Yes.

*P.* Why? Was it not because you desired to secure your own future welfare, and hoped that he might accept, and pardon you in order thereto?

*I.* Yes; I hoped he might deliver me.

*P.* Being influenced by the same selfish desires as before, this resolution was equally selfish.

*I.* Of course it was.

*P.* Again; you ought to glorify God: Will you endeavor hereafter to promote his glory, in the supreme love of it?

*I.* (*aloud.*) Yes; I will try.

*P.* Why? Was it not from a desire to secure your own future happiness ultimately?

*I.* Certainly.

*P.* And, consequently, you were selfish in this resolution also. You preferred your own happiness, and sought ostensibly to glorify God, but it was merely as a means to secure your own ends. This was from no love to the divine glory, but it was an experiment to gratify your superior love to yourself.

*I.* I perceive it; and, indeed, loving *myself* supremely, how can I love *God* supremely, except in pretence?

*P.* You cannot. The grand difficulty in the way, is your predominant desire for your own happiness, which arises spontaneously whenever you attempt any thing. If this could be removed, you might act differently. I suppose you *desire* to get rid of this selfish preference?

*I.* Certainly I do.

*P.* But this desire is itself selfish, because it contemplates the promotion of your own happiness by means of getting rid of the preference.

*I.* Yes; I perceive it is selfish. Pray, how can I discard my desire?

*P.* You *desire* to discard it?

*I.* Yes, very much indeed.

*P.* Because it stands in the way of your acting in a proper manner to secure your future safety and peace?

*I.* Yes.

*P.* And, therefore, this last desire is equally as selfish as the other. But you wish to get rid of this last desire?

*I.* Yes, I do.

*P.* But it is for the same reason—namely, it stands in the way of securing your selfish happiness; and consequently, it is as selfish as either of the former.

*I.* Truly it is so.

*P.* And every desire you might form to get rid of your selfish desires, would be selfish for the same reason; and if you could retreat to the millionth desire in the backward train, *that* would be of the same character. And if you should look forward, and interpose every thing imaginable as an object, still the promotion of your own happiness would always be a more ulterior end, and that would stamp you with selfishness in every effort. Did I not say truly that, in your present state of mind, every such effort would be selfish?

*I.* Yes. It is now as clear as the light, that I have nothing but selfish desires to start with; and I fear that every effort toward Christ will be selfish of course, and that I must remain unholy in every endeavor. I seem to have lost all recuperative power.

*P.* And herein see the total moral depravity of your heart. "O Israel! thou hast destroyed thyself." To urge you to immediate repentance would seem like requiring one to make brick without straw, and I will reserve all suggestions on that point. We are now prepared to enter upon an investigation of the obstacles to your progress, without a clear knowledge of which we can make no advance with our subject. I have therefore to request your careful and candid attention to the contents of the next two chapters; and have to urge you not to pass them over, or in any way to anticipate the subjects out of the order in which I present them, however strongly you may feel inclined to do so. The reason is, that now your views are clear so far as we have progressed; but if you should anticipate the regular natural order of our subjects you will become confused, will be unable to understand the true meaning of much that may thereafter be presented, and may bitterly regret the consequences.

*I.* Sir, you have my confidence; and in deference to your opinions and wishes, as well as for my own enlightenment, I will follow this advice.

*P.* Let me request you now to retire to your closet, and there under the eye of God to review the principles of your past life, the unholy feelings you have indulged, and the various infractions in your external conduct against the precepts of the divine law. Seek the guidance of the Holy Spirit into all truth; and confess such of your sins as rise to memory, with a determination to forsake them, rather than with your usual petitions for their pardon. Under the solemn impressions thus obtained, we will resume the general subject.

*I.* I will implicitly follow these suggestions. I feel that I have no time to lose.

*P.* Beware of grieving the Holy Spirit by any inattention, now that your mind is becoming more alive to the subject. If you now waver in searching for the whole truth, with the purpose of observing it to the best of your ability, your day of grace may close. "Reprobate silver shall men call them, because the Lord hath rejected them."—Jer. 6 : 30.

*I.* I am determined to persevere, with the divine aid.

## CHAPTER VI.

### OBSTACLES TO THE SINNER'S PROGRESS.

*Pastor.* It will be in vain for you to anticipate any useful progress, until we have investigated the various secret obstacles which lie in your path, of the injurious nature of most of which you are unaware; for their very familiarity conceals their evil character, and induces you to consider and to confide in them as proper means.

*Inquirer.* It will be a satisfaction to prosecute such an inquiry.

*P.* Since our last interview, have you resolved to obey Christ, or to live to the glory of God?

*I.* I have. Of course my desires to find the right way to succeed have been strong, and I concluded to lay aside selfishness, obey God, and live to his glory hereafter.

*P.* Which, you trusted, might prove to be the right way to please God and secure your future happiness?

*I.* Yes; I knew of no other way.

*P.* And that was a selfish way, and you remained perfectly selfish in it. It was a mere experiment of your selfish heart to succeed in its own purposes. You did not, *in fact*, lay aside your selfishness, or obey God, or live to his glory in a supreme love to it; but you merely endeavored to do so, under the influence of your predominant desires for your own happiness, and as a means to effect that object ultimately; and consequently, the hope that you had succeeded, as well as the pleasurable feelings resulting from the hope, were as selfish as ever before. You did not, in reality, prefer God and his glory to yourself; but you endeavored again to subordinate him, his service, and glory, to your own ends.

*I.* I perceive the selfishness of the whole proceeding; and I thank you for developing it to me. It would only have again deluded me, and might have destroyed my soul; for I am well aware that perseverance in selfish pursuits, under the influence of selfish desires, can never lead to holy desires, or terminate in holy pursuits. And yet, some instructors would have encouraged that resolution, and would have urged me to perseverance and hope.

*P.* Superficiality in religious instruction is the great curse which afflicts the church. We are told that "he that winneth souls must be wise" (Prov. 11:30); and in order thereto, the workings of the human mind must be well understood, together with the peculiar adaptedness of the various truths to its various states; and there must be wisdom and tact in their application (Matt. 10:16), as well as a profound reliance on the Holy Spirit to give them efficacy.

*I.* If religion is a reasonable requirement, and if the service of God is so reasonable as the apostle alleges (Rom. 12:1), then, truly, it becomes its teachers to instruct like reasonable men. To do so must require much study, experience, and honesty of heart, and they remain inexcusable for their deficiencies.

*P.* Before we proceed, let me ask whether you have become entirely convinced of your impenitency, and that you must fall under the endless wrath of God if you die in this state of mind?

*I.* Yes; I am perfectly convinced that I must be lost without repentance, and that it will be just in God to inflict upon me the penalty of that law which I have so constantly violated.

*P.* Suppose one should offer you a large fortune, on condition that you should count from one up to ten thousand in the space of one minute; would you try to count it, with any expectation of success?

*I.* No; and therefore I should not try at all, however much I might desire the fortune.

*P.* On the principle that it would be of no use to try?

*I.* Certainly.

*P.* But you might be induced, as a mere experiment, to try and see how much you could count in that space of time; and the experiment, uniting with the previous convictions of your judgment as to the impossibility of succeeding, would effectually arrest all further endeavors. Reasonable people always abandon the pursuit of any desired thing, when they become convinced, by argument and experiment, that it is impossible to accomplish it; and they can lose nothing by desisting, since they could gain nothing by persevering. But we might argue and make trials with a lunatic ever so much, and he might still persevere in his vain efforts to count ten thousand in a minute, simply because he was disordered in intellect and incapable of self-control.

*I.* I hope always to act like a reasonable being; and,

you may be sure that whatever I may perceive to be out of my reach and useless to pursue, shall be most decidedly abandoned.

*P.* In resuming our main subject, I wish, among other things, to develop various errors of opinion and practice into which you have unconsciously fallen, and which have always hindered your progress; to expose several things which you have been attempting, but which you are neither required to accomplish, nor are able to effect, and the pursuit of which has perverted your whole course hitherto; and in the end, to explain the true meaning of the principle you have often heard advanced, that "*of ourselves* we can do nothing," or, as you would express it, nothing to make ourselves deserving of salvation. And this will lead us to notice what the Holy Spirit will do. As an incident, the entire selfishness of your heart and of your past efforts, will be more fully elucidated. Of course my object in this examination is not to show how you are to succeed in your desired happiness; for an examination of the difficulties in the way, is a different thing from showing how to accomplish your purposes. From your inveterate habit of looking upon every thing with that view, you will probably commence with various plans, and will regard the whole as intended to show you how to succeed; but if you will test the various points candidly, that impression will soon be removed.

*I.* I shall understand beforehand that it is not your object to show me, at present, how to succeed in my salvation.

*P.* And that you cannot succeed by the means we shall examine, even if you try

*I.* I understand you fully.

*P.* In order to raise the various incidental points just referred to, let me state a proposition for your practical investigation. It is one on which any one can act, whether he is a sinner or a Christian, but still without any mere personal advantage. It has no bearing on religion, as you have been accustomed to regard that subject; but is an exposition of mental action on moral principle, without the intervention of the affections.

*I.* Certainly, I should never expect to derive any substantial benefit from such heartless morality as you have now described.

*P.* The proposition is this: You or any other person, whether Christian or sinner, can resolve to do, or to refrain from doing, a thing relating to a mere moral subject, where love is not excited, where no personal benefit can accrue or be reasonably expected, and where no injury will result or can be reasonably apprehended from the resolution.

*I.* Please give me some illustrations of the point.

*P.* I will. But, in order clearly to understand my proposition, you must let your own mind act upon the illustrations; and I will therefore propose questions upon them, which you will please answer aloud, as before.

*I.* With much pleasure, for I like this practical mode; it gives one an experimental, and therefore a convincing knowledge of the subject, at once.

*P.* And I have further to request that you will refrain from trying to impress on your mind the truths we may examine, and from trying to feel them, or to get good out of them, as you have been heretofore accustomed to do. That course will divert your attention from the thoughts themselves; you will lose your time and labor, and I shall have presented them in vain.

*I.* But I always supposed that the way to get good out of religious truths, was to try to feel them in my heart. Do you object to the indulgence of feelings?

*P.* Of course not, if they are of the right kind; in which case, the more there are of them, the better it will be. But such feelings as you attempt to obtain in that way, are not of that kind, and never can be made so; for they are the expedients of the selfish heart, produced for an ulterior purpose. Let the truth produce its own legitimate impressions under God, and such genuine feelings will be far nearer right.

*I.* I will exercise my understanding only, and will not try hereafter to feel what you say. I see that it would be selfish and useless, as well as a hindrance to my undivided attention to your suggestions and arguments.

*P.* My first illustration is this: Suppose a stranger is walking before you, who happens to drop his knife; and as you advance, you pick it up, and I immediately ask: What do you propose to do with that knife? What would you answer?

*I.* (*aloud.*) That I would give it to the stranger.

*P.* That would be a resolution. I ask you again: Why do you resolve to give it to him?

*I.* Because it evidently belongs to him.

*P.* That would be the reason of your resolution. His right of property would make it right for you to return the knife. Would you try to excite love in your heart toward the stranger, in order to restore it?

*I.* No; that would be foolish.

*P.* Then you would resolve to restore the property without exercising any love. Would you expect to gain any personal benefit by returning it?

*I.* None in the least; there would be none to gain.

*P.* Then you would resolve without anticipating any benefit. Would you fear any personal injury?

*I.* None whatever.

*P.* Then you would resolve without apprehending any evil. In this case, therefore, where there was nothing to hope for or to fear, and where love was not produced, you could resolve to restore the property simply under the impression of its being right to do so. This would not make you a Christian, nor would it teach you how to become one, so as to succeed in your purposes.

*I.* I am not so foolish as to suppose that such an unfeeling and ordinary act would show me that.

*P.* Being so common, it fails to raise all the mental questions I wish to reach. In order to which, let me give another illustration to precisely the same point; and you must become a party in it, giving audible answers to my questions. I introduce the name of God, not to excite your love, for it cannot in your present selfish state of heart, but merely as a being who has rights, just as that stranger had; and not to teach you how to go to Christ, or how to obtain holy feelings, or how to accomplish, now or hereafter, any thing required in the Scriptures, so as to succeed in your purposes, as you will soon abundantly see.

*I.* If I cannot act from a right state of the heart, it can do me no good, of course. "With the heart man believeth unto righteousness."—Rom. 10:10. And

Christ requires that "faith which works by *love*."—Gal. 5:6. Here I have always been deficient.

*P.* The other illustration is this: God, having given you life, and having upheld it to this time, has an unquestionable right to recall it whenever he so wills. However strong your desire to live may be, it would be wrong in you to oppose God in recalling your life in his own appointed time.

*I.* It would be wrong, no doubt; but you state an apparently impossible case, for in what way can I oppose him?

*P.* I do not say that you can oppose him *successfully;* but you can resist him in your will, as well as in the use of forbidden means to preserve life.

*I.* True; and I ought not to do either knowingly, since he has a perfect right to recall it.

*P.* He will certainly recall your life at some future period; and for our present purposes we will suppose that he intends to do so when you reach the good old age of eighty years. Now, on this supposition, you ought not to oppose him in demanding it at that time.

*I.* I ought not; but I do not know that my resolution will be observed, if formed.

*P.* You cannot tell, to be sure; but let us suppose the resolution will be kept.

*I.* And I do not know that it will be of the right kind.

*P.* You may certainly know that it will not be of the kind you wish; for you are now selfish, and every resolution you make must be done, if at all, as you now are; that is, it must be formed with the selfish heart, and must therefore be itself selfish. But you will be equally selfish if you do not resolve; and hence you may as well resolve as decline.

*I.* True. I will answer your questions.

*P.* You ought not to oppose God in recalling your life—say, when you reach the age of eighty years: Will you oppose him?

*I.* (*aloud.*) No, I will not, on the supposition that I can then observe my present resolution.

*P.* You perceive that no change of heart has occurred; and that you have derived no personal benefit from this resolution.

*I.* I have not; but I rather expect it, when I come to understand you more perfectly.

*P.* In that you will find yourself mistaken; for whatever you might accomplish otherwise, you cannot do it by means of this illustration, as I will proceed to show while elucidating the main principle in view—namely, that you can resolve on a moral subject where love is not exercised, and where there is nothing personal to hope for, or to apprehend. It is clear that your old religious habits are revived while acting on this illustration; and that you will not abandon them until you become convinced, by experiment and argument, that you can derive no more advantage by resolving upon it, than you would by resolving to restore his knife to the stranger in the case supposed. There you saw that morality was not piety.

*I.* I confess that I did anticipate some help from it.

*P.* Let us see if you can obtain it; and you will permit me to repeat the question as often as it shall become necessary to test the action of your mind upon the point. I hope you will not become fatigued, if I frequently reiterate it.

*I.* Certainly not; you know best what to do.

*P.* On the supposition that God purposes to indulge you in a long life, but to recall it at eighty years: Will you oppose him in then recalling it?

*I.* (*aloud.*) No.

*P.* Notwithstanding all your wishes and effort, you have attained to no more love for God and his glory, by this resolution, than you had before.

*I.* No, I have not.

*P.* And you never can in your present state, though you should repeat the resolution a million times. One reason is this: your love of life is constitutional and unconquerable; and you cannot love any thing that opposes it, because no one can love two such opposite things at one and the same time. Thus you cannot love to surrender your life, because you now love to preserve it; you could not love to surrender it *to me*, or love *me* for taking it from you, should you try as long as life lasted.

*I.* Of course I could not, so long as I loved to retain life, which must be always.

*P.* And on the same principle, for it matters not who the destroyer is, you could not love to have God take your life, or love him for recalling it.

*I.* I see now that I could not.

*P.* Then why will you persist in trying to produce so vain a thing? A reasonable person will abandon what he sees he cannot accomplish; but a lunatic would as like as not persevere. It can do no harm to cease trying to excite love to a holy God in your selfish heart, since to try will do no good. Wherefore, I request that you will cease;—if you do not, you will never be able fully to understand my proposition.

*I.* I shall try no more to get love to God by means of this resolution. On reflection, I perceive the attempt would be foolish in opposition to my strong love of life.

*P.* But as you cannot get love to God, surely you cannot expect to succeed without it?

*I.* Certainly not.

*P.* And you will not, as will be abundantly seen. Will you oppose God in then recalling your life, seeing that you ought not?

*I.* (*aloud.*) No, I will not.

*P.* You can perceive that you have acquired no change, or other benefit by this resolution. But did you not mean by it to determine that you *ought not* to oppose him?

*I.* Yes, I resolved that I ought not.

*P.* But I did not ask you to resolve that you ought not, but that you *would* not. You then merely *assented* to the very palpable fact that you *should not* oppose him; while I wanted something further, a *determination* of the will that you *would not* do so. If your neighbor was starving, and I should ask you whether you would resolve to give him food, you would not merely reply that you *ought* to do so; that would be taken for granted by both of us; but your answer would be that you *would* do it. So it is not necessary to resolve that you *ought not* to oppose God in this respect; but the question is, Will you refrain from *doing* what you admit you ought not to do? Will you abstain from opposing God in recalling your life?

*I.* (*aloud.*) I will not oppose him. I understand the point better now. I ought not to do it, and I will not.

*P.* I wish you to keep your mind from wandering upon other subjects, and to confine your thoughts and answers to this illustration for the present.

*I.* I will do so.

*P.* On the supposition that you will be able to observe the resolution, will you oppose God in recalling your life?

*I.* (*aloud.*) No.

*P.* You have effected no change, nor have you acquired any benefit whatever from this resolution; nor will you if you repeat it for years.

*I.* I have no different feelings, nor any evidence of any success.

*P.* But did you not merely acquiesce in his recalling your life, because of the necessity of the case? You knew that you could not prevent God, and concluded that therefore you would not try?

*I.* Yes; I knew it would be of no use to oppose him.

*P.* It certainly would be in vain, for he is all powerful. While it is immaterial what your motives are, as respects any success in your object, since you can never learn how to secure your happiness by means of this illustration, yet I want some affirmative and positive action, rather than a reluctant acquiescence, in order to exhibit the point which I have in view; and the consideration of your inability to prevent God, cannot produce such action. Besides, so far as it influences you, it becomes an immoral and unworthy motive; for, to say that you will not oppose God because you cannot do it successfully, is only to show that you would do it if you could succeed. But you ought not, even if you could. If you had the power, in the case supposed, to prevent the stranger from recovering his lost knife, it would be disgraceful to use it; for might never confers a right. Should some superior being, who was able to do so, clothe you with power sufficient to prevent God from recalling your life, the desire of life might tempt you to hinder him; but, as he has lent it to you, and preserves it for you, it would still be wrong to use the power. It would be proper to employ it as against me, for I have no claims over your life; but, as against God, it would be shamefully improper. On the supposition that you now actually possess such power, will you use it to oppose God in recalling your life?

*I.* I will not, admitting that I could prevent him. It would be wrong.

*P.* Although this is a proper conclusion in a moral sense, it has not produced any change of heart, or enabled you to secure your future safety and peace?

*I.* I am aware that it has not.

*P.* Let me repeat the question: Will you oppose God in recalling your life?

*I.* (*aloud.*) No, I will not.

*P.* And you can perceive that no change or other benefit has resulted from this last determination.

*I.* None at all.

*P.* But did you not, in answering, try to feel *willing* to die, under the hope that you might become prepared for death and future happiness by that means?

*I.* Yes; I desired that evidence of a preparation, and hoped to answer in a proper way.

*P.* But could you become perfectly willing to die, it

would be no valid evidence, in itself, that your heart was in a state of preparation for a holy existence beyond the grave. In fact, no one can be willing to die, in itself considered; for the desire of life is a constitutional propensity which cannot be obliterated. The sinner, under the temporary influence of overwhelming cares, the wasting debility of sickness, intense bodily suffering, or a hope of safety and ecstatic happiness hereafter, may become *more* willing to be relieved, or to enter upon such enjoyment, than to retain his life; but such a state of mind is purely selfish, and constitutes no preparation of heart for the scenes which await the saint in eternity. There can be no preparation for them short of a preference of God and his glory; and whoever has that is in a proper state, whether, under the circumstances, he is willing or reluctant to surrender life in itself considered. You can perceive, therefore, that could you actually become willing to die by means of resolving on this illustration, it could not benefit you in respect to your desired safety and happiness; and that it will be folly to expect or seek for it.

*I.* I am convinced of the uselessness of trying to feel willing to die, and will attempt it no more.

*P.* I ask again: Will you oppose God in recalling your life?

*I.* (*aloud.*) No.

*P.* You have acquired no change of heart by this resolution?

*I.* No, I have not.

*P.* Nor have you derived any worldly or temporal benefit from it; nor would you, by observing it perfectly.

*I.* None whatever. It never occurred to me to look for worldly advantage from the resolution; for as it has not the least bearing on that subject, there is no such good to be obtained from it.

*P.* Will you oppose God in recalling your life?

*I.* (*aloud.*) No.

*P.* You have effected no change, as you can perceive. Nor have you, as you expected, escaped from sin, so as to please God and secure your safety and peace.

*I.* I did hope to, but have not succeeded.

*P.* God has not given to his creatures the power to determine how long they shall live; and, so far as I am aware, the Scriptures do not any where present such a resolution as this for our adoption. I have taken it up for the purposes that have been suggested. It would answer most of them, to substitute Mohammed in place of God as having such right over your life; and it would have this advantage—namely, that the merely moral aspect of the point would be so clear that you would not in the least expect to escape sin, so as to please God and secure your happiness by means of it; but I will use no such supposition in respect to that imposter. Your own experiments abundantly prove that no resolution on this illustration can benefit you in that respect; while your sound judgment must satisfy you, even without an experiment, that a heartless resolution, as in the present case, must be unavailing.

*I.* I now clearly see that I cannot escape sin by it so as to please God and secure my happiness; and I shall not try hereafter.

*P.* Will you oppose God in recalling your life?

*I.* (*aloud.*) No.

*P.* No change has been secured, as you can see; but did you not endeavor to form a strong resolution?

*I.* Yes. I wanted one, as a friend once expressed it, as big as a mountain; one which would be adequate to the occasion, and which I should be sure to keep.

*P.* Of course the resolution should be observed; but the effort to make one deep and strong will no more insure that, than if it was made in a natural way. Your object was to get some benefit out of the effort; but in this you must fail, even if you could be as profound as you desire. Where the heart is not enlisted for the glory of God, no such substitute will avail. I recommend you to try it no more; for you will fail in your object, and it will prevent your understanding the point which I wish to make clear to your mind.

*I.* I shall not do any thing knowingly to hinder your opening my understanding on that subject; and will make no further efforts to form a profound resolution. I will answer naturally, just as I did in the case of returning the knife to the stranger.

*P.* That will be right, although it will effect no personal benefit. I have now proved that you cannot resolve on this illustration with love to God, or learn by it how to love him hereafter, so as to succeed. I have also proved that there is nothing personal to gain, and therefore nothing to hope for, by resolving upon it; that you cannot become willing to die so as to be prepared, nor can you escape from sin so as to please God and secure your pardon, peace, and safety. This substantiates two of my propositions—namely, that on a moral subject any person can resolve to do or not to do a thing, where love is not excited, and where there is nothing to gain or hope for. I think you must now be convinced that you cannot, by means of this illustration, learn how to love God so as to succeed; and that there is no personal benefit whatever to be acquired by means of any resolution you can form upon it.

*I.* I am perfectly convinced; and shall try no more to resolve upon it with love; and it is evident that I can reasonably expect no good that I desire from it.

*P.* One fair experiment upon any point should be as conclusive as a thousand, and will be so received by every reasonable person. You will next observe, that you hazard nothing by this resolution, because it can place you in no greater danger than you are in already. In the first place, to form it in a wrong or selfish manner, can be no more displeasing to God, than any other act where every thing you do is selfish.

*I.* Certainly God cannot be specially offended by such an act.

*P.* Again: your life is already entirely within his power. No resolution you can form will make him destroy it any the sooner; for he has already determined our days (Job 14:5), and he is neither to be so displeased, or pleased, by any thing you can do, as to change his purpose. You have nothing to fear, therefore, in respect to placing your life in his hands, or in incurring any greater immediate or remote hazard.

*I.* I perceive it will make no difference whatever in those respects.

*P.* Nor will you be punished any the sooner. You probably feared that you might be punished immediately unless you formed the resolution right, and this, perhaps, made you hesitate; but, however it may be formed, your day of retribution cannot be hastened. God is not affected in this respect, as sinners seem to suppose, by what they may please to do, or refuse to do.

*I.* I see that my punishment would be rendered no more certain, or near, by resolving on the question.

*P.* Let us test the point whether you have any thing to fear: Will you oppose God in recalling your life:

*I.* (*aloud.*) No.

*P.* Are you now any more in the power of God than before? is your life or soul in any greater or more immediate danger?

*I.* No. I am now convinced that I have nothing to apprehend in forming the resolution.

*P.* You have nothing to fear; and as I stated at first, you cannot do it with love, and there is nothing to hope for. Why then try to have love, or why expect any thing, or why fear any injury from it?

*I.* I neither expect nor fear any thing from it. I understand the subject better now.

*P.* Will you oppose God in recalling your life?

*I.* (*aloud.*) No.

*P.* You have effected no change, of course; but did you not endeavor to resolve *sincerely*, so as to become willing not to oppose God?

*I.* Yes; I did endeavor to be sincere in it.

*P.* I perceive you have introduced one of your old religious habits into this moral illustration, as I supposed would be the case; and as this is one of the hindrances which I proposed to explain, we will look at the character of that habit for a few moments. Whenever you have endeavored, in past years, to give yourself up to God, you have always tried to do it sincerely; and in order to be sincere, you have sought to produce sorrow for sin, love to God, deeper anxieties for your salvation, and the like, under the supposition that, if you could give yourself up to him with a sufficient degree of feeling, it would be done sincerely, and that he would then pardon and accept you?

*I.* Yes. I have always tried to summon sincere feelings; for I could not otherwise be accepted.

*P.* A careless resolution can be of no avail of course; for it does not carry the mind with it. But even where the mind has become most intensely interested, the way you adopted has no tendency to produce a properly sincere resolution.

*I.* Indeed! If the effort to be sincere in my feelings is wrong, pray how am I ever to resolve sincerely?

*P.* Will you oblige me by carefully reading over my last remarks, a few lines above?

*I.* Yes, to oblige you.

*P.* Then do so, before you proceed any further. * * * * *. When you consented to read those lines, was you sincere in it?

*I.* Yes; I meant to do it.

*P.* But you did not make any effort to mean it? You did not *try* to be willing to read them? You did not seek to produce sorrow, or love, or anxiety, or any other feeling, in order to be sincere in your consent to read them?

*I.* No; that would have been absurd on such a subject. I just consented without any effort.

*P.* And you became willing to read over my remarks?

*I.* Yes.

*P.* What evidence have you of being sincere?

*I.* The evidence of consciousness that I meant it; but I had no excitement of feeling. Besides, I know I was sincere because I actually read over those lines.

*P.* Your religious purposes did not any more require such efforts after feeling, in order to be sincere, than did this consent to read those lines. And such efforts were as absurd in those cases, as they would have been in this, besides being selfish and impracticable.

*I.* Will you please explain this? I always thought sinners should anxiously try to feel love, sorrow, and the like, in order to be sincere in their dedication.

*P.* To do so, is a futile effort on their part to act upon mental principles for which nature has made no provision, but which selfish persons, and some Christians in their ignorance, are always insisting upon. If you had concluded to purchase some goods because you were suited with the quality and price, you would ridicule the merchant if he should refuse to sell them simply because he doubted your sincerity from seeing no exhibition of feeling on your part. You would tell him that those motives for the purchase, rather than any casual emotions which might or might not be excited in the mind, were the best test of the sincerity of your purpose. All your expedients to mean or feel what you resolved upon, were selfish; for you acted under the impulse of your selfish desires for safety and peace in all of them, and your ultimate aim was to secure your future happiness.

*I.* That certainly was my object.

*P.* And you took a very unwise course to obtain it, if you will allow me to say so, as I will show. Suppose you had my watch in your possession, and that you desired exceedingly to retain and use it; but I come and demand its return to me as a matter of right. Instead of frankly consenting to restore it, you cast about for some plan to make me willing to leave it in your possession; and you finally conclude that if you can consent to return it with feelings of love, sorrow, and the like, and if you can really mean it, you will succeed in making me favorably disposed to your retaining the watch. Accordingly, when I ask you for it, you begin a mental struggle after right feelings, and try to mean it, as you drawl out a consent; but when I reach forth my hand to take it, you draw back and refuse, alleging that you had not consented sincerely, and that you must try again, hoping to bring me over to your designs? This would be rank selfishness, as well as folly; and only upon my peremptorily demanding the watch, declaring that in no event should it be returned to you, would you abandon such expedients, and consent, though reluctantly, to restore it to me. And precisely similar were your efforts to be sincere in giving yourself to God; you wanted at such times to consent with feelings of sorrow for sin, love to God, and the like, in order to render him favorable, so that you might get safely across that gulf of perdition which intervened between you and Christ.

*I.* I see it now perfectly. It was all selfish.

*P.* But, in addition, those efforts after right feelings were totally impracticable; for you were engaged in an expedient to produce holy exercises out of an unholy heart!—a thing which no one, not even God himself, is able to accomplish. It is a moral contradiction, and therefore a moral impossibility. "Who can bring a clean thing out of an unclean? Not one."—Job 14:4. None but unholy feelings can be exercised by an unholy heart. "An evil man, out of the evil treasure of his heart, bringeth forth that which is evil."—Luke 6:45. God requires, therefore, a *new* heart, and not a rēmodeling of the old one with its selfish impulses and exercises.—Ez. 18:31.

*I.* I am convinced of the uselessness of my efforts to acquire sincere feelings, or to mean things.

*P.* The sooner you abandon them, the better for you; for they have already made you so habitually selfish, that it is doubtful whether you can break their chains. "Can the Ethiopian change his skin, or the leopard his spots? then may ye also do good [turn to a supreme love to God in your heart, and live in a holy obedience in your deportment] who are accustomed to do evil," who are habituated to indulge the selfish heart, and to live in disobedience to God.—Jer. 13:23. To abandon them can never do you harm, since the pursuit of them can never do you good, as I have had occasion to remark before.

*I.* I will never again try in such ways to be sincere.

*P.* But further: Whenever you have thus tried to give yourself to God sincerely, you expected, if successful, to *know it*, by having some new and happy feelings occur, or some sense of pardon given to you, as an evidence that you were accepted of God?

*I.* Certainly; I always expected such a change whenever I obtained feeling enough.

*P.* When you consented just now to read over those lines, did you have any new feelings burst in upon you, as an evidence that you was sincere in the consent, and that no injury would befall you?

*I.* No; it would have been absurd to look for them in such a case.

*P.* But how do you know that you was sincere in that consent?

*I.* Because I was conscious of having made up my mind to read the lines, and because I actually read them, as I observed before.

*P.* And such is the rational evidence from consciousness and action which we are to receive in the other case also. In the first place, your endeavors after such feelings as evidences of your acceptance were purely selfish, and they retained you in selfishness. When you made the attempt, and paused to see whether any change had occurred, it was an undisguised plan to ascertain whether you had got safely across that gulf of perdition—whether you had succeeded in pleasing God, and in securing your eternal safety and peace.

*I.* Yes; I perceive that I wanted them as evidences of my own deliverance, rather than of the glory of God.

*P.* And the more anxiously you sought them, the more habitually selfish you became. Consequently, unless these plans are abandoned, the habit will be your ruin.

*I.* I will never try it again.

*P.* Such mechanical efforts must necessarily be unavailing. But, in the next place, all the feelings which you could so acquire would be selfish; for, as the efforts were those of the selfish heart, the feelings must have the same character as their source. Accordingly, you have discovered that all those which you obtained at the time of your first hope, such as the relief, the satisfaction at the thought of being in a hopeful way, the pleasure of thinking that you were actually changed, the hope of pardon and its pleasures, and the like, were all selfish and spurious, and no valid evidences whatever of a change of heart or of your acceptance with God.

*I.* Yes; I see they must be selfish still.

*P.* The Christian—he who prefers God and his glory to all other things—will eventually have those spontaneous holy affections before described; but these are far different from those you sought.

*I.* I perceive it; and shall beware of being again deluded by them. But I supposed that God would give them in answer to prayer.

*P.* We do not live in an age of miracles. Their object having been accomplished, they have ceased; and to revive and make them common, would destroy the main foundation on which the evidences of the inspiration of divine revelation rests. Revelation discloses what are the valid evidences of regeneration, as we have seen. Besides, should God give you, either suddenly or gradually, such evidences as you desire, he would become an accomplice in your unholiness by aiding your selfish projects; which, as we have seen, would most effectually destroy his own character and ruin him. But he will never thus "disgrace the throne of his glory."—Jer. 14: 21. Consequently, your attributing to him, and as his gift, those selfish feelings you cherished, was a gross insult to God.

*I.* I cannot reasonably expect them from him, either suddenly or gradually.

*P.* As all such efforts to be sincere, and to obtain

16

feelings are so useless and selfish, abstain from them hereafter; and when you resolve upon any thing, or when you answer any of my questions, do it in a natural way, just as you consented to read over those lines, and without looking for evidences. This is the only way in which the mind can act on such occasions; but you will not, even in this manner, secure your selfish happiness or learn by it how to succeed. Especially in acting upon the moral illustration I have presented, where you can derive no personal benefit under any circumstances, avoid *trying* to mean what you say, trying to be sincere or to arouse feelings, and looking for a change or evidence—for all will be in vain

*I.* I am convinced of it, and will not try again

*P.* Permit me to put these points to a practical test by repeating my question, and by your answering without any effort to be sincere, or to secure an evidence: Will you oppose God in recalling your life?

*I.* (*aloud.*) No, I will not.

*P.* Did you try to mean it, or try to have sincere feelings, or endeavor to obtain an evidence?

*I.* I did not.

*P.* But you have effected no such change or other benefit, even in this way, as I said. Still, never repeat your former useless, selfish, and ruinous plans to be sincere, or to secure an evidence of safety.

*I.* I never will.

*P.* Thus, it is shown that one can resolve on a moral subject, where love is not excited, and where there is nothing either to hope for or to fear. If I understand you aright, you have now resolved not to oppose God in recalling your life, but without being induced thereto by love, and without hoping for any benefit, and without fearing any injury?

*I.* Yes. I have acquired no love to God, nor have I been in any wise benefited or injured. It is singular that I should have expected any advantage from such a resolution. Even to the last, I hoped it would afford some valuable information how to succeed hereafter.

*P.* And this, in defiance of both reason and experience! Well may you tremble at the strength of your selfish habits, since they even pervert your reasonable conclusions. It is evident that you still suppose that this is some plan adopted to enable you to succeed in your object, notwithstanding my declarations and the abundant proofs to the contrary; and this makes it necessary to examine what you can and cannot do, on religious subjects generally, which we will enter upon in the next chapter. Let me request your patient and deliberate attention while pursuing this important subject.

*I.* You have my confidence. I will dispassionately investigate every subject you may present; and will take my position firmly upon each, as the truth shall require.

## CHAPTER VII.

### OBSTACLES TO THE SINNER'S PROGRESS.

*Pastor.* LET us now examine somewhat minutely the feasibility of your efforts, in your present state of mind, to succeed on subjects of a confessedly religious character. The inquiry will convince you that all will be entirely selfish, and therefore unavailing; and you will then be able more intelligently to appreciate the office of the Holy Spirit. I propose, as before, to ask questions for your audible answers; I wish you to answer without any efforts at sincerity or for evidences, meaning what you say precisely as you would mean a resolution on any ordinary subject. I hope you will remember my suggestion, that one good argument, or one unsuccessful experiment, is as valid and should be as convincing as ten thousand, and that by yielding to such convictions you will save an unnecessary loss of time.

*Inquirer.* I will do as you advise. I perceive that you understand my exercises and expedients far better than I do myself; and I shall hereafter be governed by your opinions in these respects.

*P.* And you may rest assured that your confidence shall not be abused. In order to be thorough, it will be necessary to repeat a question or two already proposed. You will find that the predominant desire for your own happiness will influence you in every answer; that every thing you attempt will be as an expedient or means to accomplish such desire; and that, however much you may labor to dismiss the idea, every thing, and even such labors themselves, will be done with an ultimate view to effect your own future safety and happiness.

*I.* If so, I shall be most profoundly selfish in them all.

*P.* Let us now test that fact. Will you serve the Lord hereafter?

*I.* (*aloud.*) I will endeavor to do so.

*P.* Why? You acted from a *desire* to serve him, did you not?

*I.* Yes; I should like to, if I could do so in a proper way.

*P.* And you desired to do so in order to please him, and thereby secure your future safety and peace?

*I.* Yes, of course. I have no other predominant desire than that for my own welfare.

*P.* And, consequently, you were selfish in this resolution to serve him. It was a plan to accomplish your selfish happiness.

*I.* I perceive that I was entirely selfish in it.

*P.* This desire, as we have seen, has become so habitual, and is so endeared to your heart, that it rises and influences your actions in spite of every effort to the contrary, whenever those subjects are presented which involve your eternal welfare. Should you persevere for an hour, the same desire would be excited, and would influence you each time; and should you persevere for a day, a week, a month, a year, and all the years of your life, it would be excited on each occasion; with this difference only, that on every repetition it would become more habitual and decisive, if possible, and thus insure absolute ruin. The path of safety, therefore, is far from encouraging such desires, or from relying upon any resolutions or other efforts produced under them. If you are wise, you will renounce all confidence in them, and will cease making any further experiments to succeed.

*I.* I perceive that, having only such desires to influence me, every resolution of obedience must be formed under them; and every effort to avoid the desire being selfish, the resolution must be unavailing. I do not need an hundred experiments to convince me of this; nor that the oftener I repeat the resolution, the more habitual my selfishness will become; nor that I cannot succeed hereafter in that which is impossible now, since hereafter the difficulties must be increased rather than diminished. I will make no more endeavors to succeed by such means.

*P.* Correctly said; and I repeat again that you can lose nothing by such a determination, since you could gain nothing by persevering. Still, God remains entitled to your holy service even though you have placed yourself in so helpless a position; and he will never surrender his claim.

*I.* I admit it.

*P.* Treat every other selfish expedient in the same manner, and you will speedily arrive at a correct knowledge of the whole subject.

*I.* Of course I shall not, knowingly, waste my efforts upon the repetition of any act, which it is before seen must be selfish.

*P.* Our natural sympathies always indicate that we should endeavor to promote the best good of society, of our country, and of the world at large: Will you endeavor to do so?

*I.* (*aloud.*) Yes; if it could be done in a proper way.

*P.* That is, in a way to please God, secure his pardoning favor, and thereby your own future happiness?

*I.* Yes; such was my desire.

*P.* And consequently, you were entirely selfish in it, for the reasons before given. However strong your sympathies, they belong to one's *natural* character, and your's are under the domination of your selfish desires; that is, you indulge your benevolence solely in order to gratify yourself; whereas, God requires a holy *moral* character, and the subserviency of those sympathies to his glory ultimately.

*I.* You are right. I never before so distinctly perceived the utter selfishness of those ostensibly benevolent feelings and practices of patriotism, philanthropy, and the like, on which so many rear their invalid hopes of their own future happiness. I shall try no more to succeed by such means, for I see that to repeat such resolutions is merely to strengthen my selfish influences.

*P.* Well said; but you are, notwithstanding your morally helpless position, bound by the command of God to love your neighbor, and to do unto others as you would that they should properly do unto you.

*I.* I admit it; but still it could not be made availing with God.

*P.* Will you now yield yourself up to God without question, that his sovereign will may control you and your destiny?

*I.* (*aloud.*) Yes.

*P.* Because you desire and hope that he may become

reconciled and favorably disposed, whereby you may escape his wrath and secure future peace?

*I.* Yes, such was my desire and object; I cannot help it.

*P.* And evidently it was selfish; for you sought, not the authority and sovereignty of God, but your own ends by means of them. The expectation or view with which we do a thing, forms the controlling reason of the act; so that when that fails, the act is rescinded of course. Thus, your selfish view in this ostensible act of submission having failed of being accomplished, the resolution is revoked with it; and you are now no more submissive to the divine sovereignty than before.

*I.* That is true. I fear my offended judge, and cannot avoid such desires. But I see it will be impossible to succeed by such means, and I will attempt it no more.

*P.* It would be in vain, were you to persevere all your days; but God still retains, and will insist upon his sovereign rights over you. Your inability, arising from your own voluntary, free, and habitual selfishness, does not release you from your obligations to him.

*I.* Not at all. I have myself only to blame.

*P.* Will you confide in Jesus Christ and his atonement?

*I.* (*aloud.*) Most joyfully.

*P.* No doubt; for it would be a great pleasure to secure the happiness you have in view, by that means. But in the first place, your confidence is selfish because your own safety and happiness is the ultimate object which you desire to accomplish by him. And in the next place, were he to aid you in this, he would, as we have seen, become your accomplice in sin.

*I.* I am convinced that I cannot, in my present state, succeed by means of a confidence in Christ. I have often wondered that the most irreligious men should express as strong a hope in Christ's pardoning mercy as the most devoted Christians. I was once inexpressibly pained on hearing of two naval officers who had shot one another in a duel, and lay stretched out on the field, express a belief, that through the pardoning mercy of Christ, they should soon meet each other in heaven! But I could not, before, so clearly discern the horribly depraved character of the selfish principle that could so unhesitatingly, audaciously, and confidently, subordinate Christ to its own purposes, and his atonement to such unholiness.

*P.* Making Christ a minister of sin, seems to be the current religion of the unregenerate portion of Christendom; with what ill success, eternity will painfully disclose. A consciousness of unrepented sin, will almost as effectually, for the time being, confound and dispel the true believer's hope in Christ, as though he had never indulged one. But you are aware that pardon is freely tendered to us upon condition of repentance for sin: Will you now, in heart and in life, turn away from all sin?

*I.* (*aloud.*) Yes, so far as I can.

*P.* Under the desire and hope of thereby securing the pardon and your own future happiness?

*I.* Yes; it was with such a view, of course.

*P.* But that is perfectly selfish, and is not the repentance which God requires. It does not proceed from a love to God and his glory which would make you abhor iniquity as such; but it is the repentance of the world, which we are told "worketh death;" it springs from the desire to secure your own ends by its means. To repeat the effort will be in vain, and can only increase your difficulties.

*I.* I see you are right. I shall try to succeed by this means no more.

*P.* You could not succeed, if you should try. Let me here repeat a former question: Will you hereafter live to the promotion of the glory of God, in the supreme love of it?

*I.* (*aloud.*) Yes; I should like to do so, and will endeavor to glorify him.

*P.* Because you desire and hope to please him and secure your happiness, if it is done in the manner you contemplate?

*I.* Yes; such was my wish and expectation.

*P.* And you remain as selfish in the attempt, as you were before. It was a plan to secure your own ends by means of God and his glory, you preferring those ends as before. This is living unto yourself, and not unto God. After having so often and vainly repeated this experiment, it would seem that you must be convinced of its uselessness.

*I.* I am; and will attempt no more to succeed by means of it.

*P.* But still the right of God in that respect, remains. Will you try to find the *right way* to serve the Lord?

*I.* That is the very thing I am constantly attempting.

*P.* And you are as constantly selfish in it, because you desire to find it in order to secure your selfish ends; that is, as the proper or feasible way, if that were possible, to secure your own future happiness; and such desire influences you in spite of yourself, you having no power by which to expel or overcome it. If you will consider the point calmly and judiciously, it will be evident that every attempt to do any duty in the right way, as you call it, can be conducive to nothing but selfishness. You started originally to find the supposed right way; your efforts retained you in its bonds; and you have ever since labored for the same thing, and are still in its chains; and it follows that every future attempt must produce the same result.

*I.* It looks strange that it should be so; but the fact is too evident to be doubted. I will try no more to find the right way to succeed in my desires. Nothing but some wrong way seems left to me.

*P.* And a wrong way can never enable you to succeed. Let us test this point further: Will you try to forget yourself and overlook your own happiness, and serve the Lord for the sake of his glory?

*I.* (*aloud.*) Yes; I have tried that repeatedly.

*P.* Under the thought that it might prove the right way to succeed?

*I.* Yes; such was my hope, of course.

*P.* But that was purely selfish. It was a pretended effort to abandon selfishness, as a means and with a more ultimate view to secure your selfish ends! Besides, you cannot forget and overlook your selfish happiness by trying to; for the very effort retains it in your thoughts, and makes it influence your desires and consequent actions. You never have succeeded in forgetting any thing or any subject, by trying to forget it.

*I.* That is true. It will be in vain to try to forget

myself, or to overlook my selfish object; and I shall not again attempt to succeed by it.

*P.* If you should *happen* to forget yourself so far as to have no distinct thought of your happiness at the time, it would not enable you to succeed; for, amongst other reasons, the desire would remain and would insensibly influence all your actions, under the force of habit. Thus, when you have been actively engaged in business, and your attention has been so engrossed in your occupations as to have lost all thought of yourself, you have still been selfish in every act; because your desires controlled you by the power of habit, and were even more unchecked through the abstraction of your attention to those immediate occupations.

*I.* I see clearly that, while my motive influences remain selfish, to forget myself will be of no avail.

*P.* Please to answer my question quickly, and without any forethought: Will you take the Lord's side?

*I.* (*aloud.*) Yes.

*P.* Because you wished to see whether a rapid resolution would avail you in your object? But you can perceive that you remain as selfish as before; and that it is of no use to repeat the experiment of an instantaneous, or unreflecting resolution.

*I.* I see it, and will try no more.

*P.* Will you endeavor to serve the Lord from a right motive?

*I.* (*aloud.*) Yes; if I can.

*P.* Because you think that it would certainly be the proper way to succeed in your wishes, and hence you desire to have it?

*I.* I confess such was my idea. How can I help it,

since my selfish desires arise spontaneously, and will control my thoughts and actions, do what I may?

*P.* My very object, at present, is to prove that you cannot help yourself in this respect. As your present effort after right motives is selfish, so will every future one be in the prosecution of your purpose; for the same desires will necessarily influence you. Why, then, try to have right motives?

*I.* I see that it will be of no use, I am so perfectly selfish; and I will try no more to succeed by this means.

*P.* Should you cultivate your present inclinations or disposition, it would be merely a perpetuation of their selfishness.

*I.* Certainly it would; and I shall not attempt it.

*P.* Should you try to change them, or to acquire a new disposition, it would necessarily be done with a view to your own future peace and safety; and every such effort would be selfish and vain.

*I.* I perceive it would, and shall not try. I am completely discouraged.

*P.* To recur a moment to some points which we examined in connection with the illustration respecting your life;—if you endeavor to give yourself to God *sincerely*, it will be selfish. Please try once more the experiment of producing and acting from sincere feelings: Will you now give yourself to God sincerely?

*I.* (*aloud.*) Yes.

*P.* And you can perceive that your dedication was no more sincere than before; and that you was selfish in the experiment, for your object was to find the right way to accomplish your future safety and peace. Why attempt any more to obtain such sincere feelings, since you must be convinced it will be in vain?

*I.* I am satisfied, and shall make the effort no more.

*P.* If you try *to mean* what you resolve upon, it will be equally selfish and vain. Try the experiment: Will you now, meaningly, give yourself to Christ?

*I.* (*aloud.*) Yes.

*P.* And you can see that the effort to mean it is as vain as that to acquire sincere feelings; and that it is as selfish also, being a mere plan to resolve right for your own purposes. Why, then, persevere? Failure must ever attend the effort.

*I.* I will make no further efforts to succeed by trying to mean things.

*P.* And if you look for evidences of your acceptance and success, it will be also selfish and without effect. You might set about creating some feelings, and might hypocritically, because deceitfully, pretend that they were the gift of God to prosper your selfish and unholy desires; but that, you are too prudent and honest to do. No holy emotions can spring from such an expedient, as you can see by trying the experiment: Will you give yourself now to God, so as to obtain some change or evidence of acceptance?

*I.* (*aloud.*) Yes; so far as I am able.

*P.* Which is not at all. You can perceive that no change has ensued; and there could be none, because the endeavor was selfish, your own safety being ultimately in view. Why endeavor to secure evidences of a hope, in future?

*I.* I see it will be to no purpose, and I will try it no more.

*P.* Will you try to act *conscientiously*, and obey Christ?

*I.* (*aloud.*) Yes, I will.

*P.* Because you wish, by that means, to take the right way to be accepted and rendered safe and happy for ever?

*I.* Yes; such was my desire, of course.

*P.* And by acting under it you was of course selfish; and every renewed effort to succeed by acting from your conscience must be equally vain.

*I.* I perceive that it must, and I shall repeat the effort no more.

*P.* Will you act in view of holy happiness, and serve the Lord? By which is meant, that happiness which flows from a supreme love to the glory of God, and from a supreme desire for the exercise of his Sovereign authority over his creatures.

*I.* (*aloud.*) Yes.

*P.* Because you hope, if successful, to secure your own safety and happiness ultimately?

*I.* Certainly; I desire to do so, of course.

*P.* And, consequently, you were selfish in the effort. You cannot understand what holy happiness is until you experience it; and you cannot experience it until you love God and his glory as the ultimate object of your choice. While you love your own safety and happiness ultimately, you cannot so love God; and, consequently, as every effort is under the promptings of your superior love to yourself, holy happiness cannot be pursued for its own sake, but solely and exclusively as a means to your own ends; which is no pursuit of it in any sense. In your present state, therefore, holy happiness cannot be truly your motive or object.

*I.* I see it perfectly. It is clear that the desires of the unconverted heart can take no gratification in the objects of one that is converted, and of course can never terminate on holy happiness; and that any appearance of it must be deceptive. It will, in my present state, be vain and delusive to endeavor to act in view of it, and I shall do so no more.

*P.* If you seek to obtain present relief by means of serving Christ, it will be selfish; for you will desire the relief for your own benefit now and ultimately.

*I.* Certainly; and I see it will be in vain to try it.

*P.* It is your duty to search the Scriptures (John 5: 39), and to pray, "lifting up holy hands" (1 Tim. 2:8); and from these duties God will not release you. But you are well aware that the Bible is always perused by you for the purpose of acquiring information how to accomplish your own safety and happiness; and that your prayers are all for pardon and for things which you deem essential to your present and eternal interests. Consequently, you are not heard by God; for "he that turneth away his ear from hearing the law, even his prayer shall be abomination."—Prov. 28:9. The reason, as given by James, is because such wish to use the things desired upon their own pleasure, rather than to promote the glory of God.—Jas. 4:3. And hence, all the promises to hear and answer prayer are directed to believers exclusively, who alone will use the gifts for the divine glory. In this view, as well as from your uniform experience of their unacceptableness to God, you can place no reliance upon these duties for success in your projects.

*I.* None whatever.

*P.* Should you endeavor to exercise sorrow for sin, love to God, love to Christians, or any other feelings of the regenerate heart, they would be excited merely by a view of your danger, or of favors received or desired, or of the friendly dispositions of Christians, or of those other personal causes I have before fully described. They would be the unholy emotions of the selfish heart, called out for its own purposes; and would partake of the moral character which belongs to their source.

*I.* It will be in vain to resort to such means.

*P.* If, on the other hand, you should try the experiment of abstaining from the cultivation of any feelings, and of refraining from all efforts to change or banish your desires, and of ceasing to seek after right motives and objects, and of trying to discover the right way to succeed—none of these plans would aid your purpose, for each would be purely selfish. Such abstinence would itself form a negative kind of means, by the observance of which you would hope to gratify your selfish desires for your own ends ultimately.

*I.* I perceive it would be selfish, and of no avail. But we are commanded (Jer. 29 : 13) to seek the Lord; and we are told that we shall find him, "when we shall search for him with all our heart."

*P.* True; but you are seeking not *him*, but *yourself;* you are not searching for him with a *holy heart*, but you are searching after your own future safety and pleasure by means of him and his ordinances, with all your *selfish heart.* You have perverted both the command and the promise. To seek for God implies the possession of a new heart; for the old one always pursues its own ends. Like Israel of old, "you return, but not to the Most High."—Hos. 7:16. There are various other passages which are to be correctly explained on the same principle; for, as pardon is offered the sinner only upon true repentance, so these present encouragement solely upon the condition of his truly seeking *God* with a *right heart*. An example may be found in Heb. 11:6: "He that cometh *to God* [not to his own safety and peace ultimately by means of him, as you are now doing] must believe that he is, and he is a rewarder of them that diligently seek *him*," seek his honor and glory as the object of their supreme love. He cannot, in any sense, become the rewarder of those who seek themselves; and their believing that he will reward their diligence in it, under the mistake that they are seeking God, will not only be an insult to him, but will retain them in selfishness, and bring a deserved punishment on their own heads.

*I.* I see my error. I have heretofore regarded diligent seeking as the chief thing, and have bestowed no thought upon the ultimate object which I have pursued or its moral character. Selfishness had so blinded my eyes to the truth, that I doubt whether I should have detected this fatal delusion, but for your explanations. And yet, although I am now more enlightened, when I attempt to go to God rather than to subserve my own ends, I find that every effort remains selfish and impracticable.

*P.* Suppose you try to go to God partly from a desire to secure your own pardon and peace, and partly from a desire to glorify him?

*I.* I have tried that, in order to have something to catch hold upon.

*P.* But it is impossible for you to succeed by such an expedient. It will prove a mere repetition of your original effort to serve God from a desire to secure your own happiness, and from a desire to glorify him as the *proper way* to succeed in that object. All your desires are for yourself and your own interests; and you cannot at your mere will originate any for God and his glory. On regeneration, the heart spontaneously puts forth holy desires for God. They are supreme, and often exist independent of any active desires for self; while the latter, when excited, will fix upon his glory as their chief good. Hence the two may, and do, exist together in perfect moral harmony; but obviously it cannot be so where, as at present, the desires exist as a preference for yourself.

*I.* I perceive that you are right; and I shall be careful not to be deceived again by such an expedient.

*P.* Suppose that, in your present state of heart, you should take the course adopted by many, and resort to the revealed means of grace in order to succeed in your purpose. Suppose you should endeavor to cultivate all the right feelings possible, and form all the apparently requisite purposes; and after a season should receive baptism, unless you have been baptized before, should unite with the church of Christ, partake of the communion, and observe all known duties with a peculiar strictness; so that your own hopes of safety and peace should be strong, your enjoyments great, and your reputation for piety unsurpassed. The prĕdisposition to your own happiness ultimately would underlie the whole, and would make you selfish in every particular. The false charity of those believers who Christianize every fellow-professor whose exterior conduct is correct, and whose intellectual belief is orthodox, could not relieve you from the censure of him who looks at the heart. "The sacrifice [and by implication, all the religious services] of the wicked is abomination; how much more when he bringeth it with a *wicked mind?*"—Prov. 21:27. And perseverance would only strengthen the bonds of selfishness; for, as the whole process would be in pursuance of such original selfish prēdisposition, it would tend to cultivate and perpetuate it. Those means of grace are, as the term clearly imports, designed to aid the heart already regenerated, in its progress in holiness and in glorifying God.

*I.* In my extremity, I have often contemplated precisely that course, but I see that it would have been of no avail; and if I had entered upon it, a new heart would have been just as necessary, and perhaps more difficult of attainment. I can now readily understand how baptized selfishness should become the monster-parent of spiritual pride, exclusiveness, intolerance, and worldliness; "having the form of Godliness, but denying the *power* thereof," because destitute of the new heart which gives to a profession all its vitality.

*P.* And you, together with the unconverted reader, have doubtless commenced this conversation, or are perusing this book, with the same prēdisposition to your own ultimate safety and happiness, and to discover, by means of its instructions, how to succeed in it. As a consequence, every resolution you form, and every step you may hereafter take under it, will be selfish.

*I.* I perceive it must be so of course; for, as my selfish desires prompt me in every thing else, they will in this. What is to be done?

*P.* Persevere in acquiring information, and in abandoning every useless expedient; or you may be for ever lost. "Take fast hold of instruction; let her not go; keep her, for she is thy life."—Prov. 4:13. To relapse into inattention, will be to grieve the Spirit of truth. To go on, is the path of wisdom and duty.

*I.* Of course I shall steadily attend to and follow your advice; I am determined to act upon it, whether it makes against me or not, for that cannot affect its truth or propriety.

*P.* Honestly said. Can you devise any other means of succeeding?

*I.* I do not think of any, at present.

*P.* Were it possible to devise a multitude, you would be selfish in entering upon every one of them, for your selfish desires must influence you of course. Could you now stand with angels in the immediate presence of God, your very first effort would be to propitiate him in order to bring him over to your wishes, lest he should visit you with deserved punishment.

*I.* Such is, even now, the spontaneous impulse of my heart. I am perfectly satisfied that, whatever the means, I should, at the present time, be selfish in the use of them. Even my reliance upon the prayers of others is a selfish end; and it can therefore do me no good.

*P.* We have now tested your ability in every variety of form; and the result is clear that in your own strength you can accomplish nothing whatever to secure your own safety and happiness. The love of your own welfare has acquired such an *habitual* predominancy, it has so enslaved you to its own purposes, that you have lost every recuperative power; and this must continue irrecoverable while you are under its domination.

*I.* I perceive that I cannot at present help myself; and I have myself only to blame. Had I began earlier to seek the Lord, it might have been better for me; but, alas! regrets are unavailing to retrieve the evils of the past. Could I extricate myself, nothing should hinder; no worldly sacrifice or temporal injury that could possibly be endured should prevent my escape.

*P.* The vanities of the world can have no weight under such circumstances. But truth requires me to state that you are not only incompetent to succeed *at present*, but that you can never succeed *hereafter* by your own unassisted efforts. The reason is, that every effort, even to the moment of your death, will be prompted by the same selfish desires, and must, consequently, be equally as selfish as all that have preceded. Instead of releasing, every repetition will only confirm you in selfish action by the power of a more determined habit; just as one who has lost his balance, and with it his self-recovering power, while rapidly descending a steep declivity, must, as he proceeds, be inevitably precipitated to the bottom. If you should rēcommence your efforts *now*, they would be selfish; if you should persevere in them all the day, they would continue to be selfish, as your experience has fully proved; and if you should persist day after day as long as you had life, they would increase in selfishness, with no door of escape. What have you to urge against this fact?

*I.* Nothing. I can foresee that as every successive act

must partake of the character of the preceding desire, and as such desire cannot be changed, all my efforts must be selfish. Truly, of myself I can do nothing now or hereafter to make myself good, so as to succeed. My hope is solely in the mercy and power of the Holy Spirit.

*P.* None but one entirely desperate could hope, under such appalling prospects, to succeed hereafter by his own unassisted strength.

*I.* I do not expect to, of myself. I had hoped to be able, by reading, meditation, prayer and other means, to produce a gradual change for the better in my feelings. I have supposed that a correction of my views by a proper enlightenment in the Scriptural doctrines and duties, might result in a change of heart.

*P.* That is far from a necessary result. Satan and his angels have the most enlightened views of truth, and a perfect intellectual faith in it; while their hearts remain unchanged, and are becoming more perverse, more hardened, and more profoundly diabolical. It would seem that your own experience for so many years, would be enough to destroy such expectations; for your views of truth are much clearer now than when you was first under conviction of sin, and your devotion to the use of means has been very decided, at intervals, for a course of years, and yet you have not acquired a holy heart. On the contrary, your anxieties are more profoundly selfish than before, and your feelings have been kept alive only to your own welfare, and to the persons and things which you judged might promote it; and as respects any love to the holiness, justice, and glory of God, your heart has every hour grown more hardened, until it has become as insensible as a nether mill-stone to such affections.

*I.* This is all too true.

*P.* Were there no other reasons for the continued unholiness of Satan and his angels, the principle we have before examined—namely, their being under *actual* punishment at the hands of God—will ever keep alive their selfishness, by a kind of instinctive desire for their own relief; this will necessarily remain predominant, will exclude love to their punisher, and will increase the intensity of their opposition and malignity evermore. You, thank God, are not under actual punishment; and the mere contemplation of it as future and deserved, does not necessarily hinder your loving God, since there is no present infliction to call forth uncontrollably your propensity to happiness. But in place of this, selfish *habit* has conquered and holds you in its chains by the aid of the governing prēdisposition to your own welfare; so that your change of intellectual views proves of no avail. One who is prēdisposed to the acquisition of wealth, cannot be moved by any motives which tend to reduce him to voluntary poverty, however enlightened he may become (Matt. 19:22); but he might be induced to accept of poverty, under the influence of motives to wealth, if he judged that such poverty would finally conduce to wealth. In like manner, as you are so prēdisposed to your own selfish happiness, your heart is insensible to those motives which tend to a stronger prēdisposition for the glory of God; but, if you judged that your own happiness might be finally secured by such a disposition, that consideration might incline, as indeed it has always induced you to strive for it; but the attainment of it has eluded your efforts, and you have found a counterfeit instead. And thus, under such habits, it must always be. Cultivate your views and opinions as you may, your selfish heart will always pervert them, and will lead you to embrace a counterfeit Christianity; which, however pleasant here, will end in disappointment hereafter. "Except a man be born again, he cannot see the kingdom of God."—John 3:3.

*I.* What a profound necessity there exists for that apparently arbitrary requirement!

*I.* At the hour of death the same influences will exist, though in a far more powerful degree, if that were possible, caused by the perceived near approach of the judgment and perdition. As you cannot succeed by any intermediate expedients, so you cannot prevail then; and the result is, that so far as respects your happiness, you can be no better prepared to die then, than you are this moment.

*I.* Yes; I can do nothing then which I cannot effect now; and I see that I cannot, do what I will in the mean time, become so prepared to die. Alas! I have fondly imagined that it would be an easy thing to offer up the prayer of the penitent publican and so get ready for the summons, when death should come upon me. But here again my deceitful inclinations have perverted my judgment and instilled groundless hopes.

*P.* Of yourself, therefore, you can do nothing now or hereafter to prepare for death, so as to secure the happiness you so ardently desire.

*I.* I see it perfectly. It is of no use to expect it, and I shall try no more.

*P.* But beware of the whisperings of Satan, which

would tempt you to retreat and so involve yourself in the protracted misery of that "certain fearful looking for of judgment, and fiery indignation which shall devour the adversaries." He is your greatest enemy, and his suggestions, if followed, will inevitably lead to ruin. "Resist the devil, and he will flee from you." Like the starving lepers at the gate of Jerusalem, if you remain where you are, you must die; if you falter or go back, you must surely die; the only course left is to go forward. "If the Syrians save us alive," said they, "we shall live; and if they kill us, we shall but die."

*I.* Having put my hand to the plough, God being my helper I shall go forward. While retaining my senses, I cannot deliberately turn against the truth unto perdition. Will you please proceed?

*P.* A moment's reflection will convince you that the Holy Spirit ought not to do that which both the Father and Christ refuse—namely, to become an accomplice in your wickedness; and that he ought not to counteract their known purposes.

*I.* I am not so foolish or wicked as to expect he will.

*P.* And yet you seem to have overlooked the fact that he would do both, should he gratify your wishes. The pursuit of your own happiness, as we have frequently seen, is the cause of all your sins of heart and of life. Should the Spirit in any way whatever aid you in securing this, should he operate upon you, either directly or indirectly, or assist you in the use of any motives or means, so as to enable you to succeed, he would make you the conqueror in this strife with God, and would cause the divine glory to give way to your selfish interests. He would irretrievably debase and ruin himself for your sake! I ask, whether, as a reasonable being, you can longer hope for assistance in your plans from the perfectly pure, living Spirit?

*I.* No. I have not before taken this matter-of-fact view, and am ashamed of the insult of looking for his aid in such purposes. Still I can get no other.

*P.* My friend, truth impels me to declare further, that were there any possible means left by which you might succeed, the Holy Spirit would himself block up your path! He will never use either holy or unholy means, nor will he suffer you to use them successfully, to promote your purposes. How can you hope for his aid?

*I.* I neither deserve nor expect it. I have been confiding somewhat in your aid also; but I see that no instructor can truly guide me where there is no path, and where, if there was, God himself would righteously interpose and prevent me. I have done with that trust, for "vain is the help of man."

*P.* Review your actual position. As regards securing your future happiness, you are utterly helpless in respect to any thing you can do *now* or *hereafter;* for you move in a circle, as it were, and invariably return to the starting-point of self; and you cannot break loose from it so as to succeed, for you have no self-recovering power. However it may be with others, your own consciousness declares that you have begun the work of heart-reform too late, if your purposes could ever be accomplished. You can have no valid dependence, as we have seen, on the prayers of Christians; they can never aid your projects. And God will not help you; but he, an unconquerable enemy, has set himself against you. "The wicked is snared in the *work of his own hands*" (Ps. 9:16); and an incensed sovereign holds your chains. If you will take a restrospect of your life, and note the profound unholiness of your heart, the repeated violations of the laws of God which it has produced, and your unsuspended attempts to turn him to your own purposes, you must become sensible that he is right in his disapprobation and abhorrence of you; and, under such convictions, you will justify his purposes of vengeance, however reluctant you may be to become the subject of it. "In the hand of the Lord there is a cup, and the wine is red; but the dregs thereof, all the wicked of the earth shall wring them out and drink them."—Ps. 75:8.

*I.* I am entirely convinced on these points.

*P.* You have, substantially, been endeavoring to exercise the pardoning power, and have signally failed. God reigns; and he has declared that "he will have mercy on whom *he* [not the creature] will have mercy, and whom *he* will he hardeneth."—Rom. 9:18. It is as necessary for him to punish the incorrigible sinner as it is to sustain his authority and government, and for the same reasons. Hear what he declares respecting your selfish desires and hopes: "The expectation of the wicked shall perish."—Prov. 10:28. Hear what he affirms respecting your expedients and efforts: "The eyes of the wicked shall fail, [fail to discover the means of safety,] and they shall not escape [their doom]; and their hope shall be [shall expire] as the giving up of the ghost."—Job 11:20.

*I.* I have always had a presentiment of being destined to perdition; and it is now verified. Once, after wandering for hours in a forest, I sat down bewildered, thinking, " now I *feel* lost;" and I now feel the same.

*P.* As respects your own happiness, you are so indeed; and as there is none other which you can enjoy, you are doubly lost. Indeed, the eternal happiness you have been pursuing exists only in your own fancy; it is an ideal *ignis-fatuus*, which has beguiled you into the morasses of sin and error. In eternity, nothing has been provided by a wise and holy Creator, adapted to gratify your selfish desires; and hence you could never find your happiness there. On the contrary, every thing there, whether in heaven or in hell, is adapted to disappoint them—in heaven, the blazing holiness and dread majesty of God, and in hell unbridled selfishness—so that nothing but misery can result to you. Thus has God made provision for the penalty of the law; which is, substantially, the everlasting wounding of the sinner's selfish desires, and the destruction of his selfish happiness. It must sink into that grave where is darkness for ever!

*I.* At last, I perceive the truth of all I feared! There is no happiness in eternity for me, a wretched sinner!

*P.* How useless, then, have been your endeavors to secure it? And how exceedingly absurd will be any future devices?

*I.* I shall make no more. I am like one walled up above and around, unable to move any way; and having already lost every thing I pursued, I can afford to risk all things by ceasing my struggles. I have abundance of feeling now; but, alas! of what avail can it be, since it is all selfish?

* * * * * *

*Pastor*. Let us now return for a few moments to the establishment of the points for which we have used the illustration respecting the right of God to recall your life at his holy pleasure. I beg, my friend, that you will not, under any anxiety which you may now experience, turn to any succeeding chapter before we have finished with that illustration. If you, incautiously, should do so, it will do you no good, but an injury; your mind will become confused; you will be unable to understand, in their true bearing, the things hereafter presented; and you may hereafter bitterly curse that unbridled selfishness which led you to disregard my friendly caution. But if you will take your ground decidedly on that illustration in the first instance, this confusion will be avoided.

*Inquirer*. I shall curb my anxiety, and observe your advice. I feel utterly incompetent to move a step, or mark out any course; and shall incur no worse hazards by following my deceitful heart. Wherever you lead, I will follow.

*P*. The proposition was, that you, or any other person, could determine to do, or not to do some act, where love was not excited, and where there was nothing to hope or fear. In proof, we took the illustration that God, having given you life, had a right to recall it at his will, and that he should not be opposed by you therein. We saw that, in resolving not to oppose him in recalling life, you could not act with love; that you could not become prepared to die; that you could derive from it no worldly benefit; that you could not so escape sin, or do any other act, as to please

God; and that there was, consequently, nothing to hope for. We also saw that it would not offend God any the more; that you are already so completely within his power, that your life would be in no greater danger, but that you would live as long as in any other case; that you would be punished none the sooner; and that, consequently, there was nothing to fear on forming that resolution. But you still expected to derive from it some knowledge how to succeed; and hence you did not clearly apprehend the very plain idea which I had presented for examination. Of course you cannot now indulge any such expectation; for if it is impossible to succeed by avowedly religious means, or indeed at all, surely that moral illustration cannot inform you.

*I.* I do not expect to learn by it how to succeed hereafter, and shall not try. I am already somewhat confused, and can see no use in returning to that illustration.

*P.* You are confused, not in respect to your helpless position, but how to make progress in your plans and purposes; a confusion for which there is no remedy. You must permit me to judge of the further degree of light which you can derive respecting your selfish state by means of this illustration.

*I.* I yield to your judgment, and will rëexamine it with you.

*P.* I shall propose my questions anew for your audible answers; and I do hope that we shall not be delayed by any further plans or expedients to resolve in some right way, since there is no right way for your purposes.

*I.* It is indifferent to me how I resolve; as I shall neither gain nor lose by it, I may as well resolve wrong as right.

*P.* Let us test that fact again. God has a right to recall your life, and you ought not to oppose him: Will you oppose him in it?

*I.* (*aloud.*) No.

*P.* And you have gained or lost nothing, and have no more love than before. But did you not cast about in your mind to find the proper way to resolve?

*I.* I confess I did unconsciously; but I will do so no more. Whether I resolve right or wrong, I will not oppose God, so far as my mind is concerned, and so far as I can execute the determination.

*P.* Will you oppose him in recalling your life?

*I.* (*aloud.*) No.

*P.* Did you make any efforts to be sincere in this resolution, or to mean it, or to feel it, or to get an evidence, or to do it in any other supposed right way?

*I.* I did not. It would have been too absurd with the light I now possess on the subject.

*P.* But it has done you no good to abandon these experiments, however sensible it is to do so; for your purpose cannot be accomplished in any way, as you well know. But did not the thought that you could not prevent God from taking your life, recur to your mind, and lead you to acquiesce to my proposition not to oppose him?

*I.* I confess it did.

*P.* So far as respects your plans and prospects of success, it is perfectly immaterial what your motives are, or whether you have any; for could you even secure holy motives, (which you cannot,) God would not confer your happiness on you; so that, I trust, you will seek no longer after motives. But in order to understand the point we have immediately in view, you must take some affirmative action, as I said when on this subject before. We then saw that the idea that you could not prevent him was an immoral consideration.

*I.* Yes; and an uselessly immoral one.

*P.* Then lay it aside, as you would dismiss any other objectionable thing. If you had made up your mind to go to a certain place with a view to purchase some goods, and also to have a quarrel with another, you could readily abandon the idea of the quarrel on being convinced of its impropriety, and could go there exclusively for the reason of making the purchase. This very ordinary course of action would not involve a change of heart. In like manner you can dismiss the idea of not resisting God because you cannot prevent his recalling your life, on becoming convinced of its immorality; but it will involve no change or other personal benefit.

*I.* I see that it can be dismissed if I will.

*P.* I take it for granted that there is no one in the circle of your acquaintance whom you would wilfully wrong; and that, if you had injured any, it would be a satisfaction to redress it at once. And, surely, you should not needlessly wrong God, even in principle.

*I.* Certainly not.

*P.* Suppose some venerable friend should present you with an immense fortune, requesting only, in return, that you should treat him right; your satisfaction would be great, and your gratitude might know no bounds for a season. Suppose, further, that one should suggest to you the plan of making more money by defrauding and injuring this friend; and you should decline, because you doubted your ability to defraud him! How shameful would be such a reason! You would despise yourself for harboring the thought! Indeed, you would never entertain the idea, but would despise the tempter, and refuse to wrong that friend, even though you had the power to do it.

*I.* I should not hesitate a moment.

*P.* And God has kindly given you life and preserved it hitherto; a boon which you value far above all worldly wealth. And will you treat him worse than you would a fellow-being? Will you say, I cannot prevent his recalling what is his own, and so will not try? Be ingenuous, my friend, although it will not avail your objects; take your ground not to oppose him in respect to your life, whether you can prevent him or not.

*I.* I will not oppose him, at any rate.

*P.* Suppose, as before, that some superior being had actually invested you with power sufficient to prevent God. The natural love of life might tempt you to exert it against him; but you would not be justified in using it. It would be a high-handed infringement of his rights, and an unmitigated wrong against him, and the wish should not be yielded to. In common propriety, supposing you now to possess such power, you will not use it to resist God?

*I.* (*aloud.*) No; I will not.

*P.* It would also be an act of the basest ingratitude to use such power against him; which, although a selfish consideration in your mind, can make you no worse than you are, for there are grades even of selfishness. He has hitherto preserved the life which he originally gave; and he has guarded it for you among a thousand dangers which have threatened it. It is reserved for the viper to wound the hand that feeds it; but not for an ingenuous mind so to treat a benefactor. Will you oppose him in taking it, even if you had the power?

*I.* (*aloud.*) No; I will not.

*P.* But your natural love of life would tempt you to use such power, sufficiently to protect it, without wishing to injure God; and to use it at all, would defeat him on that point. Your success would infringe on his omnipotence, destroy the foundations of his government, and plunge him and the universe into ruin. In good morals, the iniquity of the principle is the same when merely entertained, as when actually enforced. Ought you thus to ruin God for the sake of your forfeited life, by preventing his recalling it?

*I.* (*aloud.*) No; and I will not resist him, come what may.

*P.* You have made no progress in securing your selfish plans or objects; but there is an obvious propriety in your taking this position. I understand, then, that on the supposition that you now possess the power to prevent God, you will not oppose him in recalling your life in his own time, since it would be wrong, basely ungrateful, and ruinous to him to use it?

*I.* I will not, even if I could prevent him; it would be wrong.

*P.* When I repeat my question, you will observe that I do not ask whether you are *now willing* not to oppose him, for I know that you are not; nor do I ask whether you will now *become willing*, for it is mere nonsense for you to endeavor to *feel* willing. But my question is, that unwilling as you may be to die, will you *consent* yes or no, so far as the mind is concerned, not to oppose God? I refer simply to a resolution of the will, which you are aware is also on the side of selfishness, and not to any change in your willingness or unwillingness, or in your desires or inclinations.

*I.* Then my consent must be the coldest of all possible acts, and therefore the most useless.

*P.* Yes; and that is all I propose to have you do. You have been mistaken in supposing that I intended some hearty resolution, as you would express it. Once for all, you must understand that you can resolve on this subject only with an unwilling mind as respects yielding up your life; and, therefore, without any willingness in favor of God's recalling it. If there was any thing to be gained, that might make you willing to consent to let God recall it, but there is nothing; and if you understand the matter correctly, you will rather be unwilling.

*I.* I see no reason to be make me willing to let him recall my life; there is no benefit to result from it.

*P.* I can make this perfectly clear by an illustration. Suppose you are bound to spend this day in important business for me; and suppose you now receive an invitation to meet some dear friends, and spend the day with them. Your desires to accept it become very strong, and you apply to me to release you from your engagement; but I refuse, and insist upon your transacting my business immediately. Now, you could resolve to stay and do that business, but it would be a very unwilling resolution; and the more you thought of your friends the more disappointed you would feel, and the more unwilling you would become to stay here.

*I.* Yes; I see I could determine to stay. But there would be no virtue whatever in such a constrained act.

*P.* I have not said that it would be virtuous; but only that you could do it. And yet that is all you can do upon the illustration before us. You are unwilling to die, and unwilling to let God or any one else take your life; and all you can do is merely to determine you will not oppose him, unwilling as you may be. It will show you, however, that you cannot by means of it become a Christian, or get a pardon, or any evidences, or in any way please God, so as to succeed.

*I.* And I have been foolishly trying all the time to *feel* a willingness!

*P.* Test it once again, and answer without trying to be sincere, or to feel willing, or to mean it, or to have evidences, or to have right motives or objects, or any thing else. Unwilling as you are to die, will you oppose God in recalling your life in his own appointed time?

*I.* (*aloud.*) No; I will not.

*P.* And you are no more willing, or in a more hopeful position in any respect, than before. And if you resolved at all, it must have been unwillingly as respects your life.

*I.* I understand you now; and I shall make no more efforts to feel willing, or for any thing else.

*P.* Then we can soon bring this matter to a close. And that we may fully understand one another, and that you may be satisfied beyond all doubt that you cannot succeed in securing any such change, evidence, or other benefit that you desire, I wish to propose the question in two directly opposite aspects. There are only two ways in which your mind can possibly act upon it; both of which we will try, and then drop the subject. The first is that which you have supposed to be the *right way* in which to succeed—namely, by means of efforts to resolve sincerely, or in some peculiar way. The second is that which we have seen to be the *wrong* one to effect any such good—namely, to resolve just as it happens, without any effort for a motive or other experiment, just as you consented to read over those lines. You then merely made up your mind to read them, without any anxiety or plan of any kind.

*I.* If that is all you mean, I could have done it long ago. But I was so possessed with the notion of making myself acceptable, that I really could not understand you before. But of what possible use can it be to resolve at all? I can do nothing now, or hereafter, to be prepared to die, and shall not attempt it. I can in no way secure my desired happiness, for it is not to be had; and I shall no longer pursue a mere fancy. I cannot help myself, nor will God help me; so that it seems quite unnecessary to press your question.

*P.* You are right as respects any success you can derive from the resolution; but still, you can test the correctness of my proposition by acting upon it. As you are entirely selfish, and as whatever you do with your present views must be with the selfish heart, every resolution on this subject may be set down as certain to be selfish; and if you will take this fact for granted, you will understand me forthwith.

*I.* I know that every resolution I form will be selfish, as certainly as I make one.

*P.* Then try it in the first or supposed right way.

Suppose God intended to recall your life in twenty minutes; then not only your life, but your future happiness also, must be for ever destroyed; but notwithstanding it would be wrong to oppose God in it. Now, try to resolve sincerely, willingly, or in any way you can think of as right: Will you oppose him in recalling your life?

*I.* (*aloud.*) No.

*P.* Have you acquired any new feelings, or are you any more willing, or do you mean it in any more acceptable manner than before?

*I.* No; nor did I expect to.

*P.* Then you are not disappointed. Now, take the second way I proposed, that which we have seen to be the wrong one as respects your success; and answer at once just as it happens, whether willing or unwilling, or right or wrong; for in no case will you receive such feelings as you have desired. Though God should recall your life in twenty minutes, still you will not oppose *him* in it?

*I.* (*aloud.*) No; I will not oppose *him.*

*P.* You have gained nothing, as you can perceive. But you seemed to hesitate, as though you were placing your life in some greater danger than it is in already; which cannot be the case, as you well know. Please answer at once, without any hesitation: You will not oppose *God* in recalling it, at any rate?

*I.* No.

*P.* It would be wrong to do so, and you will not oppose him, so far as a mere resolution goes?

*I.* No, I will not.

*P.* In forming this final resolution, as we will call it

for the sake of a more ready reference, what did you think about, or what did you try to effect?

*I.* I thought of nothing whatever but your question. I just concluded not to oppose him, and made no effort of any kind. I did not try to effect any thing, for I knew it would be a failure.

*P.* What consideration induced you to determine you would not oppose God?

*I.* I had no motive, that I am aware of. I merely thought I would not. I summoned a resolution under an impulse, as it seemed.

*P.* Do you mean the impulse of your desire to please him?

*I.* No; I had no thought of pleasing him.

*P.* You say that you thought of nothing, except that you would not oppose him. In order to get at the fact more clearly, permit me to inquire in particular whether, in forming this final resolution, you expected to learn how to love God, or to obtain sincere feelings, or find some other way to please him?

*I.* I did not; for I thought nothing about them.

*P.* Did you not then hope to be prepared when you came to die?

*I.* No. I supposed I might die in twenty minutes, and I knew I could not be prepared.

*P.* Did you then try to resolve in a right way, or to have a right motive, or a right object?

*I.* No; I thought nothing about them. It would have been of no use.

*P.* Did you try to forget yourself, or to overlook your own happiness, so as not to be selfish in forming that final resolution?

*I.* No.

*P.* Did you then think of yourself?

*I.* No.

*P.* It would have done no good if you had. Did you then rely on Christ or on the Holy Spirit for help?

*I.* I thought nothing about aid from either.

*P.* Did you have any plan for the future?

*I.* None at all.

*P.* Did you then fear any injury from resolving?

*I.* No; I neither expected to gain any thing, nor feared any injury.

*P.* And you have neither succeeded in your plans, nor placed yourself in greater danger by it. You knew that you ought not to oppose God?

*I.* Yes; and I just concluded I would not.

*P.* God is a holy, just, and good being; every thing he does and every thing he requires is right, however it may affect our personal interests. He has a perfect right to dispose of our lives as he sees fit; and it is this fact that makes it so grossly wrong to oppose him in respect to it. As it is so wrong, you ought not to oppose him, and *must not.*

*I.* And I *will not.*

*P.* Does this fact alone seem at present sufficient to induce you to resolve not to oppose God?

*I.* It is enough of itself. It is wrong to oppose him, and I will not.

*P.* Even though he should take it immediately?

*I.* Yes; even though I am not prepared.

*P.* But, in forming that final resolution, did you not consider that you could not prevent God from taking your life, and so would not try?

*I.* I always knew I could not hinder him.

*P.* But you might know it and yet not have it influence your determination. Thus, in view of some necessary business to be done, you might resolve to visit the metropolis. You would know that, if you did go, you would also probably see multitudes of people there. But this fact would not be your *motive;* if your business called, that would move you to go, whether many people were to be seen or not; and if that did not call, you would decline going. In like manner, you was aware that you ought not to oppose God in recalling your life, and you also knew that you could not prevent him; but did that fact come in to influence you, or did you resolve that you would not do it, since you ought not, whether you could hinder him or not?

*I.* I understand it better. I did not think whether I could prevent him or not. I felt an impulse that I ought not and must not, and concluded I would not.

*P.* So that, even if you now had the power, you would not act so wrongly, basely, and ruinously toward God, as to oppose *him* in it?

*I.* I would not. It is my intention not to do it in any event.

*P.* Do you mean it in the same sense that you meant to read over those lines, after you had concluded to do so at my request?

*I.* Yes; but I can hardly consider it a resolution, at least such an one as I ought to have formed. It is not such a cordial one as I have desired to make.

*P.* But still your mind is made up, in an ordinary sense?

*I.* Certainly.

*P.* God has a right to recall your life whenever he will, whether you are prepared or not. In this affirmative view, do you now consent to let him recall it at his pleasure?

*I.* (*aloud.*) Yes; it is his right, and he may recall it when he chooses.

*P.* Even now, if he so wills?

*I.* Yes; even now.

*P.* Under the thought that you may be prepared?

*I.* No; I am conscious that I shall not be prepared. I can derive no such benefit as I formerly expected.

*P.* Although you may not be willing to die, in itself considered, yet do you feel willing, at present, to let God exercise his right over your life in preference?

*I.* Yes; as I now feel, I am willing, since it is his right, to let God recall my life whenever he may choose. I will not, knowingly, oppose God in any respect whatever.

*P.* You have at last practically seen that a person can resolve on a moral subject, where no love is excited, and where there is nothing personal to gain or lose; for you have now resolved not to oppose God in recalling your life, without being influenced by love to him, or by the idea of receiving any selfish benefit or injury.

*I.* The truth of the proposition is now perfectly obvious; and it seems strange that so plain a thing should have been so obscure to my mind.

*P.* The difficulty lay in your expecting to learn from it what it could never teach; and hence you tried experiments with it until you became convinced. In view of the importance of practically understanding this point, and of the liability of the selfish mind to mistake some other action for it, I have to request that, before proceeding further, you would rëexamine the illustration from the point where we just now resumed it, and take your position anew, while the subject is fresh on your memory.

*I.* As there cannot be too great caution exercised by one who has to deal with such a deceitful heart, I will immediately comply with your request.

*P.* Could a personal interview be enjoyed with any of those whose mistaken positions we have been examining in connection with yours, no doubt many important points relating to such individually could be cleared up, and much valuable information could be afforded, which the circumstances imperatively prevent from being now presented.

## CHAPTER VIII.

### DEVELOPMENT OF RIGHT MORAL PRINCIPLES.

*Pastor.* I PROPOSE to advance with the aid of the moral principle which we have just viewed, and which it is hoped you have, in your retrospection and action upon the illustration with which the last chapter concluded, firmly embraced. Your audible reply is desired as before to the questions I may propose, and for the same practical reason. I wish you to consent to such as you shall deem correct, in the same ordinary and natural way that you came to the final conclusion that you would not oppose the will of God in respect to your life; and I earnestly request you never to repeat those vain efforts to produce sincere feelings, or to feel willing in the first instance, or to resolve in some supposed right way to acquire evidences of your acceptance. Resolve freely, uncurbed by mental contractions or selfish expedients, since nothing can avail toward securing your selfish ends.

*Inquirer.* I am done with all such useless expedients; and hereafter I shall answer on these subjects just as I would consent or refuse to change my seat, and with no more effort.

*P.* God has the same right to direct and control you in the use of life, that he has to recall it; and you are as much bound, therefore, to observe his directions. He is our Creator and proprietor, and as such has a perfect right of property over us, a right of sovereignty which is supreme and peremptory. You never can effect your own selfish will by his means, or by means of any thing you can do yourself; but your duty to him remains, notwithstanding, that of an implicit obedience; an obedience which is to be rendered without question or regard to personal or other consequences.

*I.* It is clear that my duty to my Creator does not in the least depend upon any consequences to myself or others, whether they prove either favorable or disastrous. His mere right to command, makes it obligatory on me to obey; and I no longer expect any personal benefit from any thing I may do, for I have tested that point to my sad conviction.

*P.* Nor will you succeed in any. But God, as your Creator, having such a perfect right to control your conduct, will you obey him hereafter, so far as you may possess the ability?

*I.* (*aloud.*) Yes. It does not seem to be much that I can do.

*P.* Why have you formed this resolution? Did you anticipate the preservation of your selfish happiness by means of it?

*I.* No. I have abandoned all such expectations. I perceived that my Creator had a right to my service and that I ought to obey him, and that, indeed, I *must* therefore do it; and so I concluded I would.

*P.* That is precisely what I proposed by my question. It is said of our Lord Jesus Christ, "Him hath God exalted with his right hand to be a PRINCE," that is, a sovereign ruler: Will you hereafter obey him as your King and God?

*I.* (*aloud.*) Yes; with his aid. I have always heretofore so regarded him as the Redeemer, as practically to neglect him as the Almighty God entitled to my implicit obedience on that account only. In this, also, I have been sadly wrong.

*P.* You need not fear that your present resolutions will not be observed. I will hereafter show you upon what principles they can be executed, but yet not so as to secure any selfish ends.

*I.* I thank you for this encouragement; for these resolutions are so obviously demanded by duty, and are in themselves so proper to be observed, that it is my sincere wish to fulfil them.

*P.* Whenever you have heretofore sought to avoid transgression, it has been with a view to secure your selfish happiness; but that end, as you must now be convinced, cannot be accomplished by it. Still, you ought not to disobey God for the same reason that you ought not to oppose his will in respect to your life. Christ, as your Creator, has a right to command you to avoid all transgressions of the divine law, and you are under obligations to shun them for that reason: Will you hereafter obey the command of Christ by abstaining from all disobedience?

*I.* (*aloud.*) I will. My dependence can be only on the Holy Spirit for guidance and strength, for I can no longer place any confidence in myself.

*P.* Should a kind friend, as we have before supposed, confer on you a large fortune, you would feel inexpressibly thankful; and no consideration could induce you, knowingly or in willingness, to injure him. But if your life and all its privileges were at hazard, and could be saved only by the surrender of that fortune, you would sacrifice it; for life is the most valuable, and you could live without the fortune, but you could not enjoy the fortune without life. God has kindly given you all these superior privileges, and Israel's Keeper has ever protected you even while dashing onward in sin; and surely you will never, knowingly, oppose his will or injure his cause by disobedience while you remain the recipient of his blessings?

*I.* Never, with his help. And yet, alas! I fear that I may yet commit much that is wrong.

*P.* There is not a just man upon earth that doeth good, and sinneth not (Eccl. 7:20); and we must be watchful. Heretofore, as we have seen, you have acted as if you had a supreme right to control yourself and your actions. Do I understand you now to renounce this claim in favor of the superior right of God to control you; and that, when they conflict, you will observe his will in preference to your own?

*I.* (*aloud.*) Yes; such is my purpose.

*P.* My friend, permit me to remind you that heretofore you had set up your own selfish welfare, interests, and happiness, as objects of desire and pursuit superior to every thing beside; and that this was the parent principle of all your sins, and of that criminal state of heart which had involved you in all depravity, and which had justly made you the object of the divine abhorrence. It should be renounced as opposed to God and antagonistic to every thing holy, even though you could succeed in it, which you are aware is impossible. God forbids it; and do you now for ever abandon the pursuit of your selfish happiness?

*I.* (*aloud.*) Yes; and may God ever keep me from desiring it again!

*P.* As has been before observed, the glory of God consists in the moral excellence and loveliness of the character which he develops by means of the holy, just, and good administration of his government over his moral creatures. Every thing he is, every thing he does, and every thing he commands us to do, is right; and his glory, so resplendent in moral beauty, forms the most desirable object for his own love and pursuit which is conceivable even by God. There is nothing more noble, more exalted, more worthy of man as a creature of God, than the same object; and in making the promotion of the divine glory the ultimate aim of all our purposes and conduct, we shall do honor to our own natures. With the divine aid, will you hereafter devote yourself to the promotion of the glory of God, in his appointed ways?

*I.* (*aloud.*) Yes; I will.

*P.* In order to secure your own selfish ends thereby?

*I.* No; I had no such thought, expectation, or intention; and I would not secure them if it was in my power, for it would be in opposition to the will of God, and that is sufficient. Will you show how I am to glorify him?

*P.* Yes, hereafter. As you well know, nothing can reconcile Christ to that selfish happiness which you have yourself so properly renounced. As the Creator and Sovereign of all, it is his province to decide the destiny of his sinful creatures; and you should implicitly resign yourself into his hands, leaving at his unquestioned disposal your temporal and eternal interests, with your body, soul, time, talents, property, and every thing you possess. Do you now consent that his will may control in all these respects?

*I.* (*aloud.*) Yes. I deserve nothing at his hands; but I now leave myself entirely at his disposal for time and for eternity.

*P.* In the hope that he will secure your own happiness by means of pardoning and accepting you?

*I.* No; I thought nothing about that, and I have no wish that he should favor me unrighteously. Whatever may be the consequences, I now devote myself to him to serve and glorify him to the extent of my ability, and to have him order all things now and hereafter according to his own righteous will. With Eli of old I can say, "It is the *Lord*, let him do what seemeth him good." I fall upon him in the dark with no claim upon his mercy; but whatever may befall, I would rather be in his power and at his disposal than at my own. In the decided language of the poet, I can also say:

> "Welcome! welcome! Lord and Saviour,
> Welcome to this heart of mine;
> Lord! I make a full surrender,
> Every power and thought be thine.
> Thine entirely—
> Through eternal ages thine."

*P.* And having now voluntarily placed the reins in his hand, having resolved your will in obedience to his sovereign authority, he will henceforth and for ever exercise his supreme control over you in such manner as shall best promote his own glory.

*I.* I am perfectly satisfied to have him do so.

*P.* In consenting to obey him and to be resigned to his will, did you act from the dictates of your conscience in view of the creative rights of God over you? Did the idea of his right to your service, for example, so impress your conscience with a sentiment of duty toward him as to make you feel that you ought and that you therefore would obey him, or did some thought of securing your own selfish ends intervene?

*I.* The idea of his right to my service was, to the best of my observation, the only external consideration that influenced my determination.

*P.* I wish you would be habitually certain and decided in your knowledge of, and conclusions respecting facts; for there is neither humility nor merit in doubting things within our own observation; while to do so, evinces either an undue timidity or a want of due investigation. Consciousness is the knowledge of our own mental operations obtained by our own observation; and, next to divine revelation, it is the highest evidence capable to man, and must supersede every thing contradictory. Our own experience is always intuitively perceivable. Suppose that, for the reason of acquiring information, you determine to purchase a book. On reflection, you would be perfectly conscious that you had so resolved, and that it was for the sole reason of gaining information; and you would be so certain, that if every person you met should deny that you had formed such a purpose, or for such a reason alone, you would reject their assertions as false, and attribute to them gross ignorance at least. And you would be justified in this; for, as they could not scrutinize your mental operations, they would not possess the same degree of evidence as yourself; and to yield the point to their vehemence, would be pure folly.

*I.* Undoubtedly in such a case I should retain my belief in full confidence, though every person should affirm that it was not valid. They might be honest, but would still be mistaken.

*P.* The same principle should be applied to the subjects we are now examining; and you should receive with a perfect certainty whatever your consciousness clearly declares to be a fact.

*I.* And I will hereafter always do so.

*P.* You are conscious, for example, that you have resolved, in an ordinary way, to serve the Lord?

*I.* Yes; I am conscious of it and could as soon doubt my existence.

*P.* As you now look at the subject, does the fact that your Creator has a right to your service appear a sufficient influence of itself to move you to resolve to obey him?

*I.* It does. No other reason, at present, produces my resolution; and if there were any other, that is now sufficient of itself. But I cannot clearly see how I have reached this position.

*P.* Then you can be perfectly certain from consciousness, were the whole world to contradict you, that the idea of the right of God to your service is alone sufficient now to move you to resolve?

*I.* Yes; I am perfectly conscious of it, and perfectly confident.

*P.* And it is my advice that you always obtain and act upon the same clear perception and knowledge of facts within the compass of your own observation; and if on such evidence, then also on the higher grounds afforded by revelation. By doing so you will avoid much perplexity, darkness, and distress; and will make greater progress in those pursuits which you may hereafter select.

*I.* I will no longer fear being presumptuous when I am sustained by clearly perceived facts.

*P.* You will please give your attention to the following illustration, and make it real by supposing the facts true in your own case. You have probably restrained your feelings recently under the apprehension that they would be selfish; but I wish you to do so no more, for by repressing them you will be unable to feel on any subject. Whatever emotions may arise spontaneously, let them come, while you direct your attention exclusively to the thoughts that may be presented.

*I.* I will do so; and will obstruct my feelings no longer.

*P.* Suppose that there are many persons who are your mortal enemies and guilty of the most atrocious crimes. Rectitude demands their condign punishment; but your benevolent sympathies toward them forbid its infliction without an effort to deliver them from their guilty state and conduct, in order that, by their true penitence, rectitude may be satisfied in their pardon. But this, let us suppose, can only be done by some immense sacrifice on your part. You have a little brother, sister, or child of that tender and confiding age when they are most interesting; one who loves you with all the affections of its guileless heart, and who, in return, is beloved by you as your own soul. Here is the lamb whose slaughter alone, we will suppose, can permit you properly to gratify your benevolence toward those enemies. But how could you endure the thought of inflicting such intensity of anguish upon that beloved object! How sustain the idea of lacerating so profoundly your own pure affection for the loving and confiding child! How few of any sensibility would be competent to the sacrifice! But, moved by a view of the condition of these enemies, your soul becomes nerved to the utmost of its power; tremblingly you seize the child, and amid its falling tears, and cries, and shrieks, you nail its quivering limbs to yonder wall!—and then stand gloomily by to witness the terrible results. The blood trickles down its face pale with agony; its bosom heaves with intense auguish; and the scalding tears suffuse the eyes still cast upon you in tenderest love, while you hear its moaning complaint, Have *you* done this? as it sinks in death. You could not endure it.

*I.* No; my soul would almost expire in the anguish it had created. Thank God that such a sacrifice is not required of us!

*P.* It was asked of old, "Wherewith shall I come before the Lord?—shall I give my first born for my transgression, the fruit of my body for the sin of my soul?" No. It was reserved for God alone to make that sacrifice. He beheld a world crowded with his enemies, bound in selfishness, self-ruined, bent on unceasing sin and rebellion, and destined to endless perdition. His compassion was profoundly moved, but rectitude forbade the world's deliverance without an adequate remedy for the violated law. There was one way only which even infinite wisdom could devise, by which, on man's true repentance, the authority of the divine law could be sustained. God had a Son, an only son, a son beloved as his own glory, for he was the very brightness of that glory; and upon him the powerful affections of his great heart were immutably and intensely fixed; and man's redemption could be reached only through his sacrifice! He who spared us spared not himself, nor that beloved object! He who faltered over man's wretchedness, faltered not over the pain he was called upon, by mere compassion, to inflict on his holy child! To the persecutors he gave him; in all his obedience and sufferings through life he followed him; and when the hour for the last, sad, crowning trial was arrived, to the murderers he delivered him. Nailed to the cross, his body writhing under its pains, and his blood commingling with the tears that streamed down his haggard face, he watched him. A spectacle of shame to the deriding crowds, the Father stood aloof even while the heavens clothed themselves with his funeral pall, and the earth rocked to open, as it were, a sepulchre for him. Terrible as were then the pains of his body, they were trifling in comparison to the agony which swept over his holy soul when Christ entered under the penalty of the violated law of God, and its pains were poured down like an overwhelming torrent upon him—those pains which we should have endured instead! The anticipation of them had well nigh destroyed his life in the garden of Gethsemane; but now the reality was upon him. With uncovered head and with his bosom bared to its pitiless agonies, he passed down alone into the wine-press of the fierceness and wrath of the Almighty God! Who can penetrate those crushing sufferings beneath which Christ trembled and agonized during those fatal hours; and who can fully appreciate the deep emotions which must then have filled his Father's heart! And yet he himself inflicted the final blow; for he departed and left the sufferer alone with the powers of death, and the still more raging powers of hell. This desertion broke his heart, and with its crowning agony terminated his protracted sufferings: "My God," he cried, "hast *thou* forsaken me?" And bowing his head heavily upon his bosom, his weary spirit fled.

*I.* Thank God that, having suffered once for all (Heb. 10:10), he is never again to breast that storm of wrath!

*P.* As your voluntary sufferings with regard to the child would evince not only the extent of your compassion for your enemies, but your superior regard to rectitude, so do the sufferings of Christ exhibit those traits of God in a most eminent degree. How profound is that compassion! "God [not the Son only, but God] so loved the world, that he gave his only begotten Son, that whosoever believeth in him should not perish, but have everlasting life."—John 3:16. How devoted is he to rectitude! it is superior to his compassion not only, but also to his love for the happiness of his own Son. How disinterested is his goodness! sacrificing his beloved, and not for his friends, but for his enemies, many of whom hated him so intensely as to deride the sacrifice itself. How perfectly uncontaminated is he with selfishness! sacrificing every thing personal when it interferes with the attainment of these higher objects. Around the cross, there radiates "an excellent glory" which is lovely beyond expression, and is worthy of the everlasting praise of every moral creature in the vast universe of God; and that glory expanded by his subsequent gracious conduct toward his erring creatures, has illuminated our day.

*I.* It is indeed most lovely.

*P.* When I reflect upon the necessity that some strong hand should control the multitudes which exist in the world, and when I remember that God created, and has therefore a perfect, exclusive, and absolute right to govern all, I feel willing to have him rule, whatever may be the results to myself. And when I dwell upon his wisdom, power, and rectitude, I am glad that he does reign; and glad that no one can rightfully question his conduct or is able to destroy his sovereignty. How do you regard these things as you feel at present?

*I.* I feel entirely willing to be in his hands; and would rather have his will control than my own.

*P.* Would you withdraw yourself from his rule and power, if you were able?

*I.* I would not.

*P.* When in addition to those traits, I contemplate his unwavering justice, so indispensible to the well-ordering of the moral universe; his benignity, forbearance, and personal long suffering toward evil doers whom his single word would consign to a deserved perdition; his unrequited, yet still unfailing goodness in his blessings upon the unjust and unthankful; his compassion for his enemies; his rectitude, even in his mercy;—when, I say, I contemplate him as the Holy One, so disinterestedly kind, just, and good, I cannot refrain from loving him—would that it was more profound, more tender! In considering these traits, how do you now feel toward them?

*I.* I can like them, and him for them. I see them as it were through a glass, darkly; but the view is most beautiful notwithstanding.

*P.* The vision is obscure because it is so new; but the more you dwell upon his character the clearer will be your view, and the higher will be your regard for it. Can you now love this glory, and God for his glorious character, in the natural way in which you would love any other good object?

*I.* Yes. I can love him, as never before.

*P.* Do you know of any thing which is, in your view, preferable to God and his glory?

*I.* No; I feel that I can prefer him to any and every thing besides. And yet I do not love him as much as I perceive he deserves.

*P.* Love him all you can; no more can be required of us. Can you love his trait of justice, as well as his mercy? His justice is as important and as indispensable to the preservation and well ordering of his moral government and consequently to his glory, as the other.

*I.* Yes; I can now love God for his justice.

*P.* Under the hope that it will not be inflicted upon yourself?

*I.* I thought nothing about that; it was independent of all personal considerations. Much as I dread its infliction, I would not disarm him of it even if I could.

*P.* Can you love Christ for his holy, just, and good character, as well as for his disinterested sacrifice?

*I.* Yes; and whether he confers its benefits on me or not, much as I may desire them. You will understand that I do not value happiness the less, but that I now desire the will of God the more, or in preference to it.

*P.* As you feel now, would the observance of the divine will and the promotion and contemplation of his moral excellence and glory, afford you pleasure?

*I.* I know of nothing which would afford more satisfaction. My feelings are so new and pleasant that I can hardly describe them. I am glad that Christ reigns, that "he hath mercy on whom he will have mercy, and that whom he will he hardeneth," for it will all be right. I feel, as one has remarked, as if treading in a new world. Every thing seems to lead my thoughts to God. "God, the great—the holy God, the benevolent, wise, perfect God" seems written on every thing around me. And how inexpressibly lovely does his character appear; so pure, so just, and yet so kind, so perfectly holy and radiant with every moral beauty! There is a richness and excellence in the character of God which I have never before perceived, and which I hardly believed to exist when portrayed by others. I always knew that God was right, and *approved* of him in all he was and did; but I never before appreciated or *loved* his moral beauty. "O worship the Lord in the beauty of his holiness!" Now I can exclaim, "Holy, holy, holy Lord God Almighty, the whole earth is full of thy glory!"

*P.* Look upon the conduct of your past life in contrast with the authority and glory of God. You have rejected that authority, you have disregarded that glory, and you have done evil as you could. Under your present views, how do you feel in regard to it?

*I.* I have, as yet, thought but little of it; but I am

disgusted with myself and my conduct. The whole is stamped with unholiness; and its moral deformity is hateful to my sight. It is a luxury even to grieve over the odious selfishness of my past life.

*P.* Christians desire to imitate the character and promote the glory of God in their life and conversation. As you feel now, can you love them on that account?

*I.* I feel that I can; and the more closely they imitate their Father in heaven in their principles and conduct, the more I shall love them.

*P.* Would you love to have sinners converted?

*I.* Very much indeed.

*P.* Of course you desire their deliverance from endless misery; but would you have it at the expense of the Sovereignty or glory of God?

*I.* I would not. Now the full meaning and value of the "salvation of God" breaks in upon me; for, in fact, it was difficult to perceive the difference between that, and the selfish salvation I so much desired. I no longer wonder at the mistakes committed on that subject by professors as well as sinners. It is a far different thing to love God and his glory, and to desire to avoid sin because it is opposed to him, and to love one's own happiness chiefly, and to desire to avoid sin because it will ultimately interfere with that. I would now have all sinners converted from sin itself to God and his glory in a supreme love of him.

*P.* If I understand you correctly, your present feelings and purposes differ from those you have heretofore exercised, in the following respects: First, you always heretofore acted merely from the desire to promote your own safety and happiness by your religious efforts;

whereas, at present, although you still desire happiness, the fact that God has a right to your obedience is a sufficient motive of itself to induce you to obey.

*I.* Yes; I can clearly perceive that difference.

*P.* Next, heretofore your own happiness was chiefly prized and always ultimately in view; whereas, now you prefer the glory of God to it, and pursue that chiefly.

*I.* Such is the correct explanation.

*P.* Next, you have always heretofore employed the means of grace as instruments of sin—that is, to forward your selfish hopes, desires, and purposes; whereas, now it is your desire and purpose to use them for the more ultimate promotion of the divine glory.

*I.* Yes; I now supremely desire, whether I eat or drink or whatever I do, to do all to the glory of God. Irrespective of all possible consequences, he is worthy of my entire devotion, and shall have it with Christ's help.

*P.* Next, you have new reasons in view of which you wish to avoid sin, to have sinners converted, and also for loving Christians. Before, they were your own interests and the workings of natural sympathy; now, they are the command of God, the moral deformity of sin, and the likeness of Christians to Christ?

*I.* Yes.

*P.* What kind of happiness do you desire for others?

*I.* Not their selfish happiness at all; but their enjoyment of God, his glory and service.

*P.* In fine, as heretofore it was your general intention and disposition to subserve your own interests and happiness ultimately, it is now your general intention and disposition to promote the glory of God ultimately; and you can take your pleasure in so doing?

*I.* Yes. But I anticipated no such results.

*P.* My argument all along, you will observe, was that you could not succeed in your *selfish* happiness; that you could never secure the favor of God by any new feelings or other means whatever, so as to make him favorable to it. And it has proved true; for you have not, and never can succeed in that object.

*I.* That is true; and however much I desired it then, I would not effect it now if I could, in opposition to the will and glory of God.

*P.* I never said that you could not love and glorify God; but only that you could not do so in your selfish state of heart, and while so bent on your own ends. When you abandoned these, the difficulty was removed. Now, you can not only desire to obey God in view of his creative rights and purpose to live to his glory, but you can execute them through divine grace. It is the very course that God requires of you, and with which he is pleased. The Holy Spirit by his power brought you there, and he will aid you in prosecuting such right desires and purposes. You may now rely upon him for guidance and strength with the same confidence that you would expect him to promote holiness with any other person, or under any other circumstances.

*I.* I thank you for this encouragement. Still, I fear that I shall continue to be selfish in my proceedings, and this apprehension has hindered me all along.

*P.* I have been aware of it, but could not touch upon the point until now. You know as well as you know any thing, whether you now choose the divine glory in preference to every thing besides? Let your mind act with truthful decision on the point.

*I.* Certainly; I am conscious of that preference.

*P.* Then you need no longer apprehend that your future feelings, purposes, and efforts will be selfish. Whatever may be the religious character of the soul, it never parts with its constitutional faculties or propensities; nor with its appetites until delivered from the body. Your natural desires of life, of knowledge, of society, of esteem, of possessions, of power, of happiness, and the like, will remain more or less developed according to circumstances; but it was the indulgence of these and of the bodily appetites independently of God and to the end of your own gratification, that made you supremely selfish in heart and conduct. But you have now a *superior* principle, one by which you can control and make these *subordinate* to God, and *subservient* to the divine glory—namely, the desire and purpose to uphold the authority of God over your will, feelings, and conduct. This relieves those propensities from the stamp of selfishness, which consisted solely in their *predominancy* as motive influences. It is now proper for you to take pleasure in God, his service and glory, for it is a holy pleasure. It will not now be selfish to hope in his salvation, for it is "God's salvation" you now desire.—Rom. 5:2. It will not be selfish to take pleasure in worldly good where the means are not objectionable, where it is had in subordination to the will of God, and where it is taken under the general intention to honor him. And it will not be selfish to pursue those worldly avocations which are lawful and necessary for our own support and that of our families, and to enable us to acquire and do good with our substance in Christ's kingdom, when they are pursued with the same subordination and ultimate intention. Dismiss your fears on this point; but be on your guard lest you fall into temptation.

*I.* I now see the difference between selfishness and holiness more clearly, and can take courage.

*P.* The more pleasure you take in God and in his service, the stronger will you become.—Neh. 8:10. The chief end of man is "to glorify God and enjoy *him* for ever." Such being the salvation which you now at heart desire, it will not be selfish to seek it; for in this sense it is only another term for an eternal moral union and blessedness with God. "Let such as love *thy* salvation say continually, The Lord be magnified."—Ps. 40:16. Such a salvation implies a Godly repentance for sin, true faith in Christ, holy obedience, moral conformity to the divine character, and enjoyment of the glory of God. In all your ways devote yourself to God, and when Christ, who is our life, shall appear, then shall you also appear with him in glory.—Col. 3:4.

*I.* It is my earnest desire to honor and glorify God, so far as I can learn how to do so.

*P.* A parent who instructs his son in good morals and in strict business habits, thereby exhibits his own moral characteristics and business principles; and when the son acts upon them before the world, he exhibits to others through himself, these good traits of his parent, and thus honors him *before men.* And when he does so with the deliberate intention of making the character of his parent known, and from a love to him and a desire to obey him, he thereby honors him *in his heart.* In like manner, whoever does the same in respect to Christ's holy teachings, making it known that, in his principles and conduct, he purposes to obey

Christ, will exhibit Christ's character before the world. So far as he does exhibit it, he will honor him before men; and by his desire and intention to do so, will honor him in his heart. Thus his worship and praise become the occasions of glorifying God, because they flow from a devoted heart and exhibit Christ's goodness to others.—Ps. 50:23. Our labors for the conversion of men and in every good work honor God for the same reasons, and because, as the fruits, others also are brought to engage in the same love and duty.—John 15:8.

*I.* I perceive the principle.

*P.* In obeying and glorifying God, whatever may be our particular mental frames from time to time, we should act upon the *prëintention* to observe his authority and to promote his glory in whatever we may engage. This will habitually influence us; and will stamp the character of our hearts in all we do, even when the special occupation shall have so engrossed our thoughts as to exclude the remembrance of God for the time being. If you should start for the metropolis from an intention to do some good act, that general intention would govern your movements all the way and would decide your character in them, even though your intermediate occupations should almost entirely exclude thoughts upon the object of your journey.

*I.* Yes; the character of our governing intention, being itself determined by that of the motive or object in view, must decide our own character and that of our conduct under it. And I now see that, with such a holy intention, conduct otherwise only moral as respects men, may be made evincive of piety toward God.

*P.* You are right. But never let your immediate

occupations hinder you from securing that leisure which is necessary to the cultivation of right affections. In respect to the means or instrumentalities by which we are to glorify God in our bodies and spirits, agreeably to his command (1 Cor. 6: 20), you will observe that it is of the first importance that the divine law be made the habitual rule of our lives. As it was promulgated by the sovereign authority of God as our lawgiver, we should obey it because of his right to command us; and as it was designed to promote his glory, we should observe its precepts with that ulterior view. The law is his great instrument in governing his loyal subjects, in promoting their best good in consistency with rectitude, and in developing his own moral characteristics; and although salvation is not by the law, but by grace through faith (Gal. 2 : 16), yet it is so intimately dependent on holy character that he who rejects the law or refuses to make its precepts his guide in life, will fail of the salvation of God.—Rom. 2: 13.

*I.* And necessarily so, since his is a salvation to holiness, and in continued holiness, to an ultimate blessedness in the glory of God.

*P.* The moral law is most eminently adapted to the ends proposed by its author. But, as is remarked by Mr. Abbott in the *Corner-Stone*, we have read the ten commandments so many times, and they have been so long and so indelibly impressed on the memory, that it is difficult to get a fresh and vivid conception of their character. To obviate this difficulty he proceeds to give their substance in other language; and I now insert, substantially, his statement of them for your attentive examination and observance.

### I.—DUTY TO GOD.

1, Your Maker must be the highest object of your interest and affection. Allow nothing to take precedence of him; but make it your first and great desire to honor him and to obey his commands.

2, You are never to speak of him lightly or with irreverence, and you are not to regard any visible object as the representative of him. He is a spirit invisible from his very nature, and you must worship him in spirit and in truth.

3, Consecrate one day in seven to the worship of God, and to your own religious improvement. Entirely suspend, for this purpose, all worldly employments, and sacredly devote the day to God.

### II.—DUTY TO PARENTS.

You are placed in the world under the care of parents whom God makes his vicegerents to provide for your early wants, and to afford you protection. Now, you must obey and honor them. Do what they command you, comply with their wishes, and always treat them with respect and affection.

### III.—DUTY TO MANKIND.

Keep constantly in view, in all your intercourse with men, their welfare and happiness as well as your own. Conscientiously respect the rights of others, in regard—

1, To the security of life.

2, To the peace and happiness of the family.

3, To property.

4 To reputation.

In keeping these commands, too, you must regulate your heart as well as your conduct. God forbids the unholy desire as much as he does the unholy action.

*I.* How beautiful is the law, and what perfect blessedness on earth would result from its universal observance! I do not wonder that the Psalmist should exclaim: "O how love I thy law! it is my meditation all the day:—How sweet are thy words unto my taste! yea, sweeter than honey to my mouth!" Surely, God could never repeal such a law.

*P.* Never; and Christ came on purpose to restore and enforce it in its purety.—Matt. 5 : 17. In the two tables, as given by our Lord to the lawyer who endeavored to ensnare him (Matt. 22 : 35—40), all these commands are reduced to their fundamental principles—namely, first to love the Lord with all our heart, and second, to love our neighbor as ourselves.

*I.* I supposed the second table authorized impenitent men, equally with Christians, to love themselves, provided they loved others in an equal degree.

*P.* That is impossible. A sinner is one who *prefers* himself; and although he can like others, he cannot have a *preference* for them at the same time.

*I.* That is true.

*P.* And if he could, it would be unholy; for it would authorize him to *prefer* himself and other creatures to God; which is to put God and his glory in a subordinate position where he could exercise no holy regard for him, as we have abundantly seen.

*I.* That would be the result.

*P.* But when the sinner is regenerated, when he comes to *prefer God* to himself, his love to himself ceases as a preference and becomes subordinate to his love to God. He then loves himself for nobler reasons, and desires a holy happiness. Having taken this secondary position, he can love his neighbor *as* himself, and for similar reasons, both being held subordinate to his preference for God; and he can do him good and seek his holy welfare in reality, and with propriety. Then God has the first place and himself and his neighbor the second in his heart, according to the natural relations in which he stands to God and man, and their respective claims upon him.

*I.* This must be so.

*P.* Christ never intended to authorize that wicked lawyer to make his own selfishness the standard of his piety, as your construction would imply. He commanded him *first* to love God, which implied an abandonment of his selfishness; and this being assumed as complied with, (as is common in the Scriptures,) his self-love (now become subordinate) was, *secondly*, to be made the standard for his love to his neighbor.

*I.* I perceive the correctness of your explanation; but how many sinners have been ruined in consequence of a mistake as to that standard! Such encouragement of self-love, must prove the nursery of perdition!

*P.* In your future course, you must carefully cultivate the graces of the Spirit. Do not retain a passive state, one merely to be acted upon by the Spirit: but remember that you are to be as active and diligent in the cultivation of holy principles, feelings and deportment, as you would be in cultivating those things that pertain to temporal affairs, and, indeed, more so. As, in the latter case, you would not wait for the Spirit, nor exonerate yourself from blame for your neglects on his account, so you are not authorized to do either in the former. The command to *believers* is, "work out your own salvation with fear and trembling"—do it yourself, as if all depended on yourself, but knowing that—"it is God which worketh in you [by the efficient motives he presents] both to will [to form right purposes] and to do [to execute them] of his good pleasure," which is always for his own glory.—Phil. 2:12, 13.

*I.* Certainly, unless the graces are a miraculous gift they must be cultivated by the new heart; and even if they are so, they must be cherished, for experience proves that otherwise they will die.

*P.* If the glory of God is of any value, it is worth every thing; and, as was said by one who acted upon his conclusion, it warrants and demands every sacrifice to promote it. Live in view of death and the judgment, and it will enlarge your perceptions, and render you more dead to the world as well as more determined for God. Cultivate humility of heart, meekness of spirit, kindness and good-will to man; restrain your passions, order your conduct aright, and strictly guard against all worldly snares. Seek for religious society and counsel; acknowledge Christ before men; and use all your influence in the world for God. Establish a closet for private meditation and prayer; set up the family altar, and upon it daily dedicate yourself and your household to God; and, in fine, in every feasible way "let your light so shine before men, that they may see your good works, and glorify your Father which is in heaven."—Matt. 5:16.

*I.* I will do so, Christ strengthening me.

*P.* Be punctual in the duties of public worship and prayer; be careful to observe the Sabbath, with all your house, abstaining from every thing which is not a work of *necessary mercy* on that day; and by every feasible means, seek to bring about the conversion of your household, your friends, the community around you, and the whole world, to Christ.

*I.* My mind is fixed on these points.

*P.* And God will bless you most abundantly.

"So shall your walk be close with God,
Calm and serene your frame;
And heavenly light shall mark the road
That leads you to the Lamb."

*I.* May the Spirit guide and sustain me in that delightful path!

*P.* And you should glorify Christ by exalting him as your Saviour as well as your Sovereign Prince.—Acts 5:31. I have wished to present this subject before, but the course of our examination prevented. Can you trust in Christ for remission of your sins?

*I.* I am confident he will do right, and am perfectly willing to confide in him on that account. "Though he slay me, yet will I trust in him."—Job 13:15. I am glad he reigns and that his will will be accomplished.

*P.* You seem to have that filial, confiding spirit of adoption "whereby we cry, Abba, Father!"—Rom. 8:15. It is far better to rest there, than to pursue a systematic struggle after a mere hope of salvation. "I have been forced," said Fletcher, "by many disappointments, to look for comfort in nothing but the comprehensive words, THY WILL BE DONE. A few more trials will convince you experimentally of the heavenly balm they contain to sweeten the pains and heal the wounds that crosses and afflictions may cause." But it is due to Christ, and honorable to him, that the obedient should make a personal application of his atonement.

*I.* I am too guilty to look for this. I know not whether he righteously can, or is willing to receive me to heaven; but I will love and serve him notwithstanding.

*P.* We must take up this subject in detail, in our next chapter. In the mean time, you will please peruse the fourteenth chapter of the Gospel according to John; and then in the privacy of your closet review your past life, search out and confess and forsake every particular sin, renew your dedication to God without looking for any miraculous feelings or tokens in answer to prayer, and seek the aid of the Holy Spirit to enable you to fortify and execute your intentions for God. Then turn your thoughts from yourself, and let your heart flow out upon a sinful and dying world, and seek the blessing of God upon its regeneration. We will then proceed with the subject of the next chapter.

## CHAPTER IX.

### ASSURANCE.

*Pastor.* HAVE you complied with my requests at the close of the preceding chapter?

*Inquirer.* I have; and now feel willing to yield implicitly to the authority and commands of God. It has become the chief desire of my heart to obey and honor Christ; and the review of my past sins presents them as increasingly odious and hateful.

*P.* The exaltation of Christ as your Saviour to holy blessedness in the glory of God, was the subject reserved for examination at the present time. The hope of the believer, you will observe, is of a far different moral character from that of the sinner; for it proceeds from a loyal heart, and is directed toward objects honorable to God. God is the enemy of selfish happiness only; he delights to confer that holy blessedness in which his own heart rejoices, upon those "whom he hath made meet to be partakers of the inheritance of the saints in light."—Col. 1:12. It is fit that the subjects of his love should exercise due gratitude not only for his numberless temporal mercies, but also for the blessings of redemption, and for that sovereign grace which led them into the paths and prepared their hearts to enjoy the beauties of holiness.

*I.* As I have before intimated, I always supposed

that religion consisted chiefly in a sense or hope of pardon given us from above; and hence I always strived and prayed for a hope.

*P.* It was natural for the selfish heart to induce that mistake, since it seeks its own security only, and desires the attainment of some evidence of it. But you have since learned that Christianity consists in a supreme love to God, evinced in the conformity of our principles, affections, and conduct to those of Christ.

*I.* Should such a believer die with no comforting hope of a pardon through Christ, would he fail of the grace of God and of eternal life?

*P.* By no means; for his new relation to God as a son (2 Cor. 6:18), does not depend on his possession of a well-defined hope, but upon his having the same moral principles, affections, and objects, as God. Not a few of the most humble, devoted, and self-denying Christians have, at such a time, lost their hope through the depressing influence of bodily disease, a view of the odiousness of their sins, or an ignorance of the true basis on which they were entitled to confide in the divine mercy. Yet they have uniformly evinced to others by their deep submission to the will of God, and their lively interest in the promotion of his kingdom on earth, that they were the unconscious possessors of the Spirit of Adoption which, as we have seen, is God's peculiar gift to his children.

*I.* I shall hereafter make a conformity to the will of God the object of my endeavors, rather than the sustentation of a hope of pardon and acceptance.

*P.* And by so doing, and by acquiring clear views of the Scriptural grounds of our acceptance, you will actually fortify your hope the more, as will be seen hereafter. God never confers a sense of pardon aside from our own instrumentality. He has presented, in the Scriptures, the terms upon which he will pardon sinners; these we are to examine, and are to compare our own principles and exercises with them. If they agree, we are to take Christ at his word and draw the inference for ourselves; and by such a reasonable conclusion a foundation will be laid deep and strong in our convictions, enabling us, under the Holy Spirit, to "have boldness to enter into the holiest by the blood of Jesus, —and to draw near with a true heart, in full assurance of faith."—Heb. 10:19. 22. The feelings which may result, are such as will flow spontaneously from such new ground taken by the soul. As we shall hereafter show more at large, there is no claim of merit either express or implied, in such well-founded convictions, as the selfish mind erroneously supposes. Compliance with those terms is a mere duty; the performance of a duty cannot absolve one from a previously deserved punishment; nor can it entitle him to *claim* any recompense for the future, for the duty exists irrespective of rewards or punishments, and is to be done in fulfillment of those rights of the superior which make it a duty.

*I.* Certainly one who is bound by some obligation, can never lay claim to a recompense for fulfilling it. But I feel content to resign my soul into the hands of God, and to be governed here and hereafter exclusively by his righteous will; and I do not see the necessity of again exposing myself to become selfish, by pushing this point about a hope any further.

*P.* But you need not become selfish again by doing

so; while it is indispensable if you would fully honor Christ, and guard yourself against future bad consequences.

*I.* Then I will do as you advise.

*P.* You will please propose inquiries on such subjects as now appear most interesting or important to you.

*I.* I will do so with pleasure. What is regeneration?

*P.* Regeneration is the act of the Holy Spirit in recovering the soul to holiness, through the instrumentality of the truth.—Jas. 1 : 18. The term implies the original begetting or producing of holiness in the heart, in which the Spirit takes the initiative; and is condemnatory of that view which presents the sinner as taking that position. "Which were born, not of blood, [not by natural descent from Abraham, as held by the Pharisees] nor of the will of the flesh, [by any purposes instigated by the selfish heart] nor of the will of man, [of the prē-purpose or power of any human being] but of God," of his purpose and power.—John 1 : 13.

*I.* Consequently all the praise and glory of that work belongs to him; while it is left to us to cherish and enjoy its fruits.

*P.* Yes; and also to labor to bring others under the influence of the truth as it is in Christ.

*I.* What is conversion to God?

*P.* In a general sense, conversion implies a turning from the pursuit of one thing to that of its opposite; or a change from one state to another. In respect to God, it intends that change which consists in an abandonment of the pursuit of our selfish ends, and a turning to God in obedience to his authority and in the pursuit of his glory instead. "Repent, and turn yourselves *from* all your transgressions;—and turn *unto* the Lord your God."—Ez. 18:30; Joel 2:13. The first act of turning is known as conversion; while the continued observance of the new duties into which it ushers the soul, is called perseverance in holiness.

*I.* I see that I have heretofore been grossly mistaken in regard to the motive influence in conversion; for instead of the authority and glory of God, I had only a desire and hope of accomplishing my own pardon and acceptance by means of Christ.

*P.* In order to its possessing any moral value, conversion must be an act of duty; and as we have seen, our duty is produced by the creative right of God over us,—a motive in direct hostility to the sinner's desire for his own ends. The obligation of duty can never be fulfilled in morals, except as it is entered upon from the consideration which makes it a duty. Thus, if I honestly owed you a sum of money, the obligation would be fulfilled *in law* by my paying the debt at maturity. But if I did it reluctantly under the constraint of a threat of prosecution, purposing to retain the money if I could, it would not be a fulfillment of my obligation *in good morals.* That would be satisfied only by my repaying it because I honestly owed it; and then it would be done readily (2 Cor. 9:7), and without regard to threats or fears. Otherwise, you would justly pronounce me a dishonest and unreliable man, even though your threats secured the money. If God should fail to demand such a fulfillment of our obligations, it would be unjust to good morals, and consequently to himself and his government; while, if he should require more it would not be just toward us, since they already embrace all that we can do. Consequently in the observance of his commands, we must be governed by a sense of duty to him.

*I.* Undoubtedly conversion to God is an act of duty; and as such, it must be done in view of the creative rights of God over us.

*P.* And we can enter upon the observance of our duty to God under that motive, only by means of some *resolution of the will* which is prompted thereby.

*I.* Of course, since it is by some free act of volition that the will always directs our conduct.

*P.* As the resolutions of the impenitent will are always produced by the influence of a predominant desire of happiness, it will be impossible to accomplish a moral change therein so long as such desires retain their control.

*I.* So I have discovered by my own experience.

*P.* In order, therefore, to a proper action of the will toward God, it is indispensable, in the first instance, that the influence of such desires be suspended, at least for the time being. It is only when their *motive power* is destroyed, that the will can become liberated from their domination.

*I.* True; but how is this to be accomplished?

*P.* It cannot be effected by eradicating the desire of happiness; for that is a constitutional propensity, perverted indeed, but indestructible as the soul itself. You will remember that we saw at the commencement, that it was the *hope of succeeding* which gave to the desires for an object all their motive influence; and that when this was destroyed, the desires would exert no impulsive power over the voluntary conduct where the person was not under actual punishment.

*I.* We saw this principle developed in the case of *O.*, who ceased his resolutions and efforts to assist *P.* in extinguishing the fire at his house, when he lost his expectation of securing the desired reward.

*P.* On the same principle, the sinner must be convinced that he cannot secure the happiness which he desires. Then his hope of success will be destroyed, and with it the stimulant to exertion for that selfish end; for, as we have seen, no person under the influence of reason will voluntarily attempt an object which he is perfectly convinced is beyond his reach.

*I.* That was precisely the position which I reached in respect to my own safety and peace.

*P.* Whether this conviction is produced by arguments with accompanying experiments in proof of their validity, as has been done in the preceding pages; or whether it is produced more blindly by the repeated failure of long-continued efforts for an evidence of safety, as is the case under the ordinary preaching of the gospel; still, it is attended with an entire despondency of mind. This is significantly expressed by the apostle: "Sin revived, and *I died*" [to the pursuit of myself].—Rom. 7 : 9.

*I.* I well know, from recent experience, what is that dejection of spirits and loss of courage in view of the insuperable difficulties that were presented to my success in selfishness; it was such a failure of hope that made me abandon its pursuit as utterly useless.

*P.* Our Lord, in giving an outline of true conversion, laid down three fundamental principles as indispensable thereto. The first is this: "If any man will come after *me*, [after *Christ*, not after his own selfish ends through him] let him deny *himself*."—Mark 8:34. To deny, means to renounce, overlook, disown, and turn entirely away from the pursuit of a thing; and for the sinner to deny himself, is to withhold all pursuit of his selfish happiness and interests. It is, for example, no denial of *self*, for the inebriate to abandon his cups, at whatever sacrifice of feeling, for the sake of his own ulterior health, happiness or property; for, in such case, he gratifies himself in respect to the more important particulars, at the expense of some mortification in respect to the less important. And so it is no denial of *himself* for the sinner to submit to painful mortifications for the sake of some ulterior personal advantage. It is rather a gratification of himself in the most important points, and the degree of his mortifications proves the higher estimate he places upon them. If we suppose a person, impelled by strong desires, to be traveling southward while his business would call him northward, it is evident that he must entirely suspend his movements southward by denying his desires in the sense of entirely rejecting their influence, before he can turn about and guide his steps in the northern direction; and in like manner, the sinner must suspend his efforts for his own happiness by so denying his desires, before he can turn about and direct his steps in the opposite moral direction. You will observe that after the soul is converted, the desire of happiness will again put forth its impulses; but it will cease to be a selfish influence because it will act subordinately to the authority, and subserviently to the glory of God, and the happiness which it will then contemplate will not be independent of him, but will be taken in him, his service and glory, which will stamp it virtuous and holy. In that aspect, the desire need not be denied.

*I.* The reason for requiring self-denial of the sinner is very obvious.

*P.* And it is a primary object of the Holy Spirit, in his convicting energies through the truth, to induce this very act of self-renunciation. "He openeth the ears of men, and sealeth their instruction, that he may withdraw man from his [selfish] purpose, and hide pride [inordinate self-regard, or selfishness] from man."—Job 33: 16, 17. To accomplish this, "he reproves the world of sin, and of righteousness, and of judgment" (John 16: 8); he convinces sinners of the rightful claims of God over them; of their sinfulness in disregarding his commands; and of the certainty of their damnation therefor, as sinners. As soon as the sinner becomes thus convinced that his efforts to escape will be unavailing, he will suspend them, and not before.

*I.* I had not noticed this peculiar harmony between the command of Christ and the influences of the Spirit.

*P.* But the actual result is also in harmony with both. You can observe in your own case, that by a process of convincing argument enforced by experiments, you become persuaded that success in securing the happiness you desired was impossible. You accordingly desponded; and at last, when that final resolution not to oppose God in recalling your life was proposed, you abandoned, as utterly useless, all attempts in favor of your own safety and peace, and overlooked and even forgot yourself, in your response to it. In that process the *power* of your desires was suspended, and you denied *yourself.*

*I.* I see it now clearly. Although my desire of happiness remained, its motive influence over my purposes was then as completely suspended as if the desire itself had been eradicated. Its disappointment produced all the trouble of my despondency; but it exerted no influence toward any relief from it.

*P.* And thus you became released from the *motive power* of the selfish desires; and your mind, for the first time in your existence, was in a position to resolve and act independently of them, and in view of any other sufficient external motive which should be presented under the dictates of your conscience. And, as you are aware, the impulse of the conscience is never impregnated with desire, but is purely persuasive and mandatory?

*I.* And by such a release the recuperative power of my moral constitution was developed or restored?

*P.* Yes. The removal of this obstacle to the supremacy of your conscience left you free to act under a sense of duty, or, which is the same thing, under the monitions of conscience that you ought and must obey.

*I.* I always doubted whether one could thus suspend all action for himself because I had never done it, but I can doubt no more. Still, I would not have done it could it have been avoided; and being such a reluctant act, there could be no virtue in it.

*P.* There was no moral goodness whatever in the act of suspending your selfish resolutions. You might, as many others have done, have resumed your selfish expedients under some false encouragement. Some are so determined, that they will not refrain from them even for the purpose of seeking God the rather. And had not the Spirit, by means of the truth and your vain expedients, withdrawn you from the purpose to effect your selfish ends, your deceitful heart would have prevailed in the same manner.

*I.* As all my inclinations were opposed to that step, it must have been produced through his power, of course. But I was far from depending upon the Spirit for such a hindrance, and, indeed, was averse to it.

*P.* The Spirit always acts in opposition to the desires of sinners, and they are in fact opposed to every thing he contemplates in reference to them, whatever may be their pretensions of dependence on him. They never either desire or depend on him for the things he purposes, until after their hearts are, by regeneration, devoted to his rule. Then they will bless him for the adverse conquering power which he exercised over their selfish inclinations and purposes.

*I.* I always believed it was wrong to despond.

*P.* That depends on what we despond about. To despond of success in an impracticable thing, is reasonable, and to despond of a wicked thing, is proper; while to despond of a good and attainable object, is both improper and unreasonable. Your heart was fixed upon a wicked and unattainable, because a selfish, object; and hence it was reasonable and proper that you should despond of it. Christians often despond of the grace and glory of God; and this is unreasonable and improper, because they are both open to them and are holy. The fact that despondency sometimes runs into painful despair, neither affects its propriety nor necessity in the case of the sinner; while such a perversion in the Christian is not only unjustifiable, but is censurable in that it evinces great distrust of Christ. The fact that despondency tends to arrest the efforts of the sinner, instead of being an objection, is the very reason for which it is valuable; for, as we have seen, his steps toward selfishness must be arrested before he can turn to holiness. The sinner is at first aroused to seek his own salvation by considerations of self-interest. The terrors of the law produce them in his selfish heart; and in his efforts, his conscience becomes enlightened in respect to the claims of God, his own duty, his sinfulness, and his dreadful prospects; so that when he reaches the point of self-denial, his conscience has acquired power to withhold him from fleeing back to worldliness. His very anxiety makes him averse to doing so; while the Holy Spirit who has brought him to that point will hold him there, as multitudes can testify who have remained on the verge of self-denial for months and years before they repented. But even if such a danger of relapse existed, there is no help for it; for the sinner must deny himself here, or be damned hereafter. As a fact, however, it is those convicted sinners who have not reached that point, those who have been falsely encouraged and who have prematurely hoped for pardon in Christ, that apostatize from their profession. They have no root in them; and to sustain their own selfish eternal prospects they flee to all manner of error, seducing and being seduced, deceiving and being deceived, and waxing worse and worse.—2 Tim. 3:13. When the Christian desponds, he loses his strength (Neh. 8:10); and to *him* God speaks: "Who is among you that feareth the Lord, that obeyeth the voice of his servant, that walketh in darkness, and hath no light? let him trust in the name of the Lord, and stay upon his God."—Is. 50:10.

*I.* My aversion to despondency perverted my views.

*P.* But self-denial is only preliminary to conversion. It releases the will from the power of the selfish desires, but does not turn it to God. A second fundamental principle in the process of conversion laid down by Christ, is this: "If any man will come after me, let him deny himself,—and follow *me.*" We follow one by acknowledging and obeying his authority, and by imitating his example in compliance therewith. To follow Christ, therefore, is to acknowledge him to be the Son of God (1 John 4:15), who administers the executive power of the divine government over the world (Matt. 28:18; and 1 Cor. 15:24, 25), and to obey him as such, imitating his principles, adhering to his doctrines, and observing his examples. In order to enter upon such obedience, there must first be a resolution of the will to obey prompted by the idea of his creative right to exercise authority over us.

*I.* I understand you perfectly.

*P.* In your own case, when your mind had become released from the motive power of the selfish desires, and when you had suspended all resolutions and experiments in favor of your own safety and happiness, the sentiment that you *ought not* to oppose God in recalling your life induced you to resolve that you would not?

*I.* Yes; as I have observed, I perceived it would be wrong toward him as my Creator, to do so, and I concluded that I would not.

*P.* That resolution was the act of "following *Christ*;" it was the first act in fulfillment of your obligations in *motive* as well as in *purpose;* and, consequently, it was conversion to him. A change was then effected in both your motives and resolutions, in favor of God. The external idea of the right of God over your life, produced an internal impression that you ought not and must not oppose him, under which you yielded to his will. The conscience when duly enlightened acts as God's vicegerent in the soul. Having thus acquired the predominancy over the will for God, it proceeded to hold all your appetites, propensities, and other powers in subordination to him. It smiled in approbation of your submission, and gave you peace. It will always encourage your soul in holy obedience; and when you fall under temptation, it will rebuke and dissuade until you repent, when it will again approve, seeking, as it were, to heal the wounds it has inflicted.

*I.* For some reason not clear to me at present, I have never before appreciated the influence of the conscience, but have feared to act under its constraints.

*P.* You never before appreciated it, because you never had experienced its mild but powerful domination. You disliked it, because it always reproved your sins; and you feared its influence, because it had always before been a coercive one, under which you had been driven to things which you still disliked. You had always acted from *remorse* or *fears* of conscience, which you, as well as all other sinners, mistook for its *persuasions.* Your fears, your dread of provoking its rebukes, and the like, produced a constrained service which you felt could not be acceptable. But such is not the pure influence of the conscience itself. The Scriptures present the conscience, when enlightened by divine revelation, as the moral guide of the soul; the apostle rejoiced in the testimony of a good conscience (2 Cor. 1: 12); and it was his constant effort "to have always a conscience void of offence toward God and toward men." —Acts 24:16; 2 Tim. 1:3.

*I.* My own experience now exhibits the difference between acting reluctantly from remorse of conscience, or the fears it produces, and freely from its mandates or persuasions. But I did not look upon the act of resolving not to oppose God, as being conversion.

*P.* Your ignorance of its moral character did not alter that fact; whereas, had you supposed it would have been such, the expectation of succeeding by means of it would have been excited, and would have kept you selfish and made the act a failure. Thus, there is a good reason why God should lead the blind by a way they know not.—Is. 42:16. It would have been worse than in vain to have explained its character beforehand, for you could not have understood it, being destitute of all experience on the subject, and it would have revived the power of your selfish desires under the supposed discovery of the right way to succeed.

*I.* I see the philosophy of that course, and now understand better the mental process through which I passed. My mind was so intent on the facts and arguments presented, that I did not watch its action under them. But in that final resolution not to oppose God in recalling my life, I was actuated by no desire or love for him. Indeed, it was so cold and simple a conclusion that I placed no dependence upon it, and hardly regarded it as a resolution.

*P.* I perceive that you are still looking at the subject

through the selfish medium to which you have been so long accustomed, but which should now be corrected. You acted both voluntarily and freely in coming to that conclusion?

*I.* Perfectly so.

*P.* You could not have any desires for God *beforehand*, because all you had terminated upon yourself; and so you could not then have been actuated by any.

*I.* That is true; and I see that it was my selfish desires which I endeavored to excite beforehand.

*P.* You could not have resolved with any *accompanying* desires for God, because you had none to take along with you.

*I* That is evidently so.

*P.* It is preposterous to suppose that any sinner can be willing or desire to have God rule over him, until *after* he has *consented* to his rule. By the act of consenting not to oppose him, you became *willing*; so that when the question was presented *subsequently*, Whether you would obey God since it was his right,—you acted from a *willing state of mind* in view of such right.

*I.* Yes. I now perceive that I had become *willing* toward God generally, in consequence of my previous consent not to oppose him in opposition to his right.

*P.* You had before been accustomed to act on subjects where desires already existed, and consequently were influenced by them; but this was one of an entirely new order in reference to which you had no favorable desires, and you were under the necessity of acting from a mere sentiment of duty urged by the conscience.

*I.* So I perceive. But is such a simple and cold resolution, even though conscientious, sufficient?

*P.* Since you could not produce one from vehement emotions, it must be sufficient. But every resolution is, in its own nature, a cold and unimpassioned act, whatever may be the subject or whatever may be the attending feelings; and it is because they fail to discriminate between the antecedents and the volition produced, that any entertain a different opinion. Professor Upham remarks, "It is undoubtedly true that volitions may have aroused and excited antecedents, and may thus be closely connected with the various affections; but in themselves they are cold and unimpassioned; they are purely executive and mandatory, and are as obviously free from any actual impregnation of appetite, sentiment, or desire, as the most abstract and callous exercises of the intellect."—Upham's *Men. Phi.* vol. i. Intro. ch. 4. § 30. Thus, if you desire ever so much to visit a beloved friend, the *resolution* to do so will be a simple and cold act, one merely executive or directory, although the excitements of your desires might conceal it from your view, and when superficially observed it might seem to partake of their vehemence.

*I.* I see that I have fallen into the common error of failing to discriminate properly on this subject. But is there any moral value in such a resolution as mine?

*P.* Yes; for it partook of the character of the motive which prompted it; and that being holy, the resolution was holy also. Thus, should you *consent* to do an act which would defraud another, the simple consent would stamp your character as vicious because of the viciousness of your motive or object. In deciding thus, no reference would be had to any intervening feelings, nor indeed would men inquire whether you had any. And if you should conscientiously *refuse*, a virtuous character would attach to you for the same reason. The Scriptures require our offering to be the act of our own, or free and voluntary will.—Lev. 1:3. Of the Corinthians it is said, "they first *gave* their *ownselves* to the Lord."—2 Cor. 8:5.

*I.* But what connection has such a simple resolution (which I had almost mistaken for a mere assent of the understanding, as it was so different from what I had anticipated) with my subsequent exercises?

*P.* In connection with your observation of truth, it was the origin or source of all your new desires and affections on religion. By so consenting not to oppose God in respect to your life, you adopted, under the Spirit, his creative authority as a supreme motive influence; so that, when the idea of his right to your service was afterwards presented, it spontaneously influenced you to enter upon it; and the same idea has ever since exercised a controlling influence over your purposes, and has constantly *disposed your mind* to obey him. This is one important result of that volition.

*I.* I can see it clearly.

*P.* It also placed your will in a new and favorable state toward God; that is, it produced a *good-will* toward him in view of his rights.

*I.* It did.

*P.* It also produced a good-will to all his commands, and to every thing you perceive to be right; for the resolution of the will was substantially to do right, since God had a legal authority to command it.

*I.* You are correct.

*P.* As soon as you paused to reflect upon the rights of God, his sovereignty for example, good-will thereto and desires for the stability and extension of his government over mankind, arose spontaneously.

*I.* They did.

*P.* When you contemplated the righteousness of his character, such good-will excited love to him therefor; and as the beauties of that character glowed before your mind, a love to his glory and a strong desire to promote it as the chief moral good (Ps. 4 : 6), resulted in your heart.

*I.* Such was the train of my exercises.

*P.* *Ill-will* to every thing opposed to the rights and will of God and to righteousness in general, was the necessary result of such good-will to God. Accordingly, when you reflected upon your past selfishness of heart and sins of life, an intense ill-will and regret were excited against them, and self-hatred, producing purposes to avoid all sin. The view of the character and conduct of sinners produced similar feelings toward them, with desires for their conversion from sin. And again, the coincidence of the character of Christians with Christ, excited your good-will toward them; and your duties were prized as means of gratifying good-will to God.

*I.* I can now clearly see that the good-will for God produced by that final resolution, originated all my subsequent new exercises.

*P.* And it was the *new heart* in its primitive form.

*I.* Indeed! Pray explain this point.

*P.* The heart is so called from the fleshly organ of the body, which, by its pulsations, sends the blood, and with it life, to every part. In its spiritual sense, the heart is the *will in exercise*, sending its influences for good or evil through the whole moral system. The selfish heart is the will exercised in favor of self, its appetites, passions, and pleasures. The holy heart is the will exercised for God and his glory. President Edwards observes, "The *will* and *affections* of the soul are not two faculties; the affections are not essentially distinct from the will; nor do they differ from the mere acting of the will or its inclinations, but only in the liveliness and sensibilitiy of their exercise."—On the *Affections*. Pt. I. § 1.

*I.* Is this view sustained by the Scriptures?

*P.* Abundantly; and on so important a subject we should rely on nothing short of revelation. We shall there find that the requirement of the hearts of men is answered by the action of the will in each of its various states; which will prove that the favorable action of the will is that which God demands. 1, The Scriptures receive the action of the will in the form of a purpose, resolution, determination, or other simple volition, as being the heart. "My days are past, my *purposes* are broken off, even the *thoughts of my heart.*"—Job 17:11. "And exhorted them all, that with *purpose* of heart they would cleave unto the Lord."—Acts 11:23. "Nay, but *we will* serve the Lord."—Josh. 24:21. 2, They also recognize the will in its state of willingness, as being the heart. "Thy people shall be *willing* in the day of thy power."—Ps. 110:3. "Whosoever is of a *willing heart*, let him bring it, an offering of the Lord."—Ex. 35:5. 3, They recognize the will in its more lively state of inclinations or desires, as the heart. "There is none upon earth that I *desire* besides thee."—Ps. 73:25. "Delight thyself also in the Lord, and he shall give thee the *desires* of thy heart."—Ps. 37:4. 4, They also recognize as the heart, that fixed state of the will seen in a predominant disposition. "O God, my heart *is fixed.*"—Ps. 108:1. "The *disposings* of the heart of man is of the Lord."—Prov. 16:1, in the margin. 5, They recognize that still more lively state of the will as seen in love, as the heart. "Thou shalt *love* the Lord thy God with all thy heart."—Matt. 22:37. 6, They also speak of pleasurable emotions when connected with and evincive of desires, as the heart. "The Lord *taketh pleasure* in them that fear him."—Ps. 147:11. "I have *no pleasure* in you, saith the Lord."—Mal. 1:10. "*Delight* thyself also in the Lord."—Ps. 37:4.

*I.* The *bent of the soul* on God, is what he requires; and this is the new heart, under whatever more or less sensitive aspects it may occur?

*P.* That is it precisely; only, inasmuch as he is entitled to the *whole* bent of it, he rightfully demands all our purposes not only, but all our inclinations, desires, affections, and emotions, for himself. In the first holy act of the sinner toward God, a simple resolution of the will must take place, because that form of the heart precedes the others in the nature of things, and originates, as we have seen, the good-will from which they proceed. When the soul is thus turned toward God, as the moral excellence and glory of his character is more clearly perceived it increases its attachment to him, until the mere sense of plighted faith and allegiance is absorbed in a grateful and affectionate devotion. Conscience still acting as the guide in duty, the soul is attracted along its paths by holy love, thus "working by love."—Gal. 5:6. When, for any reason, the inclinations do not promptly move the soul in favor of some perceived duty, conscience assumes the reins and issues its mandate; the will then *purposes* that duty; the *inclinations* of the will are revived; and then the soul proceeds to execute it both from conscience, and inclination or love. In this view, how important it is to keep your conscience properly enlightened, by a constant and careful attention to the Scriptures; and active, by a wise use of your leisure hours in meditation upon the claims of God and your own duties.

*I.* It is important indeed.

*P.* Let us proceed. The Scriptures recognize such a change in our motive and purpose as a turning to the Lord, or conversion. This can be abundantly seen from the passages just cited in respect to the heart. It can be seen also from the following passages, among others: "Seek ye the *Lord* [not yourselves] while he may be found, call ye upon *him* while he is near: Let the wicked forsake his way, [his course of sinful *conduct*] and the unrighteous man his thoughts, [his unrighteous or selfish *motives* and *purposes*] and let him return [turn away from them] unto the LORD, and [then] he will have mercy upon him. For my thoughts [motives and intentions] are not your thoughts, [in respect to their moral character] neither are your ways [courses of conduct] my ways, saith the Lord. For as the heavens are higher than the earth [in altitude] so are my ways higher [more *morally* exalted] than your ways, and my thoughts than your thoughts."—Is. 55 : 6—9. In the days of Joshua, the people, in view of the benefactions and anticipated pardon and favors of God, resolved to serve him: "therefore will we serve the Lord, for he is *our* God." There was no self-denial and therefore no holiness in such purposes; which Joshua was prompt to avow. "Ye cannot serve the *Lord* [being still devoted to *yourselves*], for he is a *holy* God [requires holy motives and purposes]; he is a jealous God [solicitous to defend his rights and glory]; he will not forgive your transgressions nor your sins" [for you are still selfish]. Cut off thus from their plans, they renounced selfishness by abandoning themselves, saying: "Nay, [notwithstanding he may not forgive us] but [still] we will serve the *Lord*." Joshua here recognized a new motive and a holy intention, and he accepted *these first resolutions* as conversion. "And Joshua said unto the people, ye are witnesses *against* YOURSELVES that ye have chosen you [have brought yourselves into united action with] the LORD, to serve *him*. And they said, We are witnesses." He then proceeded to make known their duties, and set up a monument as a testimonial of their covenant and conversion.—Josh. 24:17—27.

*I.* I have been much perplexed on a point which is now clear to my mind. The resolutions to serve God formed by *careless* sinners do not accomplish any radical change in the bent of their minds, because they are neither in earnest nor have any holy motive. Those usually formed by *convicted* sinners, though intensely earnest, are deficient in respect to such holy motive and are under selfish reasons. Those formed by *self-denying* sinners are both in earnest and in view of a right or holy motive, and therefore accomplish a change in the bent of their minds in favor of that motive. A misconception here has led me to doubt the sufficiency of any kind of resolution in conversion; but I can doubt no more. Will you give me a detail of the ordinary experience of Christians who have been left to act without very clear instructions under the gospel?

*P.* I will. For want of such instruction many who have, at times, been the subjects of serious impressions, have doubtless been for ever lost; as is said by the prophet: "My people are destroyed for lack of knowledge."—Hos. 4:6. There is no material difference between the rise and progress of the first convictions of sin in one who is afterwards truly converted, and in one who is not. *Q.*, for example, is aroused to reflection by the same instrumentalities as any of those I have described in the first chapter; and it is not at all material to the final issue what they were. He starts with a heart bent on securing his own safety and peace ultimately; and with this prēpurpose, he pursues such means as he hopes will terminate in success. He aims to secure evidences of a change and a sense of pardon, in order to a hope of his own safety through Christ; and to this end seeks to make himself good and propitiate Christ. The usual course is first to correct his outward deportment; and next to obtain sincere and right feelings, as has been before fully described. In his progress he determines to forsake the particular sins which occur to him, and finally, to renounce the world and its sinful pleasures, with a view to succeed in his more selfish ultimate object. Obtaining no relief or sense of pardon, he redoubles his efforts to make himself better and to give his heart to God sincerely, so as to do it safely to himself and secure the desired change; he prays often, studies the Scriptures, consults Christians for their advice; and in increasing anxiety for his own ends casts about to find what he calls the right way to Christ. He tries to believe, but it does no good; while his thoughts, dwelling upon his sins, arouse his conscience to loud reproofs and condemnation, and he becomes more deeply convinced that God is right in his displeasure, that he ought to have served him all his days, that every thing in himself and in his conduct has been and is altogether sinful, and that he justly deserves the everlasting vengeance of God; and his reproving conscience assures him that remaining in his then impenitent state, his final and eternal perdition is certain. In his renewed efforts to escape, he usually ponders upon the pains of future punishment until his alarms are very much increased, and his endeavors become very energetic.

*I.* Are great fears of perdition necessary to a true conversion?

*P.* No; and many have no such sensitiveness about it as I have described, but are merely aware of the principle of eternal punishment, and are conscious that it will be their fate unless they repent. In their extremity, they are often tempted to flee to the world; but their conscience, fears, and the Holy Spirit prevent. In this way some continue under the convicting influences of the Spirit for months and even years, leading a life of sadness, and ignorant of the true reason of their remaining unconverted.

*I.* Better remain so, than to receive false encouragement as I did.

*P.* Yes; for the Spirit may finally drive them out of their prēpurpose for their own ends, into holiness; but if a false belief should confirm them in it, there can be no hope in their case, for with it they will resist the Spirit to the last. *Q.* at last becomes discouraged because of the fruitlessness of his prayers and efforts for right feelings; he still thinks that Christ is willing to help him, but that he cannot find the right way to go to him for aid. This inability he ascribes to the singularity of his own case; no one, as he supposes, having had such strange thoughts, wicked feelings, or so hard a heart, as himself. Perhaps he ascribes it to his having begun too late, and having so long withstood conviction, and resisted the Spirit; or, to his being too great a sinner to be pardoned. Perhaps he concludes that he has committed the unpardonable sin, and grieved away the Spirit; or that he is not elected to be saved.

*I.* The true reason, as I now see, being that which Dr. Nettleton developed when under similar convictions of sin—namely, that in all his efforts he was prompted by selfish motives; that he had no love to *God* and no regard to *his glorg* in them; that in his distress there was no godly sorrow, and that he had not hated sin because committed against God, but had merely dreaded its consequences.

*P.* Yes, that is the true reason. But under his own inferences as to the cause, *Q.* becomes convinced that all his expedients and efforts to succeed are useless, and in utter despondency he finally suspends them. He is now slain by the law; that is, he is convinced of his entire depravity, of his just exposure to the penalty of eternal death, of his inability to do any thing toward his own safety and peace, and that no help therefor is to be obtained from God or man. His hostility to God is restrained by the conviction of the justness of his doom; and he is determined never to retreat to the world, because his conscience forbids, and he perceives in it a "certain fearful looking for of judgment and fiery indignation," and he is withheld by the power of the Spirit which brought him there. He looks upon himself as a lost man, in every sense.

*I.* How clearly the subject opens to me now! As regards every thing he values, he is lost; but no more so then than before, only he has become more fully aware of it.

*P.* Yes. The loss of every prospect of success in his selfish purposes, destroys the *power* of his desires; and now for the first time in his whole existence, his will is released from their domination, and his mind is open to the influence of new moral motives. In his extremity he anticipates no benefit from any thing he can do, since he has tried every thing conceivable; so that the hope of good does not influence him in his subsequent volitions. He is aware that his situation can be made no more desperate by any position he may take; and consequently he ceases to be influenced by his fears. He is then led to reflect upon the fact that his offended Sovereign not only has power to punish him, but that he deserves to be punished; that God has a right to do with him just as he sees fit for time and eternity, and that he *ought* to let him. The Holy Spirit now reaches his heart in his regenerating influences; and *Q.*, without any efforts to be sincere, and without resorting to any of his former expedients, simply resigns himself to let the will of God be done; and under the mere impulse that he ought to, and without interposing any desires, hopes, or fears, makes up his mind or consents to leave himself entirely at his disposal for time and for eternity. This consent of the will, is the act of turning to God.

*I.* But he does not then regard it as conversion?

*P.* No. Accustomed to expect strong feelings and bright evidences, and ignorant of the true moral and metaphysical character of the act required, he passes it over as having no tendency to promote his desires. In this he is correct; but he regards it as having no tendency to true piety also, in which he is mistaken. He is conscious of being in earnest in thus consenting to the will of God, but attaches no moral value to the act; and this idea is apt to abide with him through life, hindering him from precisely understanding his own conversion, and consequently from affording others clear instructions upon the same point. Under the idea that *love* only is the heart, when he comes afterwards to exercise pleasure in God he considers that feeling to be the act of conversion or change of heart; and he consequently labors to keep up his own enjoyments and advises others to do the same, in order to preserve the new heart—a thing which cannot always be done under our present circumstances.

*I.* No wonder, in this view, that Christians have so many doubts and are often plunged into such darkness.

*P.* Many self-deceived sinners love to keep the subject in obscurity, and, under the cloak of humility, loudly oppose every attempt to make the point of conversion clear, because it will destroy their own hopes.

*I.* But they must be destroyed, in order to their own deliverance?

*P.* Yes; but their selfish hearts will not consent, and would rather abuse those who kindly attempt to enlighten them. *Q.*, in consenting to the will of God, acts simply under a sense of duty, that is, under the impulse that *he ought* to yield to him; and under the same sentiment, makes up his mind to serve him as well as he can, whatever God may do with him hereafter. It may be that, on so yielding, he expects to be punished; or it may be that he thinks of neither pardon nor punishment, but submits to God as one who has a right to do as he will, without anticipating any consequences, favorable or unfavorable. The important point is, that by the removal of all others, the right of God becomes the strongest present motive, and moves him, under the Spirit, to yield his will to God.

*I.* Is submission always the first act?

*P.* No. Perhaps when so desponding in self-denial, *Q.* first thought of his past sins; and the idea that God had a right to forbid them, and did forbid them, led him to resolve to sin no more. In this case, the same principle of the divine authority would be yielded to, and would constitute the act of turning to God. It is not material what particular duty is contemplated in the first volition, provided the authority of God is its motive; and whoever enters thus upon one duty, will find that the idea of the authority of God has thereby so obtained the ascendancy over his mind that, under its impulse, he can spontaneously comply with every other.

*I.* I see that if the right of God obtains the control of the will through the conscience, on any subject, it will exert the same predominance over all others; for it is intrinsically the most powerful of all motives, and the Holy Spirit, I suppose, will preserve its influence on the heart.

*P.* Yes. *Q.* did not anticipate any change on so yielding to God, and he acquires no such evidences of safety as he formerly endeavored to secure; yet he enters upon a new state of mind, inasmuch as he finds himself *willing* to be unreservedly in the hands of God, and to serve him because he ought to do so. By consenting, he has reached a state of willingness; but he seldom looks upon it as a change of heart—for he wants brighter evidences. Still, he feels pleased that God reigns, that his holy will shall be accomplished whatever becomes of himself, and he is satisfied to be in his hands. Conscience now approves his submission and gives peace to his soul, leaving him astonished, perhaps, that he can feel so composed and even pleased with God while, for ought he knows, his soul will be destroyed. This he regards as a degree of insensibility, instead of the power of a new principle as it actually is. Perhaps while engaged in prayer or reflecting upon the character of God, he feels a love to him spring up in his heart; and the more he reflects upon his rectitude, holiness, justice, goodness, the stronger his love becomes. And then, as has been said, he begins to indulge a hope in Christ, and dates his conversion from that period.

*I.* The difference then between a true and false convert is this: the true submits to God and loves him for his own sake, before he entertains a hope of pardon; while the false hopes for his own happiness first, and makes a pretended submission to accomplish it, and entertains a selfish love afterwards?

*P.* Yes. The false cannot conceive how one can love God, until after his regards are excited by a persuasion of his friendship and mercy to himself! By such yielding to God, *Q.* has acquired good-will to him, to all his commands, to all who imitate his character, and generally to every good word and work. This is exhibited in that love to the disciples, hatred to sin, desire for the extension of Christ's kingdom and devotion to his glory, which have been heretofore sufficiently described.

*I.* In order, then, to test our conversion, it is only necessary to decide whether the idea of the creative right of God exerts, of itself, sufficient power over our minds to lead us freely to resolve to obey him?

*P.* Yes. And in order to discover the resulting evidences of such a volition, we are to look at our exercises toward the character of God, toward duty, toward sin, toward Christians, toward sinners, and the like.

*I.* This renders the matter plain and highly satisfactory. Most Christians are seeking after some grounds for a hope, instead of contemplating their principles.

*P.* In order to show the agreement of a true experience with the principles we have been examining, I will give in a note the exercises of an artless Indian girl, substantially as they are narrated by the missionary at the Mackinaw station.*

* ME-SAI-AIN-SEE had long endeavored to dispel the alarm produced by the faithful instructions of her teachers; but the fear of dying without the new heart had induced her to correct her deportment and to live morally in all respects towards her companions. At last, under an outpouring of the Spirit at the station, she became so convicted of sin, and so distressed at her danger, that she resorted to every conceivable expedient to secure relief, and an evidence of a hope of pardon and future peace. Every effort seemed vain; while the apparent success of those of her companions who had found peace, filled her heart with envy against them, and rebellion against God. Her heart seemed to harden, until she gave up all hope of softening or breaking it; and unable to go forward she was shut up, not knowing what to do. For three days her per-

*I.* Are there no varieties in Christian experience?

*P.* There are in respect to the causes of conviction of sin, and in the occurrence of the exercises after conversion; but in respect to the fact of self-denial, and the yielding in some form to the authority of God, there is

plexity and anxiety was so great as entirely to overcome her; and at last she became unable to shed a tear. She afterwards said to her friends, "I got to my bed-room, and throwing myself upon the bed, I lay for some time unconscious of every thing but the fire within; nor durst I shut my eyes for fear I should find myself in death, actually sinking into the flames of hell. I said to myself, I have tried every way [to secure relief by a hope of peace and safety] in vain. I cannot help *myself;* neither prayers nor anxieties do any good; they lead to no relief." Under this conviction she ceased her efforts for it, and thus denied herself; and conscience then took the command. "It is right, it is just in God to destroy me; I *ought* to perish. He may do what he pleases [an earnest, but unimpassioned *consent* to God's sovereign authority]; if he sends me to hell, let him do it; and if he shows mercy, well; let him do just what he pleases [that is, a transfer of the whole question to God without dictating what he shall do, and with a previous consent to his decision, whatever it may be; the *will* thereby turning from the dominion of self to that of God]. Here, as in a moment, I had such a kind of one or whole view of myself and *willingness* to be in God's hands, that I could keep in bed no longer, and resolved to go in prayer and throw myself for the last time at the feet of my Saviour [her name for Christ], and solemnly beg of him [not, as before, to pity, pardon, and secure her safety and peace, but] to do what he would with me" [that is, to accomplish his own will, the new object which had, unobserved to herself as it were, just become chief in her thoughts, desires, and purposes.] A pious Indian woman now engaged in conversation with her. The girl said, "she told me how easy it was to believe in the Saviour [hope in his mercy], if I would. She then prayed with me; and here I lost all my burden. I felt light, a strange feeling which I cannot describe. I had no thought that I no variety. Let us take another case. *R.*, we will suppose, has yielded himself to God, and takes an unexpected peace in the idea that he is at his sovereign disposal, and that he will do right. Of course his fears and anxieties are now dissipated; but he is not aware of being in a converted state. It suddenly occurs to him, perhaps, that he has lost his convictions for sin; and in alarm he seeks to recover them. At once he passes down into a state of deep repentance for sin and of self-abhorrence and gloom, which dispel all his late comfort. This he mistakes for conviction of sin merely,

loved Christ [had no idea that she had any Scriptural evidences, and so had no hope of pardon], but I was happy [in God himself]; and yet afraid to be happy. I was afraid to give indulgence to my feelings; for it would be dreadful after all, it appeared to me, to go to hell with no feeling of distress about it! [Her submission to, and love of the will of God, had not destroyed her desire of happiness; but had for the time so engrossed her heart that the thought she might be lost gave her no anxiety.] Rising from my knees, I was conscious of a smile upon my face, which I tried to hide." Soon after another person prayed with her, and Me-sai-ain-see afterwards said, "Here I was filled with that happiness I hope to enjoy in heaven, arising from a view of the love, the nearness, and the glory of the Saviour. I seemed to see it, to feel it all in a fullness of joy beyond expression." On being asked, "Can you not love this Saviour?" the poor girl ventured to say, "I hope I do." She said, "this was the first intimation I had dared to give of my peace of soul. My joy had swallowed up all my fear, and I could not resist the answer. Now, I had such a love to all around, as well as for the Saviour, that I could have folded them to my bosom. I appeared to be in a new world; every thing led me to God; not an object did I see, but it seemed to say, How glorious and lovely is the great God!" From that memorable night her life and conversation have been such as becometh godliness.

and struggles onward in deeper darkness. Perhaps some view of God in his moral beauty may finally lift his soul out of despondency; but if not, he will spend his days with new principles respecting God and his duty indeed, but without a hope to cheer him onward, and perhaps in the vain struggle after evidences of acceptance. In sadness and doubt he serves the Lord, "faint though pursuing;" and perhaps never enjoys an unclouded hope of "God's salvation" until his entrance into the kingdom on high renders a hope unnecessary.

*I.* I think I have met with many such hopeless believers. Some persons are prone to despondency, and always look at the dark side of every subject; and well it is for them that religion consists in a devotion to God and his glory, rather than in a hope of pardon, else they would fail of final holy blessedness. I realize more and more the importance of clear and correct views, in order to Christian enjoyment.

*P. S.* belongs to a class who have never been much alarmed by a view of the eternal perdition which they know awaits them; but who are peculiarly sensitive to their sins, and whose consciences are very readily aroused in view of their guilt. Under the influence of his reflections upon the truth, and under the power of the Spirit, his conscience turns his thoughts so entirely to the subject of his sinfulness and rebellion against God, that he loses sight of all prospect of escaping the divine penalty. Suspending every effort for his own escape, he makes the struggle on the point whether he will submit to God or no, until the Spirit reaches his heart, and he yields to God to let him control as he will for time and eternity. His will having now submitted under a kind of impulse for God, he finds himself *willing* to serve him, and soon exercises those other Christian affections before described. In explanation of this subject more at large, I will give, in a note, an account of some revivals of religion under the preaching of some of the sound divines of the last century.*

* *Extract from an Account of a Revival of Religion in the township of Bristol, Connecticut, in the year* 1799.

Before the close of the year, there were about fifty who appeared to be reconciled to God, and who were rejoicing in hope.

The exercises of these persons were in some respects different, and in some similar. Some seemed to have much more pungent convictions of sin than others—some were more conscious of the strength and bitterness of the enmity of their hearts to God than others. Yet there was a great similarity in the account which they gave of themselves. That account was something like this:

At first they were principally affected with a sense of their danger of the wrath of God; they then resorted to their own works to conciliate his favor, without that submission to him, and reliance on Christ, which the gospel requires. While pursuing this course, they gradually grew more and more sensible of their guilt, and of the dreadful depravity of their hearts, till they were convinced of their entire dependence on the sovereign mercy of God for salvation. At this point many were conscious of dreadful heart risings against God and his government. Some were on the borders of despair. After continuing for some time in this state, many of them were suddenly relieved from the anguish of their souls. Of these, some were immediately filled with great joy, and with admiring views of the excellence of God's character. Every thing about them seemed showing forth God's presence and glory which they had never seen before.

Others at first experienced only a calm composure of mind, a full approbation of God's right to dispose of them as he pleased. They did not view themselves as entitled to the promises of the gospel, but even feared that they were losing their convictions, and should

*I.* I shall be obliged by your doing so.

*P. T.* is the representative of still another class, whose numbers are comparatively small. He had become con-

return to their former stupidity. This state of mind was generally followed in a few hours, or a few days, with a joyful perception of the excellency and glory of God, and a spirit of love, praise, and comfort in Him, or of the glorious work of redemption in Christ, the fullness of His salvation, or some other of the various manifestations which God has made of his perfections. These exercises caused a hope to spring up in their minds that they were born of God. This was commonly by no means strong at first, and was expressed with caution. As they were more or less obedient to God, their hopes increased or diminished.

Many of them declared that the happiness they enjoyed in religious exercises, far exceeded all the sinful pleasures they had ever enjoyed. A number of those whose experience has thus been alluded to, were formerly opposed to the doctrine of the divine purposes, and the total depravity of the natural heart. After their conversion, they had no quarrel with these doctrines. There was a man in the parish, about fifty-six years old, who had been very inattentive to religion, and had very much neglected public worship. When the revival commenced, he was at work in a neighboring township. After two or three months he returned. He found many of the people greatly changed; and this led him to reflect on his own sinful condition, till he became deeply impressed with a sense of his danger. He then constantly attended religious meetings, and soon acquired some just views of the relations between God and himself, and of the way of salvation. Not long after, he manifested a spirit of submission to God. He was asked if he was willing that God should govern all things according to his own good will and pleasure. He readily answered, "Yes, that is what I want." It was said, "What if he should cut you off?" He answered, "Well, I won't find fault with him if he does. I won't say I submit, and then find fault with him if he doesn't do with me as I wish."

He said this in a manner which indicated that he uttered the real feelings of his heart. He remained for several weeks rejoicing in vinced of his sins, of his just desert of the divine wrath, and also that he would be lost if he remained in his then state of heart; and for some time he had been

God and his government, and in the doctrines and duties of the gospel, before he had any idea or hope that he was a real Christian. This was not known to his neighbors, and one of them asked him to state the reasons why he thought himself a Christian. He replied, "I don't think I am one, I have no idea that I am, but I hope I shall be." Mention was made to him of the gracious promises made to those who will cast themselves on God's mercy. He answered, "I choose that he should do with me as he sees fit."

Some time after this by comparing his exercises with the word of God, he indulged an humble hope that he was a Christian. He continued to enjoy great peace of mind, though a sense of his own vileness and unworthiness increased upon him. On one occasion, he said, "A sense of my vileness neither interrupts my happiness, nor leads me to dread the day of judgment, for MY HOPES ARE IN CHRIST alone."

*Extracts from an Account of a Revival in New Cambridge, Connecticut, in* 1799.

When first awakened they were generally moved by a sense of danger. They then set out with the resolution and expectation of making themselves better. But the more they attended to the duties of religion and endeavored to make themselves better, the more sensible they became of their exceeding depravity and guilt. They were soon brought to see that their hearts were full of sin and opposition to God. Instead of supposing, as they formerly did, that they had no enmity to God, and that they did many things which were right and acceptable in his sight, they were now sensible that they had always been opposed to his character and government, that they had been sinning against him in all their moral conduct, and that he might justly cast them off for ever. They were fully convinced that such was their depravity, that they should never repent unless influenced by the Spirit of God, and that God might justly withhold that influence, and leave them to go on and perish seeking religion, as he supposed, by prayer and attention to religious duties. On one occasion he was listening to an interesting, because convincing discourse on the subject of the sinner's duty to God. He soon forgot himself in the subject; and when the preacher presented the idea of the rightful authority of God over the creature, he assented to it as a clear truth, without thinking about his own happiness. On the idea being urged that we ought to obey God, he thought it would be right toward him, and under the Spirit concluded he would obey him. This was done without any thought of himself, and therefore with self-denial. He continued thus to follow the preacher through his discourse; and at its close for the first time thought of himself, and of the people who surrounded him. His eye rested upon some active Christians in the assembly, and his heart flowed out in good-will and love to them as disciples of Christ. Now, said he, I can understand what these Christians

in their sins. The convictions of some were more sharp and powerful than those of others. Some experienced them for a longer, some for a shorter time. When they were very powerful, the subjects of them commonly found relief sooner.

When they found relief, it was commonly from a discovery of the glory and rectitude of the divine character, and a disposition to submit to God. They had new views and feelings toward almost every thing around. Jesus Christ appeared glorious and lovely, and such an all-sufficient Saviour as they needed, and therefore they cordially trusted in him for salvation. They could rejoice that the Lord reigned, and would dispose of all events as he saw best. The Bible appeared new and delightful, and they cordially approved its doctrines and precepts. These and other similar views and feelings were manifested by the young converts; but some manifested a much more lively sense of these things than others.

have been about, and will help them serve the Lord. And such has been his endeavor hitherto.

*I.* I see that if one happens to forget himself, he can act in view of a holy motive alone; but one cannot forget himself by trying, and *T.* must have pretty much worn out his selfish courage before then.

*P.* My object in these details has been to meet the cases of various Christian readers, in order that they may clearly understand their own exercises, decide upon their moral character, and so enjoy the blessings which an assurance will confer. If any such have been disturbed by the instructions and arguments heretofore used for sinners, it will not work the least injury; while by understanding the false as well as the true, their perceptions of the latter will be more clear, and their confidence in it will be rendered more firm. It is a received doctrine, as expressed by the Westminster Assembly, that "although unregenerate men may vainly deceive themselves with false hopes and carnal presumptions of being in the favor of God and estate of salvation, which hope of theirs shall perish; yet such as truly believe in the Lord Jesus and love him in sincerity, endeavoring to walk in all good conscience before him, may in this life be *certainly assured* that they are in a state of grace, and may "rejoice in the hope of the glory of God;" which hope shall never make them ashamed." And again: "Such may, without extraordinary revelation, by faith grounded on the truth of God's promises, and by the Spirit enabling them *to discern in themselves those graces to which the promises of life are made*, and bearing witness with their Spirits that they are the children of God, be *infallibly* assured that they are in the estate of grace, and shall persevere therein unto salvation."

*I.* I feel rëassured; for I feared that such confidence in one's good estate might be dangerous to the Christian's faithful progress, as well as presumptuous.

*P.* As to its being dangerous, we must distinguish between the sinner who has a hope, and the Christian. The sinner has no love to God for his intrinsic moral worth, to impel him to obedience. All the motive influence he possesses, is the desire and hope to secure his favor in order to his own safety and peace. Now, let him become perfectly confident of this favor, and he will be ready to plunge into any favorite sin, and to riot in every worldly pleasure which he does not apprehend will interfere with his prospects. And he is very liberal on this point, since he has no standard in his own heart superior to the love of pleasure, by which to decide the moral propriety of his conduct. Hence we find that those increasing sects in religion which substitute rites and forms for holiness, are the most popular and their devotees the most worldly. The six days of the week are spent in worldliness and the pursuit of every attainable pleasure; while the Sabbath is, as far as is agreeable, devoted to repairing damages, and to confirming a hope of eternal pleasures after the present are worn out. But as respects the Christian, who has a new, a holy, and a superior affection for God and for the things that make for his glory, a confidence in his good estate is a most powerful stimulus to perseverance, inasmuch as it encourages him with a hope of victory! Slavish fear forms no part of his motives; but there is a holy fear which will always exist, and which will tend to sustain him in his progress, however strong his *present* confidence may be. "Let us therefore fear, lest a promise being left us of entering into his rest, any of you should seem to come short of it."—Heb. 4:1. In the perfect obedience of the saints of light, may be seen the effects of a full assurance on the holy heart. The temptations of the world are never so powerless, as when the Christian rests in a holy confidence on Christ, not merely for a pardon, but for strength to glorify him here and to enjoy him hereafter.

*I.* And the constrained service of the fearful sinner under his doubts, could be no more acceptable than if rendered from a confident hope.

*P.* As respects such assurance being presumptuous, nothing can be so which is founded on the truth. To believe any truth, or to receive any correct inference from it, can never be arrogance or presumption; but not to do so, may rather evince an undue diffidence.

*I.* My fear was to apply the fact to myself.

*P.* We should never suffer our mere apprehensions to interfere with the conclusions of our judgment, or with the application of them to ourselves, whether favorable or unfavorable, when truth will authorize or require it. I therefore advise you to dispel such influences, and to open your mind to conviction on this subject.

*I.* I will do so. But will not such a confidence in my good estate, be equivalent to declaring that I am perfect in my own estimation?

*P.* By no means. The selfish mind, indeed, so regards assurance, for the reason that all its hopes are based upon its own supposed goodness, and it seeks perfection as the ground of perfect confidence in its future safety. When the standard of holy principle and of the divine law is lowered to the exigencies of his selfishness, or when his blind or seared conscience fails to reprove him for a deviation from that which God has presented as his rule of heart and life, it is easy to imagine himself to have attained a sinlessly perfect state, and to hope *professedly* in the merits of Christ, but *really* upon his own supposed righteousness. This is the key to the destructive error known as Perfectionism; an error which cannot long enthrall the true believer, because his standard is too high and his conscience too sensitive to continue the self-complacent delusion. The Scriptures every where condemn it by implication, and in many instances by express averments. Thus God pronounced Job upright, in view of his upright principles and his honest purpose to observe them; while Job himself, in view of his various violations of them in feeling and conduct declared, "If *I* say I am perfect, it [the very pretension] shall also prove me perverse," or turned aside from the truth and right.—Job 9 : 20; Eccl. 7 : 20. Still, the Christian feels that it is his duty to be perfectly holy (Matt. 5 : 48); he knows that it is his duty to exercise every right feeling toward every object toward which he exercises any moral feelings at all. But he well understands that neither perfection nor imperfection constitutes the reason why Christ pardons the penitent, and he does not look to his progress to graduate his hope. He knows that he is not accepted *because* he is holy; and he knows also that he will not be accepted *unless* he has a holy character. He looks to his principles and exercises, not to ascertain whether and to what extent he deserves a recompense; but whether he can perceive the qualifications which Christ has rendered indispensable to his mercy, so as to trust in him without presumption. When he discovers them, he does not ground his expectations upon them, or partly on them and partly on Christ; but averting his attention from his conscious demerit as well as from his holy principles, he rests solely on the mere grace of Christ through the atonement for wisdom, righteousness, sanctification, redemption, and eternal life.

*I.* I can now readily understand the difference, but never did before. I used to think and say that my hope was alone on Christ, by which I meant, as I now perceive, that I depended alone on the *power* of Christ; while I trusted in my hope and other supposed qualifications, to recommend me to him for the exertion of that power. It was mere self-righteousness.

*P.* A species which is, alas! too common throughout the whole visible church.

*I.* I have feared that such assurance would evince a want of due humility.

*P.* And so many think, whose condemning consciences drive them from its comforts. Humility of the understanding, is a teachableness of disposition under divine revelation. Humility of the will, is its entire submission to God and his word as therein made known. Humility in estimation of ourselves, consists in ascertaining and receiving the exact truth respecting ourselves so far as it can be reached, as having long rebelled against God, and as being without any just claim to his mercy, and the like. It does not require us to condemn ourselves beyond reason, nor to keep out of view those new characteristics which we may possess, through grace. Christ was meek and lowly of heart, but he did not therefore disbelieve in every thing approvable in his own character. It is pleasant to see one arrayed in robes of whose moral beauty he is unconscious—for then we are sure that pride is absent; but the loveliness and power of piety do not consist in such unconsciousness, else they would be lost in heaven, where every saint knows himself, even as he is known by others. And while such a supposed attainment might excite the pride of the sinner, it always must fail with the Christian who well knows that what he possesses is a mere gift, and that he not only falls far short of the high mark set before him, but is continually, by sin, making occasions for self-reproach.

*I.* I am satisfied.

*P.* Then act upon these principles while we recapitulate some of the points we have been investigating. I understand that you are now conscious that the right of God as your Creator is sufficient of itself, whenever you contemplate it, to induce you to resolve to obey him?

*I.* It is sufficient.

*P.* And that, when you contemplate the character of God it looks pleasant and desirable; and when you regard his glory, you have a desire and purpose to endeavor to promote it by avoiding whatever you are persuaded he would disapprove, by dispatching whatever work he has assigned you in life, and by observing his commands in well-doing toward mankind?

*I.* Yes.

*P.* Then you are converted to God, in a new purpose and new desires for him!

*I.* Yes; I will dismiss my fears, and admit this fair conclusion.

*P.* You would not doubt my promise when seriously made, and on a matter where it could be readily performed?

*I.* Indeed I should not.

*P.* How much more confident should you be in respect to the promise of Christ, the all-truthful and all-powerful! He has promised to accept those who are converted, to remit their sins, to keep them to the end, and to confer on them eternal life.—Acts 3:19; John 10:28; Heb. 5:9. Having been converted through his grace, the promise attaches to you; and you stand in reference to it precisely as though he should now address you by name from heaven, and assure you of his favor.

*I.* Yes; the promise, I do believe, applies to me.

*P.* And you do now cast yourself entirely on Christ for remission of sins, and for eternal life?

*I.* I do. I hope in him, and in him alone.

*P.* And as you cannot doubt his veracity or power, and as you are fully confident, from the evidence of your own consciousness, that you have yielded to the authority of God—you can now trust in Christ, with a *full* assurance that he has remitted your sins, and that he will give you eternal life?

*I.* I can, and do.

*P.* "He which hath begun a good work in you, will finish it until the day of Jesus Christ."—Phil. 1:6. By conversion to Christ you have now become one of his disciples, or a Christian; by receiving him and his truth with such confidence, you have reached the assurance of faith; and by undoubtingly trusting in Christ, you have attained the *full assurance of hope.* "And we desire,' says the apostle, "that you show the same diligence, to [the preservation of] the full assurance of hope unto the end."—Heb. 6:11. The subject of "growing in grace, and in the knowledge of our Lord and Saviour, [our Sovereign, and Deliverer,] Jesus Christ," will be pursued in the next chapter. In the holy confidence of your heart, ever rest upon him for strength and victory!

*I.* With his aid, I will. I cannot express my surprise, my gratitude, my love to Christ for that matchless kindness which has plucked me as a brand from the burning, which has brought me up out of the horrible pit, out of the miry clay, and has set my foot upon a rock, and has established my goings! To God be all the praise and glory!

*P.* "Rejoice *in the Lord* alway; and again I say, Rejoice!"—Phil. 4:4. And who should rejoice, if the servants of the great King cannot? Now, Almighty power is pledged that all things shall work together for your good.—Rom. 8:28. It has been truly said that the exercise of goodness, wisdom, and power by another who is pledged to use it in our behalf, and who is competent and faithful, is of the same value to us as if we possessed and exercised it for ourselves; and as the infinite goodness, wisdom, and power of God is so pledged for us, it is the same as though we possessed them ourselves. Thus have you already become an "heir of God, and joint-heir with Christ."—Rom. 8:17.

*I.* O, may I always walk in the paths of holy love and obedience, that I may ever show my gratitude for such disinterested goodness!

*P.* The Holy Spirit will aid you to accomplish that

desire. Let not the cares and evils of life press hard upon your spirits, for life is short, and its rapid flight is hastening you to the rest of eternal glory and blessedness. Be faithful; and when you reach the last of earth, Christ will enable you to say, "Yea, though I walk through the valley of the shadow of death, I will fear no evil: for thou art with me; thy rod and thy staff they comfort me."—Ps. 23:4. Christ has gone before us, marking his pathway in blood; and we shall find the footing as firm beyond, as on this side the grave. God rewards in order that, in the everlasting "ages to come, he might show the exceeding riches of his grace in his kindness towards us through Christ Jesus" (Eph. 2:7); and we may be sure that he will recompense like one possessed of inexhaustible stores! This privilege was purchased with the life of his own Son; and he is only awaiting his own good time in which to exercise it without measure. He has prepared for you a mansion—it is a glorious one! He has made ready a robe of righteousness—it is a spotless one! He has laid by for you a crown—and it is a brilliant one! In that mansion shall you ever find shelter from sin and sorrow;—within the folds of that robe shall all your guilt be covered;—with that crown shall you reign with him for ever and ever!

*I.* I can hardly find language in which to express the feelings of my overflowing heart!

"Sweet visions these that cheer our way,
And lead our weary spirits on:
As sunbeams in a wintry day—
So bright, so beautiful are they!
But not so quickly gone.

"And faith shall shortly yield to sight,
And we shall gain that pleasant land;
Shall tread those boundless fields of light,
Drink of that stream of pure delight,
And near our Saviour stand."

## CHAPTER X.

### PERSEVERANCE.

*Pastor.* MY friend, you have now entered upon the Christian warfare; and before you are the prizes of glory, honor, immortality, and eternal life.—Rom. 2:7. The pursuit of these will subject you to no charge of mercenariness, for they are virtuous rewards for a holy life;—rewards which our heavenly Father delights to confer. "Let us lay aside every weight, and the sin [unbelief] which doth so easily beset us, and let us run with patience the race that is set before us, looking unto Jesus the author and finisher of our faith."—Heb. 12:1, 2.

*Inquirer.* God grant that I may "so run as to obtain." —1 Cor. 9:24. I can place no dependence on myself for steadfastness; but "I can do all things through Christ which strengtheneth me."—Phil. 4:13. My greatest dread is to fall into sin.

*P.* A wholesome fear will tend to keep you on your guard against temptation. "Wherefore let him that thinketh he standeth, take heed lest he fall. There hath no temptation taken you but such as is common to man; but God is faithful, who will not suffer you to be tempted above that ye are able; but will with the temptation also make a way to escape, that ye may be able to bear it."—1 Cor. 10:12, 13.

*I.* How inexpressibly good is Christ! I need much instruction in the way of life.

*P.* We are free agents in all our religious conduct; due knowledge is, therefore, as indispensable to our progress in this, as in any other pursuit; and consequently when it is enjoined upon us to "grow in grace," we are also commanded to grow "in the knowledge of our Lord and Saviour Jesus Christ."—2 Pet. 3:18. As has been remarked, a reliance upon the Holy Spirit for light and strength is not only necessary for us, but is an act of due honor to him. But it is important to observe that, in the language of Arrowsmith, "the things which the Holy Ghost discovers, are no other for substance but those very things which are contained in the written word; only he affords regenerate persons clearer light to discern them by, than they had before conversion. Turn a learned man to the same author which he perused when a young student; he will find the self-same matter, but see a great deal further into it." He draws his people after God, by the use of adequate motives addressed to minds that have become sensitive to his gracious influences; or, in his own language, "I drew them with cords of a man, with bands of love."—Hos. 11:4.

*I.* And by such means, the Spirit acts in entire consistency with our own free agency.

*P.* Some, who do not understand this fact, attempt to depose upon the Spirit the duties which belong to themselves; and as he will not assume them, many, as a consequence, fail of eternal life. But others who understand that, as "laborers together with God" (1 Cor. 3:9) they have their own separate work to do, devote themselves to it as earnestly as if every thing depended on themselves; and they reap the blessed fruits.

*I.* In what does the Christian warfare consist?

*P.* It consists in the observance of the third principle laid down by our Lord, in the terms of discipleship already referred to—namely, "to take up his cross daily."—Luke 9:23. The cross was an instrument of death; and to take it up daily, is to sacrifice every selfish project as it may arise in the heart, on the altar of duty to God; to resist every inducement to sin; and to deny every evil thought, affection, and action, as urged by remaining corruption. In order to this, the authority of God must be maintained in active supremacy over the will, and his glory as a supreme attraction to the affections. Said the apostle, "I therefore so run, not as uncertainly; so fight I, not as one that beateth the air [without any clear or definite object]; but I keep under my body [my selfish desires and aims], and bring it into subjection [to the will of God]; lest that by any means when I have preached to others, I myself should be a cast-away."—1 Cor. 9:26, 27. Thus a holy fear also stimulated him as he pressed "toward the mark for the prize of the high calling of God in Christ Jesus."—Phil. 3:14.

*I.* If Paul indulged in such apprehensions, they surely will not be groundless in us; and how wary should we be! I feel like a mere child in the school of Christ.

*P.* Have a child's teachableness and docility of will in respect to the truths of revelation, and you will not fail of the kingdom of heaven.—Luke 18:17.

*I.* What is precisely intended by obedience to God?

*P.* It has been defined while speaking of conversion

in the last chapter. I will observe, however, that obedience is a peculiar act in respect to the motive that produces it. It implies a subordination to authority, to the exclusion of every other inconsistent consideration. As, if I command my child to do a certain act, and he does it for some private reason of his own, such as getting money from me; this would not be an act of obedience to *me*, for it would not be done in observance of my parental authority.

*I.* Yes; I perceive that obedience can only be where the right of a superior to command is recognized and acted upon as the motive.

*P.* And therefore obedience to God is an act done in pursuance of his commands, and from respect to his right to command. To do a commanded act because it seems prudent or politic, is not obedience to *God*, but is in observance of the dictates of *prudence* or *policy*. You will notice that the Christian, having truly obeyed in will, is entitled through grace to hope in the mercy, and for the glory of God; and as this is in accordance with the divine will, he does not vitiate any future act by observing his commands from the combined motives of his creative right, and the hope of his pardoning grace, and glory. But still, when his attention is turned to the point, he finds himself able to lay aside his hope as a motive, and to act solely in view of such right of God; for the latter remains as sufficient a motive of itself, as at the beginning of his service before he indulged a hope. Whereas, the unconverted mind cannot lay its hopes aside until compelled to do so as we have seen; and it never acts under the influence of the right of God until it reaches conversion; and hence the sinner, in doing what God commands, never acts *because* HE commands, however confident he may be to the contrary, while stimulated by hope or fear.

*I.* I am aware that the creative rights of God, and the selfish hope of the sinner, are morally opposite motives; and my own experience abundantly satisfies me that, being *exclusively* under the power of his hope, it will exclude the influence of the former. He may *know* that God commands an act, but he cannot then enter upon it in the least degree *because* he commands it. What is intended by submission to God?

*P.* Submission is the act of the mind in yielding to the authority of God, in order to obedience. The latter is the continued observance of the will of God, while the former is the consent of the will to the divine rule under which obedience is pursued. In respect to the sinner's desires for his selfish happiness, it implies their entire abandonment by self-denial; so that, in the original act of submission, they exert no influence whatever over his will. In respect to his desires to avoid punishment—desires which can never be obliterated, or made otherwise than averse to pain—it implies a suspension of their influence also, so that they shall then exert no motive power. The idea of the authority of God, standing thus alone and being consequently the strongest present motive, subdues the will; the sinner yields thereto without question or debate, and notwithstanding whatever evil may occur to himself. By these means, the authority of God acquires through the intermediation of the conscience, the supremacy over the will, and the constitutional desires for happiness and against pain are, when they revive, reduced to subordination to it; so that should God command any duty, however onerous to the flesh, and even though it led to death itself, his authority would suffice to produce obedience under the grace of his Spirit.

*I.* This explains the principle on which Bunyan acted in the Bedford jail, while in constant fear and even certainty of death, unless he renounced the preaching of the gospel. His desire of happiness and anxiety to avoid banishment from God, made him reluctant to encounter that danger, with no prospect of security; and he thought if God would only give him an evidence of his favor, he would not hesitate in following the path of duty. But no such evidence could he obtain; and he was compelled to take it for granted that God might, after all, banish him according to his deserts; and he was thrown back upon the simple question, whether he would obey the command of God, whatever might be the consequences. One of his commentators remarks, that for many weeks poor Bunyan knew not what to do; till at length it came to him with great power that at all events, it being for the word and way of God that he was in this condition of danger, perhaps in the path of death, he was engaged not to flinch an hair's breadth from it. Bunyan thought furthermore that it was for God to choose whether he would give him comfort then, or in the hour of death, or whether he would or would not give him comfort in either, or comfort at all; but it was not for Bunyan to choose whether to serve God or not, for to this he was bound. He was bound, but God was free. "Yea," says he, "it was my duty to stand to his word, whether he would ever look upon me, or save me at the last, or not; wherefore, thought I, the point being thus, I am for going on, and venturing my eternal state with Christ, whether I have comfort here or no. If God doth not come in, thought I, I will leap off the ladder even blindfold into eternity, sink or swim, come heaven, come hell. Lord Jesus, if thou wilt catch me, do; if not, I will venture for thy name!"

*P.* Well done, noble Bunyan! that commentator justly adds. Now, had he paltered with duty until he could have become assured of his own safety ultimately, this commendation would have been as undeserved as his dereliction from principle would have been evident.

*I.* Yes. And such was my own position for many years, in respect to God. I wanted my own will, in regard to myself, to prevail over his will; but now I prefer the will of God to my own, and my preferences tend to whatever he may direct or permit.

*P.* As your desires now coincide with your conscience for God, you can act under the influence of both in repeating your submission, "It is the Lord, let him do what seemeth him good." It is, as has been remarked, the peculiarity of the Christian that, when doubts and fears assail, he can retreat to the divine sovereignty and submit himself unreservedly to God, and find sweet consolation in the fact that God reigns and that his holy pleasure will be accomplished in all things.. Of all others, this state of heart is the most delightful as well as ennobling; it is one which selfishness, though possessed of all its aims, could never afford.

*I.* As I well know by experience. All my peace heretofore has resulted from a hope of my own safety; and I was so consummately selfish as to look upon the greatest afflictions, even such as the death of friends, as designed to chasten me, and so an evidence of the favor of God—and to take comfort in the thought—which was called resignation to the will of God! How different is that beautiful appeal of the Psalmist to his own soul under trials: "Why art thou cast down, O my soul? and why art thou disquieted within me? Hope thou in God; for I shall yet *praise* HIM, who is the health of my countenance, and my God."—Ps. 42:11. In submission, are we required to consent to become unholy, if it be the will of God?

*P.* The act of unreserved submission to the will of God, is itself a renunciation of unholiness; and consequently in it the sinner impliedly consents not to remain unholy. God never wills that any of his moral creatures, not excepting Satan himself, should consent to be unholy; and hence no such contingency can arise. The penalty of the law is *pain*, not unholiness. The latter is the crime for which the former is inflicted; as rebellion against an earthly ruler is the crime for which the pain of death is imposed by human laws. It would seem strange for one condemned for rebellion against a civil government, and who was required to yield himself implicitly to the authority of his sovereign, to inquire whether he was bound to consent to continue in his rebellion! And especially so, if he should so earnestly object to consenting as to make it a point with his sovereign! We should suspect that there was some secret and sinister consideration or plan in his mind, which he attempted to effect by that stratagem.

*I.* Certainly we should, for his sovereign's will and his duty would be too plain to be mistaken. His exception of remaining in rebellion would be barefaced hypocrisy, since his heart would obviously be on continuing in it. I should imagine that it was a plan to secure a present confidence of pardon, by a *seeming* prëarrangement for his future loyalty; by which he would be able, as he supposed, to bias his sovereign's will, and submit *with safety* to his authority. This would surely exclude true submission.

*P.* Your inference would be just; and it explains what many sinners mean by raising the same point in respect to consenting to remain unholy in their submission to God. Not a few, assuming that they are already Christians and that the will of God is favorable toward them, urge that they are now *bound* to except unholiness in their submission; and under color of that name, they really except their own selfish will and desires, and so remain in moral opposition to him, with a hope. And even Christians are often misled by their arguments.

*I.* I know that, in my selfish state, such an attempt would have been merely a means of excepting my *punishment* for unholiness; for I now find that I had no real opposition to the thing itself. I am glad that I gave up every thing to the will of God, making no terms; for by so doing, I have become opposed to sin in heart, and can discard unholiness in reality.

*P.* In every exigency, and indeed at all times, accustom yourself to yield your all unreservedly to him; then you will be furtherest from unholiness; and on that foundation your hope in Christ will become the brightest, your joys in the Lord the strongest, and your activity in the duties of piety the most decided. "The

LORD REIGNETH, let the earth rejoice; let the multitude of isles be glad thereof."—Ps. 97:1.

*I.* What is intended by evangelical repentance?

*P.* Repentance consists in the opposition of the heart to sin because it is in disobedience to God, and therefore wrong. It exists in two forms—namely, as a volition, and as an affection. As a *volition*, it is the honest purpose to avoid sin produced by the idea of the authority of God. The original (*metanoia*) signifies a change of mind; a change of one's mode of thinking, feeling, and acting; a pursuit of an after-thought in reforming one's life; a change in opinion followed by a change in purpose and action; attaining to a right use of one's senses. Our Lord (Matt. 21:28, 29) exemplified repentance as a volition, by the case of a parent exercising his authority over his son by commanding him to go and work; he refused to obey, but afterwards repented, that is, recognized the right of his father to command, and resolved to disobey him no more, and went to his work. He did the will of his father in respect both to his motive and purposed conduct. The repentance of the prodigal son is intimated by the expression, "and when he came to himself" (Luke 15:17), when he came to a right use of his senses in respect to his conduct, and duty to his father. Repentance as an *affection*, consists in hatred to sin when its criminality is perceived; disgust in view of its moral deformity and odiousness; dislike to selfishness in self and in others, and abhorrence of self on account of it; and sorrow over sin in view of its opposition to the infinite goodness of God.

*I.* I am reminded of the complaint of the missionaries to the Siamese, "that they had no word in their language to indicate repentance," (meaning that they have none for the *affection*,) "but that the term used by them signified only a change of purpose." It seems they had one for repentance as a *volition*, at least.

*P.* Yes; and if they should exercise it toward God in that sense, they would be saved. Repentance as a volition is the form in which repentance, when it is his first act, is exercised by the sinner; and it is always followed by repentance as an affection of sorrow for sin and the like, as soon as the true character of sin is contemplated. The latter stands to the former in the relation of an effect to a cause; and repentance as a purpose must, like every other cause, precede its effect.

*I.* On the contrary, I always supposed that sorrow for sin must precede and produce the purpose of reform, when repentance was the first act of the sinner.

*P.* Sinners take that view from the habit of being always moved by preceding selfish affections, and from the encouragement it affords them of having feelings as evidence that they may proceed with safety and in a manner to please Christ. Christians also are prone to adopt the same view, because they overlook the mode in which sorrow for sin first arose in their own hearts, and being themselves accustomed to act from the impulse of holy hatred to sin, they imagine, without reflection, that sinners do so also. Where sin is openly acknowledged by the sinner, evincing a knowledge of the command of God forbidding its commission and a consciousness of criminality in perpetrating it, and when he forsakes it by an observed determination to depart from it, from the motive of its being so forbidden, it is true repentance as a volition; and the Holy Spirit declares he shall have mercy.—Prov. 28:13. And when he afterwards contemplates his selfish heart and sinful conduct, repentance as an affection will be spontaneously exercised; for by the first act, *ill-will* toward sin is produced, which will necessarily evince itself subsequently in the livelier state of an affection.

*I.* And yet many, in explaining that passage, act as if the Spirit did not understand mental philosophy or had made a defective communication of his views; for they insist that the sinner must have sorrow in the first instance, and that the purpose to forsake sin must be produced by it.

*P.* That is, sorrow for sin must be exercised before the sinner has any ill-will toward it as sin! A secondary exercise must precede a primary! We might smile at this were it not that sinners are hindered, and many of them, doubtless, sent to perdition by it. If one was causelessly injuring you, what would you naturally require of him first?

*I.* That he should stop immediately.

*P.* And for such a reason as would always restrain him; that is, because his conduct was wrong and unjustifiable toward you?

*I.* Yes; that should and would influence him, if he was honest in forming such a determination.

*P.* That, then, would be repentance toward you as a volition. But would you not expect, if he was honest in that purpose, to see him become sorry for having causelessly wronged you, whenever you should present the subject in a proper light?

*I.* I certainly should.

*P.* That would be the resulting repentance as an

affection. This form of it, will naturally rēproduce still more determined resolutions of reform in every respect; that is, renewed repentance as a volition.

*I.* This is all very natural.

*P.* And such is the description given by the apostle (2 Cor. 7:10, 11) in his remarks to those who had already exercised repentance as a volition, and who consequently were in the exercise of it as an affection. "For godly sorrow [that which springs from a good-will to God wounded by a sense of sin, or repentance as an affection] worketh repentance [purposes of reform] to salvation not to be repented of [not to be retracted nor regretted]. For behold this self-same thing, that ye sorrowed after a godly sort, what carefulness it wrought in you, yea, what clearing of yourselves, yea, what indignation [against sin, and against yourselves on account of it], yea, what fear, yea, what vehement desire [for purification], yea, what zeal, yea, what revenge!"

*I.* Wherein does this differ from false repentance, or the sorrow of the world?

*P.* True and false repentance differ in respect to their external motives; in respect to the internal motive influences which produce the first act of repentance; and in respect to the feelings which result. In the first place, true repentance is produced by the motive of the rights of God over the sinner, or, which is the same thing, by a view of the wrong of his conduct in violating his obligations to God; whereas false repentance is produced by a view of some evil consequence of sin to himself, and by the fears thereby excited. In the next place, true repentance as a volition, when the original act, is produced by the motive impulse of the conscience, dissuading him from further disobedience because of its being so wrong against God; whereas false repentance is produced by the motive influence of his desires for his own safety and peace, to be accomplished, as he supposes, by renouncing his evil ways. In the last place, in true repentance all the feelings of regret, sorrow, hatred, and the like, described by the apostle, are exercised in view of the intrinsic impropriety of sin, and produce more determined purposes to avoid it in every known case; whereas those feelings in false repentance are chiefly exercised in view of the danger which sin has produced, and the folly of having committed it at such a risk. Conscience has not obtained the supremacy; but, though enslaved to selfishness, it still pours remorse through the soul; and such feelings produce at one time stronger desires and purposes to avoid sin in order to escape perdition, and under other circumstances, they render life an intolerable burden.

*I.* Do the Scriptures speak of this false repentance?

*P.* Very often; as in the passage last cited, where the apostle declares, "but the sorrow of the world worketh death." And such was, for example, the repentance of Judas.—Matt. 27 : 3. The term there used (*metamelomai*), intends the change of one's mind from a painful and therefore selfish motive; and also a feeling of sorrow in view of one's miserable condition, and remorse in view of his conduct. The self-reproaches of Judas, therefore, instead of leading him to renounce sin as unholy, and to submit to God, drove him into the greatest of all sins in the vain search for relief.

*I.* This makes the selfish and morally worthless character of his repentance perfectly evident. Alas! what multitudes are, I apprehend, depending upon similar false repentance for their eternal welfare!

*P.* And by scrutinizing your own experience, you can discover the reason why repentance is so apt to be selfish and spurious, and why true repentance is, comparatively, so seldom reached. Every effort to excite sorrow for sin, was in vain for the reason before given—namely, that it is a secondary exercise, one which must be preceded by ill-will to sin produced by a right purpose to abstain from it. And again, every effort for such a right purpose was prompted by your desires to escape punishment by means of it; and even when you placed the idea of the rightful authority of God before your mind and endeavored to act from it in resolving, you was actuated in that very endeavor by those more remote selfish desires, which necessarily prevented that idea from becoming a motive.

*I.* And yet every sinner imagines that the only way to obtain a holy motive is to present one before his mind and endeavor to act from it.

*P.* When the desires are already enlisted in favor of the general subject to which the motive relates, it will become influential, on such a presentation of it, in consequence of the power of the desires; but when no such favorable desires exist, the idea thus presented and urged will be powerless to move the will. A failure to notice this radical difference leads many persons to think that they have adopted holy motives, while in fact they are influenced, as before, by their selfish desires, and the supposed holy motive is merely a new channel through which they are gratified, and from which it derives all its supposed power. The influence of the opposing desires must be suspended, before the new moral motive can successfully control the will; and until then every purpose and feeling will be worldly and selfish. And what is more, no sinner can ever deny himself *purposely* to obtain such new motive, for the effort will be dictated by his selfish heart, and so effect no self-denial;—its ulterior influence must be destroyed by some hand and power more mighty than his own. As a general thing, he must be *driven* to self-denial by a conviction, under the Spirit, that he can never make progress in that direction, or he will never reach it.

*I.* I feel distressed at the vast numbers of Christendom who will find themselves cut off from eternal life by this principle. I do not wonder that the disciples asked, "Are there few that be saved?" And what is, if possible, more deplorable still, the creeds and systems of many neither contemplate such self-denial nor are calculated to produce it, nor is it usually urged upon inquirers; so that they fail of it, notwithstanding the command of our Lord. Will you please explain what is intended by evangelical faith?

*P.* Faith, in its most general sense, is the assent of the mind to the truth of what is declared by another, resting on his authority and veracity without other evidence. This, when exercised in the truths of divine revelation, is *intellectual* faith in God; for it receives the Scriptures as true upon his authority and veracity. The faith of the *heart* in God as a Sovereign, as required by him (Rom. 10: 10) is the resignation of the will to his authority, and the reception of him, his word, his character, his glory, and his commands, as the subjects of our desire and love. It presupposes that, (selfishness being removed by self-denial,) divine truth when honestly received and properly applied to one's self, will, through the Spirit, move the will to obedience and ultimately excite its affections. Thus, Jesus is presented as the Son of God, and as such invested with the rights of divine sovereignty. When one believes this, he exercises intellectual faith in Christ; and selfishness being truly renounced, if he yields to him by resolving to obey him on that account, he will thereby exercise faith of the heart, and his affections will promptly respond to his character and glory. "But these are written, that ye might believe that Jesus is the Christ, the Son of God; and that, believing, ye might have life through his name."—John 20:31; Acts 8:37.

*I.* And hence Christians are called believers? And the cause of so much spurious faith lies either in mistaking mere intellectual belief for heart-faith, or in purposing obedience without self-denial, and consequently from selfish motives, as is the case with the Campbellites and others?

*P.* Yes. But we are not to imagine things and act upon them as the truths of God, under the idea that simple belief *in any thing* is gospel faith. It is not competent for the sinner, for example, to imagine that Christ has promised or is willing to save *him*, and to act upon it in ostensibly yielding to his sovereignty, as though it was a fact, and he had faith in the divine veracity and promise.

*I.* I fear that many do not reflect upon the validity of what they believe, but imagine things which have never proceeded from God.

*P.* The term faith is often used to express hope in

Christ. But the Christian's faith in Christ as a Saviour, is rather his confidence in the *general* declaration, because it proceeds from him, that all who are born again, converted, truly penitent and the like, shall have remission of sins and everlasting life through his atoning grace. His hope is the appropriation of this promise to himself, inducing a confidence that Christ has remitted *his* sins, and will receive *him* to eternal life. This distinction is important; for if sinners confound the one with the other, they will be liable at the first to seize upon a hope of their own salvation, instead of simply believing that the *penitent* shall be accepted, and instead of resigning themselves to the sovereign rule of Christ and renouncing sin—whereby only can the terms be complied with. Faith and hope, are radically distinct exercises: "Now abideth faith, hope, charity, these *three*" (1 Cor. 13 : 13); and faith in God, or in Christ as the sovereign God, (for these are considered the same in the Scriptures—see Tit. 3 : 8, and John 11 : 45,) leading to absolute submission and obedience, must always precede a valid hope, both in the order of the divine arrangement and of correct mental action; for true love to God cannot be exercised before such faith, nor can a hope in the blessings of grace, but they always flow from it. Hence faith, and not hope, is made the condition of pardon.—Mark 16 : 16.

*I.* I always used faith and hope as alike; and can see how my deceitful heart led me to misconstrue the declaration of Christ, "no man cometh unto the Father but by me." Anxious only for a hope, I understood it to mean that, in order to secure the favor of the Father, the sinner must first hope in the pardoning mercy of the

Son. As going to the Father means submitting to his creative authority and devoting our hearts to his glory, so to come to him by means of Christ, must mean submitting to Christ as our Sovereign and devoting our hearts to his glory,—for the Father and the Son are one and the same in substance; and then we shall be in a state to indulge a valid hope in his mercy.

*I.* Yes; and that declaration had a peculiar force with the Jews to whom it was addressed. They indulged selfish hopes in the Father in consequence of the covenant of God with Abraham "to be a God unto him and unto his seed" (Gen. 17: 7), which they misunderstood to mean his natural instead of his spiritual descendants. They looked upon Christ as one who would not favor their selfishness; and they knew that if they acknowledged his godship and submitted to his authority, it must be at the expense of the denial of their own ends. Hence, they resisted the conviction of his claim to divine authority; and he, on the other hand, warned them of the selfishness of their religion, and that they could not in reality bow to the Father except as they believed in his own divine authority, renounced their selfishness or the works of the flesh, and submitted to his rule. And to this day they deny Christ simply because of this requirement; for had he required them only to hope in *his* mercy rather than in the Father's, in order to salvation, they would have immediately received the evidence of his divinity with gladness. But then it would have produced no radical change; for the selfish heart with its hopes and pleasures would remain, terminating on the Son rather than on the Father, as its minister of sin. It is impossible for the

Jews of the present day to be truly converted otherwise than by the method which Christ and his apostles adopted with their fathers; and the same resistance will be made by that peculiarly selfish and stiff-necked people, who, "uncircumcised in heart and ears [unbelieving in the godship of Christ against all evidence, and unsubmissive in will to his authority] do always resist the Holy Ghost."—Acts 7:51.

*I.* The tables seem to be turned in our day, and men are seeking, by a precipitate hope in Christ, precisely the selfish salvation which the Jews sought by a hope in the Father, and for which Christ denounced them?

*P.* It is even so; and they love to consider it the Christian religion.

*I.* I have been much puzzled by the taunt of a person, that he had rather be selfish with the Apostle Paul, than be the contrary with others. I now see that the apostle reproved selfishness in all its forms; that the salvation he desired and urged upon the pursuit of believers was not selfish happiness, but the glory of God, conformity to his image, and the blessedness flowing from enjoying him and his glory for ever. But being then inexperienced in the difference, such remarks weighed much with me and endangered my soul. It seems to me that Paul, after his conversion, was the most unselfish person that ever lived.

*P.* Yes, next to his Master. In your progress through the world, you will find many whose opinions you would be prēdisposed to respect, but who will evince a lamentable deficiency in clearness, if not in experience, on many points. You must become well persuaded in your own mind, not from mere whim or feeling, but from examination and conviction, and must stand to those convictions in the face of all the world; and if you find any who would dissuade from this course, be sure that they wish to domineer over men by retaining them in ignorance, or else are afraid of disturbing their own hopes by having such truths examined. Rather obey Christ, who for this very purpose commanded the Jews, "Search the Scriptures, for in them ye think ye have eternal life; and they are they which testify of me."—John 5:39.

*I.* Your counsel shall be observed, with God's blessing. As I must stand or fall to my own master, I will form and follow my own opinions upon the Scriptures of truth. What is intended by sanctification?

*P.* It is the progress of the Christian upon his new principles of submission to the authority of God, and devotion to his glory ultimately. "The path of the just is as the shining light, that shineth more and more unto the perfect day."—Prov. 4:18. Its efficient cause is the Holy Spirit (1 Pet. 1:2); the instrumentality is the truth, a knowledge of which enables us to exercise our reason, judgment, will, and affections in the right channels and in reference to right objects.—John 17: 17. A change in our moral state before God involves a change in our opinions and feelings in respect to him, ourselves, and mankind, wherever they have been defective. I must refer you to the Scriptures, and especially to our Lord's sermon on the mount (Matt. 5, 6, and 7), for the necessary instruction in those duties, by the observance of which we are to grow in grace. But permit me to remark that if you are in a gracious state you will so carefully govern your temper and control your conduct in respect to those around you, that observers will take knowledge of you that you have been with Jesus.—Acts 4: 13.

*I.* I used to think that, in the process of sanctification, we aimed indeed at the attainment of the divine authority as a superior influence over the mind, but still as the last thing to be acquired, say, at death; but the Scriptures place it at the very beginning.

*P.* It is natural that the unconverted heart should always take that view of sanctification. It knows nothing practically of that principle; all its warfare consists in observing questions of policy as to what on the one hand is necessary to its hopes of happiness for the future state, and on the other what indulgences may be enjoyed in the present without materially endangering those hopes. That principle seems to be so high, so far beyond what he has ever reached, that the unconverted person is apt to conclude that no one can reach it in this life, at least before the hour of death; and hence, he makes *conversion* the end of *sanctification!* The very act of the mind from which the believer derives his characteristic principle and the moral weapon with which he is to contend with selfishness through life, is made by the sinner to be the last attainment of perfection in the Christian course! All his efforts for it are selfish, of course; and if his selfish hopes continue to be sustained by his erroneous view of sanctification, there can be no ground to expect he will ever reach the point of regeneration; and if he has so perverted the Scriptures as to be beyond correction on the subject by them, and as he has never acted on the new principle so as to have the evidence of consciousness that the idea of the authority of God may be of itself enough to move the will to obedience, and if he will not receive the testimony of others who have practically tested the fact, it will be vain to try to deliver him. The most we can hope for where the infatuation is so complete, is that he will abstain from making "the heart of the righteous sad, whom God has not made sad, and from strengthening the hands of the wicked, that he should not return from his wicked way" (Ez. 13 : 22): and from opposing others whose scriptural sentiments disturb his own repose.

*I.* I see by my own experience, that up to the period of attaining that principle, the process of what I sometimes called sanctification was pure unholiness enlivened by a hope. But when we start on the principle of the divine authority of the Son of God, are we bound to observe it perfectly in heart and life?

*P.* God requires not only that we embrace perfectly upright principles, such as the creative authority of God, but that we observe them perfectly in respect to the feelings and purposes of our hearts, and in our external deportment. And our consciences, acting upon this divine standard of perfection, always reprove us for every perceived departure therefrom.

*I.* But is such perfection attainable even in kind, in this life?

*P.* The sanctification of the believer is imperfect in this life. In the words of the Westminster Assembly, "there abideth still some remnants of corruption in every part, whence ariseth a continual and irreconcilable war, the flesh lusting against the spirit, and the spirit against the flesh:—and so that saints grow in grace, perfecting holiness in the fear of the Lord." And such is the testimony of Scripture, "There is not a just man upon earth, that doeth good, and sinneth not."—Eccl. 7:20. "Not as though I had already attained, either were already perfect; but I follow after, if that I may apprehend that for which also I am apprehended of Christ Jesus."—Phil. 3:12. In the kingdom of heaven the saint will reach perfection in kind, and will ever be approximating to the moral excellence of God in degree.

*I.* Who, then, can be saved?

*P.* All true believers. The disciple is regarded as a saint, not because he is as perfect in holiness as are the saints in heaven, but because his principles are upright and godly, and because perfection is his aim.—Job 1:8. Your selfish views formerly induced the error of supposing that absolute perfection was the condition of pardon; whereas repentance, and obedience with that aim, is made the condition by infinite grace. On the same ground Christians are prone to abandon their hopes in sadness, when they discover any sin in their thoughts, hearts, or conduct; and are apt to conclude that they have never been regenerated, on the singular supposition that there is some peculiar power in true regeneration, which, had they possessed it, would have of itself kept them from all future sin, whether they are themselves watchful or no;—a most grievous error indeed. These accusations of conscience are its reproofs for our failure to act according to the standard of right or perfection in those particular instances, and not for our want of those holy principles of heart, which, duly cultivated, would have prevented those deficiencies; that is to say, the conscience admits the believer's regeneration, but reproves him for a deficiency in its legitimate fruits, through his own fault. It is as if you had started with the view of prosecuting a journey, and while on your way are occasionally drawn aside by various inducements, so that your progress toward your journey's end is devious and slow. A view of your wanderings might make you sorrowful, and you might hastily conclude that it could not be possible that you ever really commenced that journey; whereas, the true inference would be that you started, but that you progressed criminally slow. Apply this principle to your Christian course, and it will save you much distress and trouble in respect to your regeneration, while it will make you more anxious to persevere.

*I.* I will remember to do so. But with such a defective service, will Christ accept the true believer?

*P.* Yes, where his aim is to glorify God in every thing. "Like as a father pitieth his children, so the Lord pitieth them that fear him. For he knoweth our frame; he remembereth that we are dust."—Ps. 103 : 13, 14. The ground of the believer's acceptance, as before remarked, is not at all upon any desert of a beneficial recompense on his part; nor partly upon his works or deserts, and partly upon Christ to make up his deficiencies; but is exclusively and altogether upon the righteousness of Christ, as manifested in his obedient sufferings in the atonement. If it depended in any degree upon any such merit of the believer, he would be lost beyond remedy, for he has none whatever.

*I.* Will you explain the exact mode or principles of

the acceptance of the true believer, by virtue of the atonement?

*P.* Yes; and in the first place will notice the nature of imputation. The term imputation was borrowed by the old writers from commerce, and properly signifies to set a sum down to somebody's account; as if one had made a contract by virtue of which a debt accrued from him to another, the creditor would impute it to the debtor, or set it down to his account and make him answerable for it. To impute an action to a person, is to attribute it to him as its real author. It implies a free agent, who may be reasonably and truly regarded as the author of his own actions in such a sense as that they may be justly charged to him. In this sense it is used in the Scriptures: "Blood shall be imputed unto [charged upon] that man;" and the reason is given in the fact that "he hath shed blood."—Lev. 17:4.

*I.* I was always under the impression that, in a religious sense, to impute a thing to a person was to make believe it was his, or to consider it his *as it were*, even though it actually belonged to some one else.

*P.* One may have the *benefit* of another's act, and it may be placed to his account in respect to such benefit, but never in respect to the act itself. Like his character, every person's act is his own.

*I.* I see the distinction clearly.

*P.* Imputation was held to be of two kinds—namely, simple and efficacious. *Burl. on Nat. Law.* pp. 24. 170. *Simple* imputation consists only in ascribing a person's own action to himself, and in approving or disapproving him on account of such action; insomuch that no other effect arises from it with regard to him.

Thus, one gives food to a hungry mendicant; we spontaneously attribute the action to him as his own, and attach to him also a desert of approbation on account of it; and we esteem and praise him accordingly. It would be the spontaneous attestation of our own hearts to his goodness; and his refusal, in such a case, would elicit our imputation of disapprobation. One who freely and voluntarily observes the rights of his Creator in his actions, is denominated righteous in the Scriptures; as it is said, "The Lord loveth the righteous."—Ps. 146:8. However the Almighty energy exerted by the Spirit to induce the sinner, in conversion, to bow to the authority of God, and to walk in the paths of holy obedience, may be exercised, and however clearly all the glory of it belongs to God, yet they occurred from the resulting free and voluntary act of submission by the sinner himself; as such it was *his own action*, and should be imputed to him, with all its moral consequences, as certainly and truly as we would place to one's account the gift of that food. And if he had refused, the same principle would apply to his condemnation. Accordingly we find that God, in the Scriptures, does attribute the evil actions of the sinner to himself, with his disapprobation on their account: "Behold, thou hast spoken and done evil things as thou couldest."—Jer. 3:5. "A man of wicked devices will the Lord condemn."—Prov. 12:2. And we also find that he imputes to believers, as their own act, their observance of his creative rights, and also all the moral consequences. "And a great number believed, and turned unto the Lord."—Acts 11:21. "Not he that commendeth himself is approved, but whom the Lord commendeth."—2 Cor. 10:18.

*I.* On reflection, it is obviously correct to impute to a person his religious as well as his secular, his pious as well as his sinful, actions; for in either case they are really his own; and if they are his own, then he is either approvable, or censurable, according to his moral character in them. Only it savors of a want of humility to do so in respect to our pious conduct; it looks like boasting or claiming some desert of the divine favor.

*P.* I repeat that true humility, different from that which is simulated, is always based on the truth and is never inconsistent with it; and you will find, ere we finish this subject, that there is no ground for any such fear. As has been heretofore remarked, one who has done a right action has merely discharged a bounden duty; and he has no *claim* upon others on account of it, and no right to *insist* upon their approbation or commendation. These are rendered spontaneously, if at all, by the observer; and however deficient in moral goodness he may show himself by refusing to approve and commend a good action, the agent cannot rightfully compel him to it, were it in his power.

*I.* Yes; I perceive it is so. But as God does not act from any obligation of duty toward his creatures, he has a claim to our approbation and praise.

*P.* It is said, in respect to believers, "that God was in Christ, reconciling the world unto himself, not imputing [not charging to their account] their trespasses unto them" who are brought into a state of moral agreement with himself.—2 Cor. 5:19. It is not said that they are not tresspassers; but only that their evil deeds are not attributed to them as calling for censure.

*I.* Its meaning, in this passage, is very evident.

*P.* The second kind, or *efficacious* imputation, is not confined to praise and blame; it produces, in addition, some good or bad effect upon the agent, some real and positive good or evil that befalls him; and it seems to be the office of those who are directly concerned in the performance or omission of the action. It is the beneficial recompense or reward over and above simple approbation and commendation, which is bestowed by a superior upon an inferior, in consequence of his good conduct. Thus, where one has faithfully served an employer for a course of years, he would not only commend him for his good conduct, (which would be simple imputation,) but, if he so pleased, he might also present him some money, or render him some other recompense as a token of his esteem, (which would be efficacious imputation;) a donation, which the inferior could not insist upon as a legal right, or *claim* as his merit in any respect; but it would be an act which all observers would approve, notwithstanding, as indicative of the benefactor's capability to appreciate rectitude and faithfulness, and of his good and generous feelings toward the beneficiary, and consequently of his own upright character. And, on the other hand, punishment may be imputed to one who is unfaithful and grossly violates the duties devolved upon him; and this is in addition to the simple imputation of blame and censure. Thus, it is said, "For mine eyes are upon all their ways; they are not hid from my face, neither is their iniquity hid from mine eyes: And first I will recompense their iniquity and their sin double."—Jer. 16:17, 18.

*I.* But this imputation of punishment proceeds exclusively on the ground of the sinner's ill-desert.

*P.* Yes. You will permit me here to repeat for the sake of clearness, that a duty is an act to be done in pursuance of some obligation; the right of the person to whom it is owing, is the motive to the act of duty; when the action is thus performed the matter is terminated, and the person bound can make no further claim, can rightfully demand no beneficial recompense for the discharge of his duty; and if he receives one, it will be of pure generosity. And besides, in the case of the converted sinner, the penalty of the divine law (except for mere grace) hangs over him for his former misdeeds; no future obedience, however perfect, can answer in the place of his former derelictions so as to remove it, for a perfect obedience is required to answer the present demands of the law, to prevent its penalty from falling upon him anew. And, in addition, his present and future obedience while on earth will be more or less imperfect; so that he cannot deserve or rightfully claim a removal of the penalty for the future on the ground of fulfilling his duties, and much less a beneficial recompense therefor.

*I.* I see it is impossible for the believer, inasmuch as he was once a rebel against God, to merit pardon and salvation, although his principles are holy and his conduct is ever so much guarded.

*P.* Our Lord requires of his creatures the performance of every duty to him, and will punish sinners for their *neglect of any*, to say nothing of their positive misdeeds. "And cast ye the unprofitable [useless] servant into outer darkness."—Matt. 25:30. But while blame and punishment are thus imputed to the undutiful, he does not, in any form, impute a desert of a beneficial recompense to the dutiful, on the very principle that they have done only what was their duty. "So likewise ye, when ye shall have done all those things which are commanded you, say, We are unprofitable [unmeritorious] servants, [for] we have [only] done that which was our duty to do."—Luke 17:10. "Doth he thank that servant [as if he had placed him under an obligation] because he did the things that were commanded him? I trow not."—v. 9. And yet, if he will, God may, by some beneficial recompense, properly express, both to the individual and to the public, his esteem of a character which is an humble, though imperfect imitation of his own. By so doing, he will exhibit his own love to holiness, indulge his compassionate mercy, and evince the exceeding riches of his grace; and by the amazing brilliancy and value of the recompense, as compared with the former ill-desert and the present no-desert, to say the least, of the believer, he will afford to the world some adequate measure of his own goodness and moral excellence, and will make such a development of the glory of his grace as will satisfy even the benevolent longings of him who purchased the privilege with his life upon the cross;—for it is said, "he shall see of the travail of his soul, and shall be satisfied."—Is. 53:11.

*I.* Certainly it would be all of grace, and ultimately to promote the glory of God. I can now see that the objection which some have made is groundless—namely, that faith, understood as implying such holiness of principle, heart, and deportment in the believer, takes the place of *good works* as a qualification of *merit* of the *reward* on his part, since in fact it is a moral excellence of the first and highest kind. Although it is an excellency, it lays no ground for a legal *claim* either to approbation, thanks, or beneficial reward, since it is a mere compliance with an acknowledged duty to God; and this, however praiseworthy it may be in God generously to make such imputations.

*P.* Yes. This objection is ably answered by the editor of the *Works of Prest. Edwards*, (London Ed. 1835, Intro. Essay, p. 51.) Prest. Edwards, he remarks, distinguishes between what faith is in its own nature, and what it is in relation to the privileges for which it is a qualification. He distinguishes between such qualifications as *entitle* a man to certain privileges, and such as have merely a *natural tendency* to fit him for receiving them. It is not as possessing a moral qualification which entitles its possessor to certain privileges, that he who possesses faith is justified; but because he who possesses faith is in a condition to receive the benefits of the gospel. Without such a qualification, therefore, those blessings could not be granted. Though faith, then, is in its own nature a moral excellency, yet it is only as a proper qualification for partaking in the privileges of the gospel, that it avails the believer. Let us take a simple illustration. A man designs to grant to another certain great benefits, not in the least degree *deserved*, in no sense the price of moral desert. Yet he may demand certain qualifications in the object of his bounty, and those qualifications may be of a moral nature, though it is only as natural qualifications that they are demanded. For instance, he might demand that he shall be found *honest;* a good moral trait to be sure, and qualifying him to receive it virtuously, but not at all entering into the ulterior motive with which it is conferred. In like manner the blessings of the gospel are not in any degree conferred because of any merit in those who receive them; yet they may be justly confined to those who possess a proper natural qualification.

*I.* This seems to be perfectly conclusive. But upon what principles can God be properly generous toward believers, since they have heretofore violated his laws and incurred the penalty of eternal death?

*P.* In the first place, as regards the recipient, it would not be rewarding him for evil, or while in disloyalty; for they are not conferred because of his past conduct, nor imparted to any who have not become truly loyal. In the next place, the example of the believer will not thereafter be deleterious to the rest of God's holy subjects; so that his blessings will not be perverted to subvert the general good. In the next place God may, if he will, so far as concerns himself *personally*, overlook the believer's previous injuries and evil conduct and his present short-comings, and may relinquish his private right of redress therefor, and may even impute blessings instead of punishment. And so he does; for we never hear him reproach the penitent for their past iniquities, but on the contrary, in the language of our Lord (in a parable intended to explain this point, among other things), pardon is conferred immediately and without rebuke: "But when he was a great way off, his father saw him, and had compassion, and ran, and fell on his neck, and kissed him."—Luke 15:20.

*I.* I have thought that *some* rebuke would be a relief to my soul! but such spontaneous, uncomplaining kindness overwhelms me

*P.* But before he can indulge his generous kindness to the believer with safety to the permanence of his moral government in heaven, and to the perpetuity of the obedience of his holy subjects there, some provision must be made to sustain his authority as a ruling principle over their minds, whereby their perfect obedience and blessedness may be insured. Revolt once occurred in heaven; his authority as the ruling principle was rejected there by Satan and his angels to the endangering of his whole moral government; and to fail to impute sin and the penalty of the law to creatures who deserved both, at the hazard, and indeed certainty, of so undermining his own authority in consequence over others as to hazard their continued obedience and everlasting well-being in holiness, would be unwise, discreditable to God, and surely productive of infinite mischief. For you must observe that saints and angels in heaven are moral agents, free to obey or disobey, to love God or to refuse; and a sad experiment has proved that none can be so exalted there as to be beyond the power of temptation. They are there bound to God by a supreme love to him and his glory, which is produced and sustained by a perfect recognition of his authority in their wills and conduct; just as your submission to his authority produced, and its continued observance perpetuates your love to him. Their service, therefore, is neither compulsory nor mercenary, but is free and holy; while a filial fear of God suppresses all presumption. Still, they are acquainted with the same motive influences which overthrew Satan and his angels; they are moreover familiar with all the insidious considerations which he and his followers can present; and as free moral agents bound to obey God, they are equally bound to resist temptations. To enable them to see the deformity of sin, and thus to hate it more and more; to enable them to appreciate the evil of punishment, and thus to prize the holy blessedness they enjoy; to enable them to understand the full evil of unholiness, and thus to love God and his glory the more in the contrast; and by means of the whole to guard them so effectually against the power of temptation that they will never yield to it, but ever retain their obedience, God has made the perpetual punishment of Satan, his angels, and all incorrigible sinners, with all its reasons as developed in their depraved hearts and conduct, to stand out before them as a beacon-light for ever. The saints well know that God will never forgive sin committed in the eternal state, and that if they sin there, the doom of the fallen angels will be theirs; and this producing a holy fear, shelters them effectually from temptation, and they doubtless praise and glorify God for its protection. God will have a perfect government and perfect blessedness in the future state, and in order thereto he must have a perfect obedience; and while respect to his authority and holy love, bind his adopted children to his throne, the *certainty* that eternal death will follow disobedience will disarm temptation of all its power. Then "the Lamb which is in the midst of the throne, shall feed them, and shall lead them unto living fountains of waters; and God shall [ever] wipe away all tears from their eyes."—Rev. 7:17. Thus, you perceive, that the safety of heaven from temptation depends upon the profound conviction that God's holy law is so honorable in his sight and that his authority is esteemed of so much importance, that the disastrous consequences of any violation of either these will be irretrievable.

*I.* Yes; I perceive it now. Not being accustomed to regard saints in heaven as such free moral agents, I have not thought of the necessity of guards for their preservation from transgression. But they must be free agents there in order to have any moral character of their own, or any virtue or praiseworthiness; and as free agency implies a *natural* possibility of revolting, it is wise and good in God to make it a *moral* impossibility for his children to do so. And it is very clear also that a firm persuasion of their endless moral and natural ruin upon the perpetration of sin there, would form this safeguard. No one could deliberately renounce the authority of God, with such a prospect in view; while his love to him would retain him in willing bonds.

*P.* But if God should, by any act of his own, settle the principle that a transgressor can be pardoned on mere repentance, then this persuasion and safeguard would be removed; for the same plan might be laid there that is usually resorted to by mankind here—namely, to repent, after having tried self-indulgence sufficiently, and thereby escape the penalty and recover their position.

*I.* That is true.

*P.* And the pardon of any one person on mere repentance would settle this principle for ever; for it would be assumed that God would be consistent with himself. Such an act, therefore, would not only endanger the stability of the redeemed in respect to his authority, but in the lapse of interminable ages under the various incidents of so vast a universe, would undoubtedly produce a repetition of those scenes once before exhibited; and in the mean time, God would be subject to the reproach of a want either of wisdom to devise, or of a heart or power to accomplish a remedy, and of leaving the creatures of his hand, once delivered from sin and death, constantly exposed again to fall.

*I.* Such must be the results, in the view of sound reason.

*P.* Before, then, God could forgive a penitent sinner (for an unloyal one he can forgive under no circumstances) with safety to his moral government in the eternal state, he must, by some act of his own, produce such a conviction of his superior regard to his law and of his determination to preserve his authority inviolate *there*, as will prevent their inferring that temptation may be yielded to without certain ruin. If he can do this, evincing that the penitent is not pardoned *because* of his penitence, but because of the demands of the divine glory under the exigency, and showing in the very act that he respected his law and authority beyond any and every other good, then he can safely pardon him.

*I.* Certainly, no creature in heaven would dare to sin while under the impression that God regarded his law and authority supremely, even though, for temporary purposes, he should seem to have acted otherwise by the pardon of penitent sinners on earth.

*P.* But this impression can be produced only by his own act. Actions speak louder than words, and "even a child is known by his doings." And besides, the seeming surrender of his law by the act of God in pardoning a sinner, though penitent, cannot be explained away satisfactorily by mere declarations, though these are important; actions must be met by actions to preserve the equality of evidence. And moreover, the actions or declarations of angels or men could not decisively exhibit the sentiments and purposes of God, or of any beings except themselves. God must act for himself, in order to have the impression necessary to sustain his authority go forth with equal power with the act of himself in pardoning the penitent sinner, which endangers it.

*I.* True. No one's actions but his own can decisively prove his own sentiments and purposes.

*P.* Now, could God in some public manner become obedient to his own authority and the precepts of his own law, that act would exhibit a regard to them superior to that for himself; for it would be a practical admission that he considered them as of higher importance than his own pleasure. Should he do this, he would accomplish every thing necessary to make his authority and law most highly honored by his loyal creatures, under whatever circumstances; so that not even the pardon of a penitent sinner could shake their confidence.

*I.* Such would be the certain consequence.

*P.* And further, if he should himself come under the pain and suffering which the penalty of that law denounces, it would express beyond all doubt, his regard to the penalty as just and proper, even beyond that for his own personal happiness, and of course beyond the personal happiness of any and all creatures.

*I.* Even hell itself would become convinced.

*P.* And it would produce such an indelible impression of the truth of his declared purpose to inflict the penalty in that eternal state on all transgressors there, that the safeguard would remain in the face of his seemingly contradictory acts in this world.

*I.* Beyond all doubt.

*P.* And precisely this has been accomplished, in order that God might be just toward his holy subjects in sustaining inviolate his authority as the basis of his moral government over them in the eternal state, and yet might justify him who believed in Jesus, and declare his rectitude in remitting his sins.—Rom. 3 : 26. God, the second Person in the trinity, the Word, was made flesh and dwelt among us.—John 1 : 14. By a perfect obedience to the precepts of his own law, and by baring his own bosom to its penalty, "he magnified the law and made it honorable" (Is. 42 : 21); or, as it may also read, made *him* honorable. He thus proved his superior devotion to it, and consequently his determination to maintain the authority of God inviolate. And he restricted the application of the benefits of his obedient sufferings to those who transgressed in the present state of existence, excluding those who had done so in the eternal state.—Rom. 2 : 6—10; Jude 6. Now, no one can construe his mercy to a penitent sinner here, into a virtual repeal of the penalty of the law or into a purpose not to maintain his authority inviolate in eternity; but the contrary is so fully established that the safeguard is rendered perfect. God can now indulge his compassion and goodness to the penitent, and can exhibit the amazing depths of his grace to them, and at the same time display his care and love toward those holy spirits which already worship in his presence-chamber and cast their crowns before his heavenly throne.

*I.* The remedy is perfect! But at what a cost to himself was it provided!

*P.* Now he can righteously and safely decline to impute their trespasses to believers (2 Cor. 5 : 19); not by making believe that they had never violated God's law, but by not so charging them to their account as to make them punishable therefor. And further, God can as safely charge these sins of the believer to the account of Christ, or, in the figurative language of the Scripture, "make him to be sin for us, who knew no sin."—2 Cor. 5 : 21. "The Lord hath laid on him the iniquity of us all."—Is. 53 : 6. And he can impute to him the punishment due to us, not as deserved by him in any real or mystical sense, but as charged to his account in our stead; "He was wounded for our transgressions, he was bruised for our iniquities: the chastisement of our peace was upon him; and with his stripes we are healed—for the transgression of my people was he stricken."—Is. 53 : 5. 8. He can also safely charge to our account the righteousness of Christ in his obedient sufferings: "that we might be made the righteousness of God in him" (2 Cor. 5 : 21); not by a transfer of moral character from Christ to us which we have seen to be impossible, and besides we must have a holy one of our own, but by graciously imputing to us the benefit of his atonement the same as though it had been our own act, and by treating us in consequence the same as though we had, like the angels who kept their first estate, been always righteous. Hence, when the believer "shall make his soul an offering for sin, he shall see his seed" (Is. 53 : 10),

—"to the praise of the glory of his grace wherein he hath made us accepted in the Beloved."—Eph. 1:6. Thus God can be generous toward believers only at the cost of the life of his own Son, and in the act, evinces his respect to his own authority.

*I.* O how good is God! I used to distinguish between the kindness of the Son and the Father, but now I can understand that it was "God who *so* loved the world, as to give his only begotten Son."

*P.* As this world is minute when compared with the other and innumerable worlds of God's creation, so is the period allotted for the existence of mankind upon it short, compared with eternity. Our race occupy a parenthesis, as it were, in infinite duration. An eternity of the past is pressing onward to an eternity in the future; and the occurrences during this interruption will serve to explain hereafter the holy principles and rectitude of God in reference to all events that have transpired during the entire course of his administration through eternal ages. When enough has been done to accomplish that fully, the parenthesis will be struck out; and the angel of the apocalypse, standing upon the sea and upon the earth, shall lift up his hand to heaven, and swear by him that liveth for ever and ever, "That there should be time no longer." Then cometh the end, and Christ will deliver up his mediatorial kingdom to God, even the Father (1 Cor. 15:24); and in the firm establishment of the divine government there, in the perpetual holiness and blessedness of his blood-purchased heritage, and in the full development of his Father's glory, he will "see of the travail of his soul and shall be satisfied."—Is. 53:11.

*I.* I have always heretofore most strangely confined my views of the atonement, as designed to affect this world chiefly; and the evident perversion of it which men make to encourage a hope of impunity in sin, has made its efficacy somewhat doubtful; but regarding it as designed to operate chiefly and ultimately upon the eternal state relieves the difficulty. I can now see also, how it is that God can accept the believer, even though he dies despairing of pardon; for it is his own character and rectitude, and not the believer's, that is to be justified, and others can now justify him, whatever may be the believer's apprehensions about himself.

*P.* Yes. Christ ever liveth to make intercession, by the presentation of his own obedient sufferings in behalf of all that come unto God through obedience to himself.—Heb. 7:25.

*I.* What is intended by the doctrine of election?

*P.* Mankind are in a state of hostility to God, are entitled to no favor at his hands, and have, of their own fault, so lost their recuperative power that they will not, and of themselves cannot so deny *themselves* as to recover it and turn to God; and all must be lost unless God shall interpose. Now, the doctrine of election exhibits that wonderful kindness and goodness of God toward such helpless and hell-deserving creatures, whereby, with an ultimate view to his own glory, he, from the beginning, selected many to repentance, holiness, and eternal life.—Eph. 1:4—6; 2 Thes. 2:13, 14. You are well aware that, left to yourself, you would never have devoted your attention to the subject, nor have denied your selfish heart so as to have turned to God; you dreaded and avoided self-denial to the last moment, and would then have sought refuge in a selfish hope had not God prevented. To you, it was the chief offence, or impediment of the cross.—Gal. 5 : 11.

*I.* Yes. I am as satisfied as of my existence that, but for the interposition of God by his providence, his word, and his Spirit, I should never have denied myself so as to have reached true repentance. It is to sovereign grace that I am a debtor for it.

*P.* And in like manner all true believers are indebted to the electing grace of God for their deliverance from the power of selfishness, and entrance into holiness. In the Epistle to the Romans (ch. 8: 28—30) the apostle gives a detailed view of this doctrine. He proceeds upon the assumption that mankind are free moral agents, unreasonably unwilling to discharge their obligations to God, and so bent on sin that, if left to themselves, none would ever turn to him. God knows all things (John 21 : 17), for he can foresee the results of causes and effects to the end of time; he foreknew all with whom he had to deal, what influences they would exert upon themselves and upon one another, and what course of conduct would be pursued by each in consequence. He could anticipate what instrumentalities he could put in operation, what counteracting influences he could bring to bear upon each, and what good results he could produce, if he would, without trenching upon the best principles of moral government, and without infringing upon the free action and consequent accountability of his rebel subjects.

*I.* Of course he could, since nothing is too hard for the Lord.—Gen. 18 : 14.

*P.* Benevolence necessarily dictated that he should accomplish whatever of good could be thus safely effected; and the purpose was immediately formed by him to bring to holiness all those who could be thus reached. In the words of the Scriptures, he "predestinated them to be conformed to the [moral] image of his Son."

*I.* My impression in the days of my selfishness, was that men were elected from perdition to eternal happiness; I now see that it is from sin to godliness, and that whatever blessings result are consequences thereof.

*P.* Yes. His own glory was the ultimate end designed; and he selected *many* to whom Christ might, as an elder brother, be the chief and head.

*I.* Here again I was in an error. I supposed that but few were selected, while the many were rejected; and this made me doubt somewhat.

*P.* If you only take into view the mass of adults who have refused the gospel in the present and past ages of the world, the many would indeed seem to be rejected and the very few elected. But it will appear different if, in addition to the myriads of adults who have already gone to heaven, or who are now serving God on earth, you include all the infants who have been and who shall be saved by preventing grace, and all persons who shall hereafter be converted, and especially the vast population of the millenial era foretold in the Scriptures, when the earth shall be full of the knowledge of the Lord.—Is. 11:9.

*I.* I see that our ignorance should not sit in judgment upon God's benevolence.

*P.* Those whom he thus wisely and safely selected he effectually called by his providence, word, and Spirit. To call, is to command or summon another to come;

and to call sinners effectually is to draw them into a moral union with Christ. He has sent forth the invitations, denunciations, and commands of the Scriptures; he has established his church on earth to present them, has sent abroad his ministers to proclaim them, and has employed a most wonderful combination of instrumentalities to reach mankind. Under the special supervision of his Spirit, the work of reclamation has gone on from age to age; those who could thus be brought to "ponder the path of their feet, and establish their ways" were effectually called and received; and those who proved incorrigible under such means, were rejected.

*I.* But could not God change the hearts of all mankind by whom the invitation is received?

*P.* It cannot be shown that he could not; but it can be shown that to work miracles apart from the truth or to impart private revelations in these latter ages, in order to do so, would destroy the force of the evidence on which the divine origin of his public revelation is based, and leave mankind a prey to every fancy and every mysterious imposition, thereby counteracting the very object of a general revelation. No doubt greater faithfulness and knowledge on the part of the church and ministry would enable the work of God to prosper far more than it ever has done; and this very thing is promised in the latter days: "Many shall run to and fro, and knowledge shall be increased."—Dan. 12:4. "Behold, the days come, saith the Lord, that the plowman shall overtake the reaper, and the treader of grapes, him that soweth the seed;" so rapid shall be conversions under clear truth.—Amos 9: 13. The missions of the church to the heathen world are, among other instrumentalities, evidently destined to hasten that period when "the kingdoms of this world shall become the kingdoms of our Lord, and of his Christ."—Rev. 11:15. And God himself asks, "What could have been done more to my vineyard, that I have not done in it?" To allege that more could *properly* have been done by *him*, is to charge him with a deficiency in benevolence; and "let the potsherds strive with the potsherds of the earth; [but] woe unto him that striveth with his Maker."

*I.* Of course he cannot be expected to contravene the wise and good principles upon which he acts toward all his creatures, for the sake of the ill-deserving.

*P.* Those who respond to his effectual call to repentance, he justifies. He remits their sins and treats them as though they had always been righteous, on account of what their elder Brother has accomplished in their behalf. And, in pursuance of his purpose to finish the work begun in their hearts, he proceeds to discipline, chasten, and prepare them for his own presence and to enter into his own glory.—John 17:22.

*I.* O how glorious and good is God as exhibited in these principles! He has a right to reign, and he ought to "work all things after the counsel of his own will." I can now understand that election does not depend upon any foreseen repentance by the sinner himself, because he never will deny himself and repent of himself; that it is not partial, since the offer is to all mankind, and none are selected because they deserve it more than others, all being totally depraved; and that none are made reprobates who are not incorrigibly perverse under the circumstances, and so have none to blame for it but themselves. If the sinner would avoid reprobation, he must "acquaint himself quickly with God;" if he declines, he should not therefore blame God or deny his electing grace which alone makes it certain that any will be saved. The inquiry of the apostle strikes me with peculiar force: "Why doth he yet find fault?"

*P.* Some find fault because they hate the sovereignty of God which is implied in the doctrine of election; and others, because they apprehend that they themselves are not included in its provisions. Many entertain improper views of God, looking upon him as unreasonable or arbitrary in his selections, and inferring injustice toward those who shall not be saved. But he has the best of reasons, his own glory; provision has been made for all (1 John 2:2), and none of the lost will fail to see that they might have been saved had they made a proper use of the privileges which he afforded them.

*I.* What is intended by the doctrine of the final perseverance of believers?

*P.* It does not import that believers are not exposed, of themselves, to fall into much sin and even into final apostacy. The Scriptures contain statements of the weakness and transgressions of some of the best men, such as Moses, David, and Paul. That there is nothing to render a final and total apostacy *naturally* impossible, is evident from the fact that many in heaven, who were far more holy than saints under the discipline of this probationary state, apostatized from God into supreme habitual selfishness and continued sin. And so the Scriptures assume, as when they urge believers "to work out their salvation with fear and trembling;" and when Paul declares "I keep my body [my selfish impulses] under, and bring it into subjection; lest that by any means, when I have preached to others, I myself should be a cast-away."—1 Cor. 9:27. And there is the express declaration of God, "When a righteous man turneth away from his righteousness and committeth iniquity, and *dieth in them*, for his iniquity that he hath done shall he die."—Ez. 18:26. If any one, presuming upon his forbearance and mercy, shall take such forbidden courses, he has just ground to apprehend that a holy God will fulfill his declaration and cast him off for ever. Under no circumstances can religion be safely made an apology for sin, or a cloak or aid to it.

*I.* How indispensably important, therefore, is watchfulness, prayer, and firmness of purpose on our part in the service of God!

*P.* Yes; "Keep thy heart with all diligence, for out of it are the issues of life."—Prov. 4:23. To be found wanting when the bridegroom comes, is to meet a certain exclusion from his presence.—Matt. 25:1—13.

*I.* But will not God receive the penitent backslider before the hour of death?

*P.* Yes. "Again, when the wicked man turneth away from his wickedness that he hath committed, and doeth that which is lawful and right, he shall save his soul alive: Because he considereth, and turneth away from all his transgressions that he hath committed, he shall surely live, he shall not die."—Ez. 18:27, 28. But for one who is in the constant perpetration of heinous offences against God, to rely upon impunity from perdition because he thinks that he was once converted, and that he will return to God some time or other before he dies, is the strongest evidence he can have that he is still in love with sin, that his *heart* never glowed with a true love to God or holiness, and that "he has neither part nor lot in this matter." I do not speak of the feeble frames into which Christians often fall, nor of those occasional false steps which result from sudden temptation, and which, as exceptions, prove that holiness is the rule of their lives; but of those known, willful, heinous, and habitual courses of sin which, were it not for their profession, would class their perpetrators with avowed unbelievers. The offences of the one are the errors of a loving child, bitterly repented of when realized; but those of the other are the outbursts of the hostility of a secret but determined enemy.

*I.* The Christian warfare then is for his eternal life! I do not wonder that the apostle was so anxious to impress on his converts in the churches the necessity of perseverance. Amid the temptations, dangerous influences, and habits of the world, is it not a miracle that any are kept from finally falling?

*P.* Yes; it is indeed a miracle of divine *grace.* The doctrine is, that true believers, being kept by the power of God through the workings of their faith or their devotion to the authority and glory of God, will neither *totally* nor *finally* fall away from the state of grace; but shall persevere therein to the end and be eternally saved. "And I give unto them eternal life; and they shall never perish, neither shall any pluck them out of my hand. My Father which gave them me, is greater than all; and no one is able to pluck them out of my Father's hand."—John 10:28, 29. "Who are kept by the power of God through faith unto salvation, ready to be revealed in the last time.—Receiving the end of your faith, even the salvation of your souls."—1 Pet. 1:5. 9.

"The righteous also shall hold on his way, and he that hath clean hands shall be stronger and stronger."—Job 17:9; Phil. 1:6. Your whole dependence must be placed on God, who will have the glory of your preservation as well as of your regeneration and adoption; but you must not therefore intermit your own watch and full purpose of heart after obedience. With such a course as respects God and yourself, you may look forward to the end with rejoicing. The grace that elected and effectually called the believer, will not ultimately fail through any want of ability in Christ to accomplish its purpose.—Jude 24.

*I.* Surely not. That this blessed doctrine is from God is, to me, a fact beyond all doubt. But why is it objected to by many?

*P.* It is impossible to give all the reasons. When an impenitent sinner who has embraced a false hope eventually falls back into the world, he is reduced to the necessity of concluding either that such class of hopes with their pleasures are invalid, and that he had no true religion; or else, that they are Scriptural, but that he has fallen from grace. His selfish heart assisted by the notions of others being the judge, decides him to the latter opinion of course. It is more agreeable to his selfish feelings, and affords more encouragement that he can retrieve his position by renewing his evidences when it becomes convenient; and so the doctrine of perseverance is denied. The testimony of Scripture is easily disposed of; for about the last thing the sinner will ever do will be to admit a truth or doctrine that he hates, upon the simple declaration of God in his word. Some Christians have been led to doubt this doctrine, from observing so many, who once had bright hopes and great joys and who for a time seemed to run well, relapse into sin and worldliness with a peculiar zest sharpened by their late abstinence. Honestly supposing that their hopes, like their own, proceeded from a love to the glory of God, they are dismayed at such results; whereas, they were selfish, worldly, and sinful, such as you first started with years ago. And such is the testimony of the Scriptures: "They went out from us, but they were not of us; for if they had been of us, they would no doubt have continued with us; but they went out, that they might be made manifest that they were not all of us."—1 John 2: 19.

*I.* I confess that I used to doubt this doctrine for the reasons you first gave; but I am corrected. O, how it encourages my soul to enter upon the Christian race with ardor and hope! And my own feelings testify that it can never become an occasion of lukewarmness in Christ's cause, for it opens a sure prospect of success in the very things on which my heart is most prominently fixed;—as well might the opening of the cool fountain before the thirsty soul, endanger his efforts to drink of its waters!

## CHAPTER XI.

### PERSEVERANCE.

*Inquirer*. Is there no danger of anticipating the will of God or the guidance of his Spirit, by devising and entering, of ourselves, upon measures for the promotion of his kingdom and the welfare of mankind?

*Pastor*. So far from it, that precise thing is made our duty when, in dependence on him, we take care to enlighten our minds in his will by studying his word, noting his providences, and exercising all the wisdom we can summon. "Whatsoever thy hand findeth to do, do it with thy might; for there is no work, nor device, nor knowledge, nor wisdom, in the grave whither thou goest."—Eccl. 9:10. The Scriptures no where require us, as some of the slothful suppose, to delay in our endeavors until some special or signal providence shall indicate the supposed will of God; but they rather inculcate the principle that, as a general rule, we should lay our plans and enter upon their execution precisely as worldly men would in respect to their pursuits, but yet with different motives, nobler objects, and by the use of divinely sanctioned means. It should not be suffered that "the children of this world should be wiser in their generation than the children of light" (Luke 16:8); and especially that we should make the absence of some special divine indication the apology for our neglects in laboring for God. If you would render to him those works of gratitude as well as of love and duty, which are his due, do not fear to run before the Spirit; but remember that it is when "a man's heart deviseth his way" and he thereby puts himself in motion, that "the Lord directeth [the course of] his steps."—Prov. 16:9. The last thing to be feared is that you will do too much for God.

*I.* This is, beyond doubt, the true principle; and with the divine aid it shall be my rule the remainder of my days. I am well aware of the necessity of not only overcoming vicious and slothful habits, but of substituting good and active ones in their place, so that habit as well as every other power shall be enlisted on the side of Christ. Among the various things I propose, one is continually to lend out for perusal some books calculated to effect immediate good, as well as to make personal appeals when expedient.

*P.* By the plan you propose, many persons can be reached by the means of grace; and by steadily prosecuting it rather than by suffering it to expire as a mere purpose, you can have no conception of the number of souls that may be converted to Christ or may be enlightened and strengthened in their faith and works. The kingdom of God when found, is seen to be an exhaustless treasure; and he who has secured the true riches is glad to guide the needy to them, that their souls may be supplied with its blessings. There was a special command given by our Lord to the immediate disciples, which applies as decidedly to *every* other disciple in every age and country, whose age, sex, ability and aptness to teach, and other circumstances, indicate that the path is open before him—namely, "Go ye into all the world, and preach the gospel to every creature."—Mark 16:15. Thousands of young men who, had they given due attention to the subject and sought by prayer and meditation to be directed from on high, would have burned with anxiety to unfurl the gospel standard, and as ambassadors of Christ would have proclaimed his reign to the people, have failed in securing that glorious privilege, through their neglect of such examination.

*I.* I can conceive of no higher privilege and no more desirable avocation in life.

*P.* There is none, God himself being the judge; for he had but one Son, and him he gave to be a preacher of the gospel. Apart from its tendency to relieve one from the temptations to which those are exposed who are compelled to follow some worldly business, it is a *professional* devotion to the glory of God and the good of our race; and none but those who have entered upon its cares and trials, can appreciate the blessedness and sweet rewards which are constantly flowing in upon the faithful pastor. If every ambitious project is carefully excluded from his bosom, if the desire of emulation and worldly honor is discarded, if pecuniary emolument is held subordinate to duty, and if to a warm heart is added the single purpose to honor God (Matt. 6:22) in his profession by the diligent use of the wisest ascertainable means, a degree of success will crown his labors and a store of riches will be laid up for him in heaven for the repast of everlasting ages, beyond his largest conceptions. God in his providence is still inquiring, "Whom shall I send, and who will go for us?" Will the designated reader solemnly and truly respond with him of old, "Here am I; send *me!*"

*I.* I will make the subject my careful study, will seek the light and guidance of the Holy Spirit, and will decide according to my best judgment. I am entirely the Lord's; I hope to dwell with him for ever hereafter as a "King and Priest unto God" (Rev. 1 : 6); and shall esteem it the highest honor to which a mortal can attain, if he shall permit me beforehand to proclaim the unsearchable riches of his grace to dying men.

*P.* And may he give you a multitude of deathless souls as your everlasting reward! In respect to the providence of God, it is an encouraging reflection that he guides the minutest as well as the most important event, overruling even sin to the development of his justice or his grace, and directing all things in righteousness to the ultimate promotion of his own glory. Even the general laws of nature, as has been remarked by a recent writer, are made to benefit those who love God, by becoming the occasions of his special providences toward them. There is, he remarks, something very beautiful and encouraging in the doctrine of particular providences. This would be a lonely, dismal world indeed, to a devout soul, if there were not some intercourse with the Father of Spirits; and we know not what could be more perfectly adapted to the heart's great wants, than the Scripture assurance that God is in every thing—that all life, history, and experience are but an account-current kept between the soul and its Maker. The course of events goes on according to general laws which were constructed ages ago, without reference to any individual in particular. Yet each one of these events has as direct a reference to each individual affected by them, as if he were the only being in the world besides the Creator, and the whole system of things were constructed for his special admonition and instruction. The hairs of our head fall to the ground in obedience to the general law of gravitation, created millions of years ago, and without any reference to any particular individual; yet every hair falls by the particular act of God in each case, as much as if the great law of gravitation was created for no other purpose. An accident may take place—a train may run off the track, and startle some thoughtless passenger by the terrible peril of instant death. The crash and ruin are the result of physical laws, laid down without any reference to any individual, which might have produced this result if the periled passenger had not been on board. His presence or his absence, in one sense, had nothing to do with the causation of the event. Yet in another and interior sense, the whole event was brought about with special reference to him. The general law inclosed a specific design; there was as much a particular purpose in the accident, as if the whole circle of causes by which the accident was effected, had been originally and from all eternity, created solely for him. The moral purpose of summoning his thoughts, with a terrible urgency, to the consideration of his spiritual interests, may have been an express reason for bringing about the result. We cannot tell *how* it is that this harmony of general laws and specific Providential interposition is effected—*how* an event which would apparently have taken place at any rate, nevertheless takes place only with reference to a particular end. Yet it is none the less true that in all events there is a special reference and design, however brought about; and the thoughtful mind can read in every thing that takes place, no matter by what means, a particular message to himself—a voice which no one else hears, but which speaks to him as distinctly as if the event had no other meaning or intent, and no other being were affected by it. The world may not see the invisible autograph written upon any particular calamity that overtakes a Christian; it may be nothing but a general result of general laws. The world sees nothing in the occurrence but the operation of the laws of natural philosophy. But the poor victim sees written the lessons of fearful personal instruction—an individual message from the Infinite Source of all laws to his spirit, as clearly and rationally, as if the event took place for no other purpose. It is only an accident to the world; it is a special providence to the man himself. Thus, underneath and within the visible flow of events in this world, there are electric streams of thought proceeding from God to men—a perpetual secret correspondence going on, by means of events that occur, that mean nothing to the public, but are full of significance to the individual. The Christian has thus a kind of account-current with his Maker; a system of checks and admonitions—a perpetual lesson, taught by every-day occurrences, and written in the face of all nature, history and experience. They all have a meaning to him who sees God in them—sometimes encouraging and consoling—sometimes admonitory and frowning. Beyond their general significance, the events of his life have a special significance to him, which demonstrates the presence and care of his God, and peoples the world with a holy ministry. Life becomes a great sermon—the universe a whispering-gallery, transmitting perpetual messages to his ear.

*I.* It is a matter of great joy that God will condescend to communicate thus with his creatures. Surely "all things shall work together for good to them that love God." Will you explain how holy affections are to be called into exercise by the believer?

*P.* They are never to be produced, even in the regenerate heart, by any mental struggles to excite them; but they must arise according to the established laws of mental action. The converted heart being favorably disposed toward holiness, a contemplation of the various objects toward which its desires tend will produce spontaneously the corresponding mental affections, which will exist in greater or less power according to circumstances. This principle is exhibited in the declaration of the Psalmist, "while I was musing [silently meditating and contemplating divine truths] the fire burned."—Ps. 39:3. You will observe also that the intensity of the mental interest excited, rather than the degree of pleasure produced, is the true measure of an affection; for emotions of pleasure are adjuncts to the excited desire, and it may and often does exist in a powerful degree where no pleasure is present, and even when painful emotions are aroused,—as where some great evil is apprehended to some branch of Christ's cause for which we feel particularly solicitous.

*I.* I have always heretofore been accustomed to measure the degree and even the existence of a supposed religious affection, by the gratification it produced; but I see that even here my selfish heart betrayed me in favor of its cherished object. It is clear that the degree of our interest in or solicitude for an object on its own account, will be the measure of our attachment to and love for it.

*P.* To reduce the principle to practice: If you would excite the affection of love to God, (good-will to him having been previously formed by regeneration,) reflect calmly on his principles, character, and holy conduct. Seek the aid of the Scriptures, and the works of that class of pious men who, like Baxter, Payson, and others, show themselves familiar with God; and your affection of love will arise in purity and comfort.

*I.* On the same principle that reflection upon his creative right or rightful authority, will induce me to resolve anew to obey him or to submit implicitly to his will, the contemplation of the moral excellence which he develops in the exercise of that authority will draw forth the affections of my heart?

*P.* Yes. In order to exercise gratitude, reflect upon what God has done for yourself and for your fellow-creatures; recall to mind the sufferings of Christ, his kindness in permitting you to return to him, his forbearance, the gift of the Spirit, his remission of your sins, his preservation and preparation of you for endless life, and the like. These, and particularly when your own ill-desert is contrasted with the condescension, grace, and holy benevolence of God in them, will arouse the sentiment of gratitude and make it an habitual exercise.

*I.* The very enumeration of his mercies reminds me that I can never be sufficiently grateful.

*P.* True; and we shall always remain his debtor, for eternity will not be long enough to enable us to repay the debt of gratitude we owe to Christ. In order to exercise repentance toward sin as an affection, reflect deliberately and without any effort to produce feelings, upon the course of your past life; upon the habitual selfishness in which you indulged, producing hostility toward God; upon the evil thoughts, passions, and purposes which you harbored; upon the evil conduct in breach of his holy law which you have perpetrated; and upon your accustomed neglect of every duty you owed him. Contrast these with the fact that his authority should have been observed, and you will highly *disapprove* of your conduct, and of yourself on account of it. Contrast them with the rectitude, purity, holiness and glory of God, and ill-will, and even *hatred* toward yourself on account of your former moral deformity, will arise. Contrast them with the kindness, grace, and pardoning goodness of Christ, and with the various other motives to gratitude, and *sorrow* will arise in your heart and regrets will fill your soul in view of their ingratitude and baseness. And the result will be a renewal of your purposes to abstain thereafter from every known sin, through Christ strengthening you.

*I.* Yes; I see the principle throughout. My own properly directed agency is employed by the Spirit to produce godly repentance. My sins, at times, look so very criminal and odious that I am almost disheartened and led to doubt whether I truly love God. I have heretofore supposed that when a person became truly converted he would have no more sense of sin.

*P.* Unconvicted sinners with a hope, may avoid such a sense, but not the Christian. So far from it, he will then for the first time arrive at a true sense of its guilt and enormity; and if he continues to dwell on his past sins, their criminality and his abhorrence of them will increase. In his own view he may seem to be becoming more and more guilty in consequence, whereas he is but just discovering the degree of guilt which has always been imputable to him; just, as it has been said, as one who has been long shut up in the dark with venomous reptiles, and who first discovers them on the light being admitted, may imagine that they are new companions because they were not noticed by him before.

*I.* I see it must be very much so.

*P.* The apostle, when speaking of the worshippers under the law having "no more conscience of sins" (Heb. 10:2), means that, had the law been availing, they would have been delivered from sin itself. But this implies neither a loss of a sense of past guilt, nor freedom from future sin. Sorrow and hatred for sin, and particularly the latter, with the accompanying disapprobation of conscience, are very disheartening feelings indeed; but they are, notwithstanding, as good evidences of a converted state of the soul as is love to God itself.

*I.* How can that be?

*P.* They imply ill-will toward disobedience; that is the converse of good-will toward obedience, which is conversion itself. Besides, sorrow in view of an injury which has befallen another, for example, is evidence conclusive that we have a kind regard for him; just as indifference on the occasion would show that we felt no interest in him whatever. On the same principle sorrow for having wronged God as our benefactor, and hatred to ourselves for having violated our obligations, evince a deep regard for him; just as the indifference of sinners on these subjects shows that they have no interest or love whatever for him.

*I.* I see the principle now, for the first time. But it seems as if I could never recount all my sins to God.

*P.* It would take at least as long a life to do it, as it has to commit the sins themselves. We ought to confess our sins so far as we can, and to forsake them also; but a constant dwelling upon the subject is calculated to repress your other exercises and to hinder your activity and enjoyments, as is to be seen in the cases of many pious persons who constantly brood over their past sins and present short-comings. Ezra enjoined an opposite course on the penitent people; he forbade their further mourning and weeping, and bade them to rejoice in the Lord, in order that they might be encouraged in his service: "for the joy of the Lord is your strength." —Neh. 8 : 9, 10. Watching does not consist, as some suppose, in dwelling upon and mourning over the past; but in guarding our feelings and conduct for the future, in endeavoring to act unselfishly by holding others' rights and interests on a par with our own, and in ordering our conduct in heart and life aright before God.

*I.* That certainly must be the most profitable course.

*P.* In order to produce an interest toward the disciples of our Lord, reflect upon their new relations to him and to yourself, and contemplate their holy principles, their desires for the glory of your heavenly Father, their efforts to put on his moral image, and their labors to advance his cause, overlooking those defects to which frail human nature (including yourself) is so liable. Thus an attachment to them *as disciples* (John 15 : 17) will be elicited and become habitual, and you will receive in return the blessing of God in your own soul. We can now hardly comprehend the extent of mutual love which Christians exercised in the early days of the church.—John 15:12; 1 John 3:16.

*I.* I thank you for this advice; and it shall be my constant study to observe it. I can foresee that it will produce almost incalculable comfort and usefulness.

*P.* In order to produce an interest in behalf of impenitent sinners, reflect calmly upon their unholy character, their evil conduct toward God, and upon their horrible doom. Then holy sympathy in view of their prospects, will unite with right desires for their conversion to holiness and their devotion to the service and glory of God. But of what practical use can such feelings be, unless you are impelled by them to labor for the conversion of sinners to Christ?

*I.* Of none. Whatever I can do, shall be done.

*P.* If you would cultivate zeal for God, and energy in active benevolence or in any other good work, you must deliberately examine its character, weigh its claims, and address yourself to it with a whole heart; then your feelings will flow forth. In order to derive benefit from studying the Scriptures, or from prayer, you should avoid those preliminary efforts to force the mind to feel, or to place it in a supposed holy frame, or to make mechanical impressions upon it, which many suppose to be indispensable. Peruse the word of God with becoming gravity, but with the simple purpose of acquiring information, precisely as you would any other book; and your interest in its truths will be gradually excited, as your understanding becomes enlightened in respect to them. When you retire to pray, let your thoughts turn calmly toward God and the various subjects on which you feel interested; dedicate yourself anew to Christ and his service; and humbly present to him those things which you desire; then the duty will be a source of pleasure.

*I.* What is prayer?

*P.* It is the expression before God of our actual desires.

*I.* What is meant by the prayer of faith which the Scriptures represent as prevalent with God?

*P.* There is, perhaps, no subject on which men's fancies have more prevailed, than on this; and yet the true answer will be perfectly obvious upon examination. Every Christian has, it is believed, exercised it at some period, though he may have been unaware of the character of his feelings at the time. If we draw our answer from the Scriptures, we shall find that it is there presented in two, and somewhat different aspects. In its primitive sense, it is the belief of the disciple that God will glorify himself in respect to the request presented, and his entire and cordial consent that he may do so whether it involves a grant or denial of his petition. Said our Lord, "All things whatsoever ye shall ask in prayer, believing, ye shall receive."—Matt. 21:22. The condition here expressed, *believing*, (*pisteuontes*) does not refer to the assurance of the petitioner that he shall receive the specific thing requested, but to the exercise of Christian faith in respect to it, or that which constitutes one a Christian. It intends his reception of Christ as God not only, but also the submission of his petition to be decided by him as his glory shall dictate, implying a preference of that to the thing requested.

*I.* Then every true Christian can exercise the prayer of faith in this sense.

*P.* Yes; and it is as obviously his duty as it is to love God. But our Lord, in reference to the prevailing dereliction on this very point, inquired, "When the Son of man cometh, shall he find faith on the earth?"—Luke 18:1—8. It is presumptuous to have a devotion for the things we desire for ourselves, superior to the demands of the divine glory in respect to them.

*I.* Then every believing prayer will be answered either in the specific thing desired, or in the more important end of the glory of God in respect to it?

*P.* Certainly. The Christian may, when he commences his prayer, be so fixed upon having the particular boon conferred, that he may lose sight of the more important consideration of the exigencies of the divine glory; a thing which is very common, as in the case of Paul, who was on that account denied his petition thrice presented.—2 Cor. 12:8. When the Christian, by reflection and the tendencies of prayer itself under the Spirit, comes to realize that the glory of God is concerned in the matter, his preference thereof will be elicited, and he will soon be able through the Spirit to give it the ascendancy over the specific object of his petition; and he will, while anxiously desiring that, readily superadd the request for God to glorify himself the rather, whether his specific request is granted or refused. Thus Paul came to rejoice in the glory of the grace of Christ as manifested through that very thorn in the flesh, from which he had so earnestly desired to be delivered. The Christian will, after all, receive at the hands of his heavenly Father the very answer which he would himself select, could he in a proper frame of mind survey the whole field and ascertain all the considerations which should govern his case; for he would decide then, just as God will now under his perfect knowledge of the whole subject. And should God lean in his favor at the expense of his own glory, he would be eventually disappointed and dissatisfied.

*I.* I can now understand somewhat of the force of that assurance, "Delight thyself also *in the Lord;* and he shall give thee the desires of thy heart," which will then terminate on him and his glory.—Ps. 37:4. What a sweet encouragement is this to cast all our desires and cares upon him who careth for us!—1 Pet. 5:7. And how intelligible as well as proper is that declaration, "Ye ask, and receive not, because ye ask amiss [not for the divine glory], that ye may consume it upon your lusts" or selfish gratifications.—Jas. 4:3.

*P.* The second aspect of the prayer of faith includes this idea of deferring the subject to the divine glory, and adds the firm persuasion that the glory of God will be best promoted by bestowing the specific good desired, and that *such good will certainly be conferred on the petitioner.* Thus, our Lord declared, "What things soever ye desire when ye pray, believe that ye receive them, and ye shall have them."—Mark 11:24.

*I.* Are we to understand from this, that by a simple and successful effort of the disciple to believe that his specific request will be granted, he will secure a favorable answer? If so, it seems that Christ has placed himself in the hands of his servants, and that the facility with which any one can believe things is the measure of his power over him and his providence.

*P.* Christ has not thus endangered himself, or placed his glory at the hazard of fallible creatures. In their extremities, the disciples are prone to believe in those things which they consider the best for themselves; but these are not always the most worthy of God.

*I.* What is the ground, then, for believing that the specific thing will be granted?

*P.* The determination of God to confer it.

*I.* Of course; but how are we to ascertain such determination?

*P.* In one of two ways, when it exists, and when he condescends to inform us in either. The one is by his particular promise applicable to the case; and the other is by the intervention of the Holy Spirit. With regard to the former, you will remember that many specific promises are made to the praying disciple; these, on complying with the conditions, he may and ought to apply to himself the same as if God had spoken to him personally; and on so doing he will *believe that he receives them;* and then he shall have them, for he honors God by confiding in his veracity. Thus, the aids of the Holy Spirit are promised him (Luke 11:13); every necessary worldly supply (Ps. 37:3); the supervision of providence for his best good (Rom. 8:28); eternal life. —John 10:28. To expect a favorable answer, and indeed to anticipate it with entire confidence on such grounds, is reasonable and also safe to the divine glory because authorized by God himself.

*I.* Certainly I can unhesitatingly confide in such an answer in that case. But how can I reach it in cases where there is no particular promise?

*P.* You cannot, unless the Spirit brings you there; your

own efforts will be of no avail in such cases, or rather will tend to an unauthorized confidence which will surely be disappointed. It depends solely on God then to grant the persuasion that we shall receive the thing asked for. It is our duty to exercise the first kind of faith, by yielding the whole matter into the hands of God, willing to have his will and glory promoted whether our desire is granted or not; and then, if he sees fit, we shall know beforehand what is his will, otherwise we shall not. It is the Spirit who "helpeth our infirmities, for we know not *what* we should pray for [nor how to pray for it] as we *ought;* but the Spirit itself maketh intercession for us with groanings which cannot be uttered. And he that searcheth the hearts knoweth what is the mind of the Spirit, because he maketh intercession for the saints *according to the will of God.*"—Rom. 8:26, 27. Prayer when thus dictated by the Spirit, may well leave on the mind of the earnest petitioner a sweet and perfect confidence that his request is secured! for if it was from God the Spirit, it is surely granted. "The effectual fervent [the urgent and strenuous] prayer of a righteous man, availeth much"—that is, is prevalent with God.—Jas. 5:16.

*I.* I confess that I have not before observed the pertinency of that passage in Romans, having always confined it to some mysterious influences in the apostolic days. I suppose prayer is often answered upon our compliance with the condition in Matt. 21:22, and where this persuasion of receiving the thing desired does not exist?

*P.* No doubt, for they are independent conditions. Both include a superior regard to the divine glory as their chief moral element; while the last adds thereto a present conviction of the answer being received, which in the first is to be known only when the event actually occurs. In either case, the immediate effect is contentment with the will of God on the subject, and an impression that further urgency with him is uncalled for.

*I.* Just as I felt, when I first resigned myself entirely to the divine will. I then had no heart to ask God for any thing merely personal, but preferred to let all rest with him. But are such prayers common among Christians?

*P.* Yes; more common than their mistaken views of humility will permit them to allow. Let me mention an occurrence which, amongst many others, fell under my own observation, to illustrate this whole doctrine of the prayer of faith. A few years since, a pious lady was called to witness the rapid decline toward the grave, of a lovely but unconverted daughter of seventeen, under the incurable progress of consumption. Aware that God required the use of adequate means for her conversion, she procured the advice of a clerical friend in whose ability to impart right instruction she had confidence. He found the daughter engrossed in selfish alarms at her impending death and perdition, and spending her time in endeavoring to deepen her feelings and trying to produce good desires and affections, in order to obtain encouragement to hope in Christ for pardon from punishment, and for future peace. In this she had been aided by the mistaken zeal of an anxious but impenitent father; who being himself ignorant of self-denial, and looking upon a sense of pardon and a hope with its pleasures as religion itself, very naturally supposed that he was advising her in the right way in order to a valid hope. The imminence of her death so increased the anxieties of the sick girl for a hope of her own happiness, and made her so reluctant to abandon the pursuit of it, that her clerical instructor almost despaired of her conversion. She was ready to resolve upon the performance of every duty and to promise all faithfulness, but every effort was made under the promptings of her selfish desires, and consequently her heart remained unchanged. Appalled at her obstinacy and fearful prospects, her mother fled to her closet; and there, where no eye nor ear but those of God could see or hear, she fell prostrate before him, and "with groanings that could not be uttered" confessed her sins and the sins of her daughter, and entreated for the soul of her child. But no help came; and again and still again in her agony her cry went up to God, until an exhaustion of strength compelled her to desist. A moment's calm reflection then recalled her to a sense of the superior importance of the divine will, and showed that her anxiety in her petition was more for the benefit of her daughter than for the glory of her God. Conscience-stricken at her presumption in loving her child more than her Creator, and in pressing her suit for an idol, she yielded the point, and solemnly dedicated her unreservedly to God to be disposed of according to his will, and not her own; and she besought him to glorify his own name in whatever way he should see fit in respect to her rebellious daughter. The work was done! for, in the language of our Lord, she had asked *believing*, or in the spirit of a true believer in God (Matt. 21:22); she had come to prefer God and his glory to the personal good of her child. She *knew assuredly* that, whatever he might do with her, he would glorify his own holy name; and satisfaction at that result flowed in upon her soul, and peace with the will of God absorbed her anxieties for her daughter. Her prayer being thus answered in respect to the most important point, the glory of God, she arose composed and contented; for she found that she could pray no more, since she had nothing further to ask on that subject. As she returned to the sick room of the sufferer, a sweet confidence in God spread through her soul, and she felt assured that her daughter was safe in his hands! This was the "believing that ye receive" referred to by our Lord.—Mark 11:24. It came from no reasonings or efforts of her own, but flowed from her devotion to the glory of God, and from the breathings of the Spirit who had made intercession for her, in her heart, *according to the will of God*. Possessed thus of an answer in her own soul, she entered that room to behold it verified in the heart of her daughter; for upon a renewal of the counsel and efforts of her spiritual adviser, the Holy Spirit most evidently withdrew her from her selfish purpose, led her in a despair of success to suspend all her selfish endeavors, and touching her heart as He only can, turned her soul into repentance for sin. Then, with bitter self-reproaches for her stubborn resistance of her duty to God, with tears in view of the past selfishness of her heart, and with a perfect loathing and abhorrence of her sins as morally depraved and odious, she cast herself unreservedly on God, consenting that his will should be done with her in preference to her own, and preferring his reign and rejoicing in his glory. The answer was accomplished!

she too had now become a *believer*. She grew rapidly in love, humility, and every Christian grace, a wonder to herself that she had ever escaped the snares of a selfish heart, and blessing God that he had withheld her from those selfish hopes which she had so eagerly sought. The moral beauty of her new character charmed those who saw her, and gave great power to her affectionate counsels to her friends to prepare to meet their God. In a few weeks she girded herself up for the passage through the dark valley of death, for the Messenger of the Covenant was come to take her to her heavenly home. The calm serenity of that death-scene, her quiet endurance of the last pangs, her humble submission, her glowing love and confidence in God, her assured hope, produced impressions upon her father's mind which never subsided until, after the lapse of years, he was brought to turn his own feet into the paths of God's testimonies. And that conversion, in answer to the earnest and faithful prayer of that mother, proved to be the commencement of a work of grace such as has seldom, if ever, been witnessed in our day, and the results of it bid fair to be marked on the historic page of piety to the remotest time. Such is the prayer of faith; a prayer unknown to the backsliding heart, and one which can be comprehended or enjoyed only when the soul is near its God.

*I.* This explanation of the proper method of going to Christ in prayer, encourages me to discharge that duty with increased pleasure. And I thank you especially for describing the way in which parents should dedicate their children to him.

*P.* Christian parents no doubt often fail of the blessings of the Covenant, by not fulfilling the implied condition on their part. Many, when they professedly dedicate their offspring to God, are impelled simply by an anxiety for their eternal welfare. This is a natural feeling, but they err in making their personal good the ultimate object of the consecration; and they also dishonor God, by displacing his glory from its supremacy, and by impliedly dictating to their Sovereign in the matter. It is often more difficult for the parent to make an unreserved surrender of his child to God, that God may be glorified in whatever way in preference to its personal welfare, than it was to surrender his own soul. But obviously he cannot reasonably expect Christ to accept the dedication at his hands while he prefers it as a cherished idol; while, by a full surrender in a superior regard to the divine glory, with the purpose to train up his child for God, and with a diligent execution of it under whatever embarrassments and difficulties, he may rest assured that he will be found to be Christ's in the day in which he makes up his jewels. The proofs of faithfulness on the part of God to his covenant, are too numerous to have escaped your observation.

*I.* Yes; and I now perceive the secret of the intelligent and devoted Christian parents' success; and also, as "whatsoever is not of faith is sin" (Rom. 14: 23), the cause of the sad failure of others. Would to God that all believing parents, instead of prizing their offspring more than God, would thus truly consecrate them to him, and carefully educate them for his service! Then the courts of Zion would be crowded with the children of the covenant.

*P.* In proceeding I will observe that there is a variety

in the motives presented in the Scriptures, a misapplication of which produces much obscurity and embarrassment. You should bear in mind that the Scriptures, in dealing with mankind, always contemplate one of two things—namely, either to produce conviction of sin with its attending mental states, or to produce conversion and growth in grace, or sanctification; and that they always present the motives adapted to the accomplishment of these respective ends. Thus, for example, the terrors of the law are presented, not as a motive by which to convert sinners, but to arouse them to reflection on their dangerous state and so prepare them for a realization of their guilt; the catalogue of their sins is arraigned before their minds by the Spirit, in order to convict them of sin and of the certainty of their judgment; and the promises of the gospel for *regenerated* souls are made known to sinners, not as motives to conversion or that they may embrace them *before* regeneration, but that they may know the rich grace of God, so that their selfish hearts may not reject the means of enlightenment and conviction before the conscience is aroused with sufficient power to hold them, under God, and bring them to submission as soon as they find the promises beyond their reach. And on the other hand, the authority of God is presented not only to convince and convict the unconverted mind, but as the motive which is ultimately to break his will into submission; the character of Christ and his offices are given to engage the confidence and affections of the submissive heart; and the promises and hopes of the gospel, to cheer him onward in his holy and heavenly course. Every gospel truth is adapted to produce its peculiar impression under attending circumstances; and a careful observation of the subject may make you an adept in the use of truth as a motive influence; and you will discover that when God sends forth his truth to accomplish his will (Is. 55 : 11) it is always such truth as is adapted to produce the results he previously contemplated.

*I.* It is clear to me now that truths designed for specific classes or objects, will be entirely out of place when indiscriminately applied. The most melancholy perversion, it seems to me, is the presentation of the promises of the gospel as the motives under which impenitent sinners are to turn to Christ. It was that which well nigh ruined my own soul; for, so far from leading me really to God, they were seized upon by my selfish heart and perverted to an encouragement of its own purposes, under the guise of a change. And I was sustained in my delusion by the cherished belief that we could not be expected to understand, in this world, how sinners were converted.

*P.* It is true that no one can understand how the Holy Ghost reaches the heart in regeneration, because even were we capable of comprehending it, God has not seen fit to reveal the mode to us. In some passages he merely declares the fact that he will give a new heart (Ez. 36 : 26); in others, he states the same fact, with the addition that he does it by the instrumentality of the truth (Jas. 1 : 18); but in neither case does he inform us how he grasps or renders efficacious the sword of truth to accomplish that result. As respects one's voluntary action in conversion, it is impossible for the impenitent mind to comprehend it beforehand, for the same reason that no one can understand any moral or mental exercise which he has himself never before experienced. And this was the purport of our Lord's remark to the impenitent Nicodemus, in answer to his request for information on the subject. "The wind [representing, here, the truth] bloweth where it listeth, and *thou* [Nicodemus, a sinner] hearest the sound thereof, but canst not tell whence it cometh [how it is sent by the Spirit,] and whither it goeth," or what it is designed to accomplish.—John 3:8. He must first experience the change, and then he can understand the process in the review, just as he would know from observation, memory, or consciousness, any other voluntary act.—1 Cor. 2:11. 14. Thus, in your own case at first, you did not understand what the duty of conversion was nor how it was to be performed, because you had no experience on the subject; and I did not undertake the vain task of explaining it to you, for you could not have been made to comprehend it. But after you had yielded to the simple mandate of conscience by consenting to obey God, whereby you gained an experience of the duty, you was able to understand it as clearly as any other voluntary act of your life. The only reasons why true converts are ever at a loss to comprehend the exact process of their own conversion are, that they do not preserve clear perceptions of their own exercises at the time; or that they become confused on the general subject by imbibing the errors of selfish or ignorant teachers, and they become afraid to scrutinize too closely, lest their own actual experience (supposed to be defective,) should conflict with these errors, supposed to be sound. I have known even ministers of the gospel feel sad at contemplating their own holy exercises in conversion, not because they did not love them, but because they conflicted with the erroneous views they had adopted on the same subject; and in a perverted conscientiousness, they wrongly condemned themselves while presenting such opposing views.

*I.* I have always thought that mere authority, and especially the authority of dead men who have already rectified their own errors in the eternal state, has had too decided an influence on living intellect.

*P.* In religion, as in every other branch of knowledge, it is both our privilege and duty to "prove all things, and hold fast that which is good."—1 Thess. 5: 21. It has been my endeavor to do so in the fear of God, even to "holding fast the form of sound words" which are given in the sacred pages (2 Tim. 1:13); for you will have noticed that I have always preferred the phraseology of Scripture when it could be adopted, as well as the ideas it presents, to that of any of the schools.

*I.* Will you explain the difference between legal religion, the religion of the gospel, and natural religion?

*P.* True religion, viewed in whatever aspect, has for its essential element the submission of the will to the creative authority of God; and from this, as we have before seen, spring all the affections of the renewed heart and all the excellencies of the Christian deportment. The things *purposed* to be observed are the commands of God as variously made known in the precepts of the divine law, in the writings of the prophets and inspired men of the Scriptures, in the manifestations of his will contained in the works of creation, in his providences, in the dictates of our consciences when enlightened in respect to our relations to him and to one another, and the like. The original *motive* for such purpose is the sense of duty arising from a knowledge of God as our Creator, which is subsequently combined with the influence of love. The *end* is always the promotion of the divine glory. Thus in the Old Testament we are told to "fear God and keep his commandments; for this is the whole duty of man."—Eccl. 12:13. And in the New, "In every nation he that feareth God, and worketh righteousness, is accepted with him."—Acts 10:35.

*I.* Certainly, if right motives and purposes are excluded, I cannot conceive how there can be any thing left besides a dead form divested of every thing lovely or valuable. My former ideas of religion made a hope in Christ the essential element; but I have learned by a sad experience that holy principle is the chief element, and that a valid hope can exist only when authorized by it.

*P.* Legal religion, or legalism as it is usually called, is that which is confined to the law in respect to its purposes and motives. The law consists of two parts —namely, the precepts or things to be observed, and the penalty or the pains to be inflicted for their non-observance. Legality consists, first of a *purposed* observance of the precept of the divine law and of the commands of God as otherwise discoverable; and second, in the formation and execution of such purpose, from the motive of the penalty of the law;—that is, from a fear of its pains exciting the selfish desires to employ such means in order to escape them, or, which is the same thing, from a hope of safety therefrom.

Although there is an ostensibly good purpose, yet legality knows of no radical reformation, but is a mere modification or extension of the selfishness of the natural heart. A confirmed robber plunders you of your watch; and in doing so evinces the superior power of his desire for his personal interests over the dictates of upright principles. He comes to fear detection and punishment, and purposes to refrain from robbery in future and to live orderly in society; and in doing so, he evinces as clearly as before the superior power of the desire for his own interests, only it operates in a different and less injurious form. Again he is tempted to plunder your property; he becomes persuaded that he will not be detected or punished if he should do it; and this check being removed he perpetrates the act, showing the same superior influence of the selfish principle, and that his good conduct did not proceed from any reformation in his principles, that is, in the motives of his purposes. And such is the religion of the law, under whatever disguise. It is the operation exclusively of the natural heart under the selfish principle.

*I.* I see that regeneration forms no part of it, notwithstanding its hopes and pleasures.

*P.* This form of religion prevailed among the Pharisees. It is not a *free* service; for the legalist renders it under the constraint of fear, as the least of two evils —namely, to serve God, which he dislikes, or to be damned, which he dislikes more. When this constraint is temporarily removed, he will as naturally revert to his own ways, as will the dog to his vomit.—2 Pet. 2: 22. Again, it is pure *self-righteousness;* for the legalist purposes right actions indeed, but his motive in observing them is self, or his own interests. Again, it is purely *mercenary;* for the legalist discharges an acknowledged duty for pay; he observes an obligation because it will be for his interest rather than from principle. In his view, "*gain* [of selfish happiness] is godliness."—1 Tim. 6:5. He attempts a compromise with God, as if wrong existed on both sides, and barters present duty for future impunity from evil.

*I.* You have described the very religion which I formerly had, and upon which I sometimes prided myself as being so exclusively that of the gospel, because it rested entirely on a hope in Christ for salvation! My hope of pardon from the penalty of the law was the motive to all my obedience, and the source of all my joys.

*P.* Instead of having the religion of the gospel, you was a legalist of the first order;—and needed only a stubborn resistance to every truthful principle and argument, to make you a Pharisee. The legalist rests, at *heart*, on his own works for salvation, however loud may be his *profession* of trusting in the merits of Christ.

*I.* True. I used to graduate my hopes by my supposed *merits;* I endeavored to think that I was becoming better as I advanced, and I felt more confident accordingly. As the ancient Pharisees professed to depend upon the Father, so I depended for aid upon the Son in those respects where I had failed in my observances. When you referred some time since to the subject of our dependence on Christ, I felt convinced that, like Bunyan's man, I had hoped to be justified through Christ's acceptance of *my obedience to the laws;* or, that Christ should make *my religious duties* acceptable to the Father through his merits;—thus taking justification from the righteousness of Christ and applying it to my own, and making myself accepted through the goodness of my own obedience instead of through the Beloved alone. Truly, "the law worketh wrath."—Rom. 4:15. I fear that there are many legalists in Christ's church, who ignorantly apply that designation to almost every body except themselves.

*P.* The apostle in speaking of the legalists among the Jews, gives such a clear delineation of their character that none *need* mistake. "For I bear them record that they have a zeal of God, but not according to knowledge. For they being ignorant of *God's* righteousness, [of that right conduct which proceeds from a supreme regard to the rights of God, and of that holy state of the affections which flows from a true love to his glory,] and going about to establish *their own* righteousness, [to observe a correct deportment, under the motive influence of the love of their own happiness or the fear of their own punishment, and cultivating the selfish affections which flow therefrom,] have not submitted themselves unto the righteousness of God [unto the rightful authority of God, and that obedience which flows from that motive]. For Christ [as God, that is his authority and glory] is the end of the law [is the ultimate object designed to be accomplished by the law], for righteousness [to produce true righteousness] to every one that believeth" [that receives Christ as God, and cordially yields himself to obey and love him as such,]—just as he is the end of the gospel for redemption, as the Saviour of every believer.—Rom. 10:2—4.

*I.* What is the religion of the Gospel?

*P.* The term Gospel [*evangellion*] means glad-tidings, or good and jôyful news. These did not consist in the development of new principles in relation to moral character; for a holy character is always essentially the same, and had always been required.—Lev. 11:44. Nor did they consist in the revelation of new ultimate objects for our love and pursuit; for God and his glory had always been presented as the great end of man, as we have abundantly seen. Nor in opening new paths to heaven unknown to holy men of old; for Abel, Enoch, Noah, Moses, and all the redeemed of old, though with less clear light than now exists, entered in under the same principles as do saints under the new dispensation. The gospel was preached to the Israelites in the desert. —Heb. 4:2. Christ, as we have seen, was the Jehovah who appeared to Abraham, who led the Israelites in their wanderings, and who spoke to man through the prophets. A new heart had always been required, as now.—Ez. 18 : 31, and John 3 : 7. Repentance and faith were formerly as essential to the divine favor as now.—Ez. 18 : 30, and Matt. 23 : 23. And the atonement was both prēfigured in the sacrifices of the temple, and foretold in the most explicit language. —Is. 53.

*I.* Of course, then, Christ did not come to destroy the law as it was originally given, or to effect any radical change in true religion; but to correct our views of them, and to have the law disseminated and its true objects more successfully accomplished than the perversions of the Pharisees would allow?—Matt. 5:17.

*P.* Yes. In the gospel life and immortality are more clearly exhibited, and the way of deliverance is perfected, through Christ.—2 Tim. 1: 10. The apostle thus explains the reasons of his advent: "For what the law could not do [in the promotion of the glory of God, not because it was unadapted to effect it, but] in that it was weak [made incompetent] through the flesh [through the selfishness of its professed observers,] God, sending his own Son [to obey it] in the likeness of sinful flesh, and for sin [by a sacrifice for sin], condemned sin in the flesh [by reproving men's selfishness of heart and depravity of conduct, and by exhibiting and exalting the holiness of the law in his own obedience and sufferings]: That the righteousness of the law [that which it was designed to accomplish] might be fulfilled in us [true believers], who walk not after the flesh [who are not impelled by selfish desires to the pursuit of personal ends], but after the Spirit [under his holy impulses, to the promotion of the divine glory].—Rom. 8: 3—5. Christ designed, in the gospel, to produce such a kind of obedience to the law, as would exalt God to the chief place in the hearts of his people, and by his instructions to render clear the way of salvation, and by his atonement to make that salvation possible to man.

*I.* Such, evidently, is the purpose here indicated by the apostle.

*P.* And such is precisely the religion of the gospel in one of its chief elements. Laying aside the penalty of the law as it were, and looking behind its commands, it rests upon the authority of the lawgiver himself as its motive. Love to Christ is the heart-impulse of its obedience. Under this indomptable principle, it honors Christ and overcomes every obstacle to duty.

*I.* Do the Scriptures give us any account of a conversion from legalism to the religion of the gospel?

*P.* It does in several instances. Saul of Tarsus was a selfish, mercenary and compromising legalist. He believed that as a descendant of Abraham he was born at friends with God, and consequently needed no new desires or new heart. He had doubtless seen Christ in Jerusalem (Acts 22:3); had heard him declare that the Abrahamic covenant did not authorize such a belief; that it referred to his *spiritual* seed only, or to such as had been regenerated (John 8:39, 40); that he was the Son of God, equal with the Father, and that consequently his construction must prevail. And he had heard him denounce the religion and hopes of his brethren as false, and even Satanic (John 8:44), and command them to repent on pain of eternal death. This had aroused his wrath against him, and made him eager to persecute his disciples. While on his way to Damascus he again beheld Christ, but now in his heavenly kingdom. This convinced him that he was God; that he was therefore authorized to denounce that construction of the covenant on which all his hopes were based; that his own hopes were selfish and invalid; and that he was then an impenitent sinner bound to perdition, and actually engaged in the work of persecuting his Creator! He looked upon Christ as his enemy, as well he might; in utter despair of escaping (for Christ had denounced him as self-ruined) he died to *himself* (Rom. 7:9), that is, he ceased to be under the power of self-interest; and then yielded his will unreservedly to the authority of Christ, as God. "Lord [owner, proprietor, master,] what wilt *thou* have me to do?"—implying a purpose to obey. And upon being commanded to proceed to Damascus, he obeyed accordingly. There he remained several days repenting, as was meet he should, in dust and ashes over his selfish depravity, and horrible wickedness as a persecutor; and so profound was his self-condemnation, and so deep his self-abhorrence, that hope entered not into his heart nor did he either eat or drink for three days.—Acts 9 : 1—20.

*I.* How incongruous it would have been for such a butcher to have immediately leaped up (according to modern usage), rejoicing in a hope of pardon and heaven!—evincing, that his heart was still fixed chiefly on his own happiness. But had the Holy Spirit then regenerated his heart, and was he in a converted state previous to indulging a hope of pardon?

*P.* Certainly. He remained in the same dejected state until Ananias instructed him in the duties and hopes of the gospel. Previous to which, God had declared that he prayed, which is never said in a favorable sense of any except believers, and that he was a chosen vessel to promote his glory; and Ananias accordingly saluted him as a Christian brother. After he was instructed in the gospel, he hoped in Christ; "and straitway he preached Christ in the synagogues [not to urge the sinners there to hope in his mercy rather than in the Father; in the first instance, but] that he is the Son of God," entitled to the same obedience from them which he himself was rendering.

*I.* I am much obliged for this delineation.

*P.* As supreme love to Christ is the motive principle of the religion of the gospel, it will find a moving power in him and his glory to make it permanent through everlasting ages. Plighting its faith and duty under the impulse of such a pure affection, it cannot but be approvable and acceptable to one whose distinguishing trait is love.—1 John 4:16. Although it contemplates the strictest obedience or righteousness, it is not *self*-righteous, but *God*-righteous; for its right conduct does not spring from a love of self, but from a love God, and it has in view ultimately, not the ends of self, but the glory of God. It is a *free* and *voluntary* service; one rendered of free choice, with fear indeed, as well it may be in view of the awful majesty of God, but not with the fear of the slave, but with that of the affectionate and reverential child, which deters his love from running into familiarity and presumption. It is *not mercenary;* for its service is rendered from principle, and the pleasure it takes in God is a resulting virtuous pleasure, a fitting reward at the hand of God to encourage the believer onward in holiness; but which, if it were removed, would not impair his holy purposes, however it might affect his strength under the manifold temptations of the world. It is the acquisition of that holy character, in kind, which God demands of all his creatures. It is a disallowance of every thing as good previous to its first love, and of course of every thing like merit in the previous life. It is a disallowance of future merit also, because it is rendered from affection, and in pursuance of an acknowledged duty only. In fine, the religion of the gospel is "faith which worketh by love."—Gal. 5:6.

*I.* What a perfect contrast it presents to legalism!

*P.* But there is another element in the religion of the gospel. Christ is not only elevated thus as a Prince to rule and to be loved by his creatures, but he is also presented as their Saviour. "Him hath God exalted with his right hand, to be a PRINCE, and a SAVIOUR."—Acts 5:31. "Of this man's seed hath God, according to his promise, raised unto Israel a Saviour, Jesus."—Acts 13:23. The necessity of an atonement, together with the objects to be accomplished by it, have been heretofore explained. Humble submission to the will of Christ, an active devotion to his glory by means of the observance of his commands as made known in his law and in his personal teachings, and an implicit trust and hope in his pardoning grace through the atonement alone, constitutes the whole of the religion of the gospel; and when it is observed perfectly, as it will be in heaven, it will constitute the very perfection of character.

*I.* Beyond all doubt. But I have supposed from the encouragements to hope for pardon in Christ, that that was *the* great, and indeed *only* essential of the gospel.

*P.* Many sinners, as well as many Christians, imbibe the same error. The Scriptures, in the first place, when speaking of Christ as a Saviour, always refer to him as a saviour from *sin* as well as punishment, and only from punishment as one is delivered from sin. Consequently, as a hope in Christ for deliverance from punishment merely is no where authorized in the Scriptures, it cannot be such an essential as you have supposed.—Matt. 1:21. No one can validly hope in Christ for deliverance from sin as well as from perdition, until after he has heartily renounced his sins, that is, has been converted; consequently no impenitent sinner can justly hope in him in the first instance. Again, the hope of the Scriptures further contemplates the permission to enjoy the glory of God (Rom. 5:2), which no sinner can truly indulge until, by regeneration, he has come to desire and love that glory; and if even that hope was made a condition to be fulfilled before regeneration, it would be an impossible one.

*I.* Why then is it urged upon us?

*P.* Hope of mere deliverance from punishment is never urged upon impenitent sinners, but the very reverse; for God has said, "woe unto the wicked! it shall be ill with him" (Is. 3:11); and it would also be derogatory to his character to urge it upon his wicked enemies. But it is pressed upon the penitent, humble, faithful child of God as an indication of his Father's gracious love, and an encouragement to honor God by a perseverance in his spiritual warfare. Thus you will observe that whenever hope is enjoined in the epistles, or where encouragement is given to rejoice in the Lord, believers, and not impenitent sinners, are invariably addressed. And when Paul speaks of the manner of his public preaching, he assumes the position before described: "For I determined not to know [and of course not to proclaim] any thing among you, save [first] Jesus [the saviour from *sin*] Christ [the anointed, or set apart as King], and [second] him crucified [him, as an atoning sacrifice for such believers].—1 Cor. 2:2. As we have before seen, when the Scriptures present a principle of action, they often make its fulfillment the foundation for the presentation of another; as, in the present instance, the submission of the sinner to Jesus Christ as King, and his thereby renouncing sin, is prēsupposed as the ground of the offer of him as a crucified Saviour.

*I*. Yes. As with Christ came first the crown and next the cross, so it is proper that in the order of grace he should be practically recognized as the lawful wearer of the crown, before he is confided in for the blessings flowing from his cross. Still, I am not quite clear as to the meaning of the apostle in his directions on the day of Pentecost.

*P*. The attention of the people was attracted by unusual indications from heaven, the appearance of cloven tongues as of fire, and the astonishing fact that the apostles were enabled to speak intelligibly in twelve or more languages. Taking advantage of their curiosity, Peter delivered a most admirable argument, proving from those Scriptures which they all received as the revelation of God, that "God hath made that same Jesus, whom ye have crucified, both Lord [Ruler by right of ownership] and Christ," the Messiah or set-apart, whom they had for so long a time expected.—Acts 2:1—40. The moment they came to believe in his God-ship, they felt self-condemned for causing or consenting to his death in the body; they realized that they were his adversaries, the enemies of God; their former confidence fled, and they gave themselves up for lost. Under such compunctions and despondency, and like all other unregenerate persons ignorant what to do, since all they had before relied upon had proved unavailing, they inquired of the apostles, "Men and brethren, what shall we do?"—an inquiry which has been repeated by every convicted sinner since their day. The first direction given was "Repent," abandon all your former selfish purposes and wicked courses in obedience to the rightful authority of this Jesus, the Lord and

King. This, if observed, would turn them from sin to holiness, from themselves to Christ, as we have heretofore abundantly seen. Being thus converted, the supposed fulfillment of the command is made the basis of a further direction, "and be baptized every one of you in the name of Jesus Christ, for the remission of sins;" by means of this ordinance, make known to the public that you believe that Jesus is the Christ, the Son of the living God (John 6:69), and that you purpose to obey him as such and to devote yourself to his glory; —then your sins shall be remitted.—Rom. 10:9. Other counsels he gave; but this is sufficient to explain the point which you had in view.

*I.* Will you explain the case of the jailer at Philippi?

*P.* Paul and Silas had been preaching Christ for many days at Philippi, when they were arrested and thrust into prison.—Acts 16:12—34. The earthquake, the miraculous opening of the prison doors and the unloosing of the bands of the prisoners, together with their refusal to fly, deeply affected the jailer. He had, no doubt, become acquainted with their doctrine and was in a position to become convinced of the presence of God with them, of his own want of the true religion, and of his being dead in trespasses and sins. This is evident from the perplexity, as well as anxiety, evinced in his inquiry, "Sirs, what must I do to be saved?" If he was not before converted (as some suppose) he could mean only how to secure his personal or selfish safety and peace. Their reply was, first, "Believe on the Lord Jesus Christ," receive and obey him as God, and devote yourself to promote his glory ultimately; for "they spake unto him the word of the Lord, and to all that were in his house." This, you will observe, is true conversion or the new heart. Upon doing which, they declared to him, secondly, "and thou shalt be saved, and [they doing the same thing] thy house." The apostles intended "the salvation of God" or such as he would only then desire,—the salvation not of selfishness, but of enjoying God and his glory. To have proposed any other would have been wicked not only, but it would have been rejected by him; for we are afterwards told that he and they were truly converted, "believing in God [in Christ as God] with all his house." In his extremity under that terrible condemnation, like other convicted sinners he abandoned himself by the very act of yielding to Christ as God to subserve his authority and glory the rather; and then he could understand, appreciate, enter into, and appropriate the holy "salvation of God."

*I.* Will you please explain what is meant by natural religion?

*P.* The religion of nature in its purity, intends first the observance of the will of God so far as it can be deduced by reason from his works, our relations, and the operations of the natural conscience; and second, doing it from the *motive* of the creative rights, and to the end of the glory of God, so far as his existence, character and glory are discoverable from the material and moral worlds which he has produced. So far as it goes, it is similar in principle to the religion of revelation; for that consists in obedience to God from the same motive, and to the same end. The apostle (Rom. 1:19—21) declares that God has shown to the Gentiles that which should be known concerning himself; that his existence, eternal power, and Godhead or right to rule over them, though invisible to their senses, were to be inferred from the things he had made; so that they were without excuse for not glorifying him as God. And he speaks of some (Rom. 2:14, 15) who, from the observation of the works of nature and the dictates of their own consciences, might learn and do the things commanded in the revealed law of God; these, not having revelation, have notwithstanding a law unto themselves.

*I.* I always supposed that natural religion was something very objectionable.

*P.* So far from it, the apostle places the condemnation of the Gentiles solely on the ground that, having these opportunities of knowledge, they rejected them, and "worshipped and served the creature [with his selfish lusts and pleasures] rather than the Creator, who is blessed for ever."—Rom. 1:25. Had they used their light, renouncing the creature, and worshipping and serving the Creator, they would not have been rejected. Their service would have been correct as to its governing principle, though imperfect in the details of conduct; but this would not have produced their rejection, for it is a rule in the divine government, that "if there be first a willing mind, it is accepted according to that a man hath, and not according to that a man hath not."—2 Cor. 8:12. And it is a just one, as is that other, applicable no doubt to the Gentile world according to the degree of their willfulness, "But he that knew not his lord's will, and did commit things worthy of stripes, shall be beaten with few stripes."—Luke 12:48.

*I.* Do you suppose the heathen, if thus converted to God, could be saved without the gospel?

*P.* I will answer in the language of Doddridge and Newton. The truth, says Dr. Doddridge, seems to be this, that none of the heathens will be condemned for not believing the gospel, but they are liable to condemnation for the breach of God's natural law. Nevertheless, if there be any of them in whom there is a prevailing love to the Divine Being, there seems reason to believe that, for the sake of Christ, though to them unknown, they may be accepted by God. And so much the rather, as the ancient Jews and even the apostles during the time of our Saviour's abode on earth, seem to have had but little notion of those doctrines which those who deny the salvability of the heathen are most apt to imagine. Mr. Newton asks, Who will prove that such views and desires can arise in the heart of a sinner, without the energy of that Spirit which Jesus is exalted to bestow? Who shall take upon him to say, that his blood has not sufficient efficacy to redeem to God a sinner who is thus disposed, though he has never heard of his name?

*I.* This view relieves my mind from an irrepressible sense of the injustice of the heathen being punished for not hoping in a Saviour who had never been made known to them. I see now that my false notion that a hope in the pardoning mercy of Christ was the chief thing in religion, and that it was the very faith unto salvation required of us, gave me incorrect views upon that point; but regarding belief in God, submission to his will, and devotion to his glory as the chief in his view, the matter is sufficiently plain and just. But do you suppose that the heathen do ever make such a proper use of the light of nature?

*P.* It is very doubtful indeed. I have studied the religious characters of some of the most enlightened, with a view to form an opinion on this point. Their codes of morals are in many respects proper, they evidently having had the advantage of reports at least from some of the Jewish sacred books; and some seem to have cultivated their consciences in respect to their relations to, and the rights of their fellow-creatures. Whether conscience, under a view of these rights of their fellow-beings, controlled them in their conduct we know not precisely; but I could never discover the least evidence that any had reached the point of true self-denial, that the creative right of God exerted a controlling influence over their purposes, or that their hearts were devoted to his honor and glory as the chief moral good. Much appears to show the contrary, and that they exhibited the spectacle of enlightened judgments and correct conduct on many of the abstract rights of man, with perfectly selfish hearts toward God.

*I.* A system of morality, which is often mistaken for piety in our day. How do you reconcile the fact of God's pardoning a penitent sinner, with his veracity in previously declaring that he should be punished?

*P.* Very easily. In the first place, the denunciations of his displeasure are directed to the wicked as such, while his offers of mercy are to the righteous as such; and upon a change of character that consequence, in either case, becomes inappropriate and ceases. Thus it is said, "When the wicked man turneth away from his wickedness, and doeth that which is lawful and right, he shall save his soul alive." "When a righteous man turneth away from his righteousness, and committeth iniquity, and dieth in them; for his iniquity that he hath done, shall he die."—Ez. 18: 26, 27. But in the next place you will observe that God does not speak and act in this matter merely as an individual, but as a magistrate enacting and executing laws for his creatures; and as in him is combined the legislative, as well as the judicial and executive powers of the divine government, it is competent to him to regulate the execution of the laws, or to substitute such other legislative provisions as the exigencies of that government may require; and in this view no question of personal veracity can arise.

*I.* I am satisfied on that point. But how do you reconcile his immutability, with his change of feelings and purpose toward the penitent sinner?

*P.* From the very nature of things, every moral being must feel, purpose, and act according to the existing facts as they are presented to his observation. Thus, suppose we should see a man, under the instigation of revenge upon its parents, plunge a dagger into the heart of a lovely child, and should hear its death-shriek and witness its death-agonies as it expired at his feet. Profound indignation, disgust, and abhorrence would arise spontaneously in our bosoms against the felon; and we should seize him in order to have full justice inflicted upon him. None but a brute could fail to feel and act thus. Now, if we knew beforehand that, by visiting the wretch in prison and faithfully presenting divine truth, he could be brought to true repentance and profound self-abhorrence for his act, it would make no difference in our feelings toward him at the present time; and if we should resolve to take that course, it would effect no change in our present purposes toward the guilty wretch in his hardened state.

*I.* I see it could effect no present change in either respect.

*P.* But, behold him now in the cell of the condemned, awaiting his appointed hour of death. He has truly repented; in the deepest disgust at his own former character and conduct, he weeps bitterly; he mourns over the irreparable wrong he has done to that child, and to its friends, and to society, and to God, and resigns himself to the sentence of the laws of man and God as perfectly just. Now, while we would condemn his former character and conduct no less than before, this change would so affect the existing facts that we would approve his present penitence and character, and would purpose good toward him, provided the ends of justice could be perfectly answered in some other manner than by his execution. These feelings and purposes would be called out by the occurrence of this new state of facts; and hence they would not evince any versatility in our moral sentiments or characters.

*I.* They certainly would not.

*P.* There was a vast period during which, under the then existing facts, God approved, loved, and purposed to bless Satan and his companions; for they were then eminently holy. God foreknew what would eventually be done by them, but their perceived apostacy did not affect their then present character and purposes, nor his feelings toward them; he did not hate them before they deserved it. After their unauthorized rebellion against his government, and their descent into pollution and all moral deformity, the facts changed and his feelings and purposes necessarily accorded with them.

*I.* It must have been so, as nearly as we can comprehend God.

*P.* As respects the immutability of God, you will observe that it is of two kinds—namely, natural and moral. His natural immutability consists in the essential unchangeableness of all his natural faculties, so to speak, such as his existence, power, capacity of feeling, purposing, and the like. These he possesses unalterably from his very nature. But his moral immutability relates exclusively to the perpetual right or holy use of these faculties. It consists in the preservation of a consistency of moral character under all circumstances, by the exercise of holy feelings and purposes according to the existing facts in each particular case; in other words, it consists in the unchangeableness of his purpose (with the corresponding feelings) to do every thing demanded by his own glory under the circumstances.

*I.* Certainly his moral immutability must be seen in the unwavering purpose, as exhibited in his various feelings and conduct, to promote his own glory; and should he fail there, mutability, and that of the worst kind, must be imputed to him.

*P.* One may seem to casual observers to be fickle-minded and changeable in the extreme; and yet when he is correctly understood, the very reverse may be seen to be the fact. Thus, suppose we notice one seemingly intent on his own affairs, go rapidly some distance east ward; soon he returns as rapidly toward the west; again he goes southward, and finally at a great distance we see him turn about, and pass away off northward.

We might very fairly infer that he was as changeable as the winds in his purposes, and that versatility was his chief characteristic. But on inquiry we ascertain that he is remarkably firm of purpose; that his general and chief purpose in such conduct was to reach a certain point to the northward; and that all his counter movements were caused by meeting with insuperable obstacles in each path, until with indomitable perseverance and by changing his subordinate plans and purposes, he had at last accomplished his grand object. Here, we would impute to him an immutability of will in that respect; and would refer to his subordinate changes as the chief evidence of that immutability, since he evidently submitted to them in order to subserve his ultimate end.

*I.* I perceive the principle. His immutability would not only be consistent with subordinate changes of feeling and purposes, but would demand them in order to its own preservation.

*P.* An earthly sovereign, we will suppose, contemplates and purposes the best good of his subjects; and as one plan of effecting this general purpose determines upon acquiring certain new territory. But other nations interpose, and he perceives that the welfare of his country will be destroyed should he prosecute that plan. Now, to persist in it would be mere obstinacy, and it would evince a disregard of the welfare of his country, and amount to mutability in that respect; whereas, to abandon the plan under this new state of facts, would be a persistance in his general purpose for his country's good.

*I.* It is perfectly evident what consistency of character would require.

*P.* On the same principle, the immutable desire, love, and purpose of God for his own glory and its promotion, leads him spontaneously to disapprove, dislike, and threaten to punish those whose present moral character and conduct conflict therewith; and to approve, like, and offer to bless them whose present character and conduct conforms thereto. And in each case he is perfectly open and sincere; while his foreknowledge and benevolent purpose in respect to eventually bringing many of the unholy to repentance can produce no present complacency in them. But the sinner, we will suppose, repents and devotes himself in heart and life to the promotion of the divine glory. Now *he* has shown himself mutable, *he* has changed his governing purpose from himself to God; but God remains unchanged in that respect, immutable as his own existence; while that very immutability of love and purpose for his own glory leads him, while he still condemns that person in respect to the past, to approve and like him for his new character, and to purpose to pardon and bless him for the future. Such new subordinate feelings and purposes are dictated by and made subservient to his own glory. Thus, it is the sinner and not God that changes radically. And the principle is the same, as seen in the case of the once holy but now fallen angels. It is thus, indeed, that God exhibits his glory; his forbearance with sinners, his sovereign goodness in subduing their wills, his remitting their sins, receiving them into his love, and admitting them into his presence at last, all develop the riches of that grace which will form the topic of their praise for ever and ever.

*I.* Will not this explanation throw some light upon

the alleged repentances and changes of purpose in God mentioned in the Scriptures?

*P.* Keep steadily in view that he proposes his own glory ultimately in every thing; that his moral immutability consists in his exercising feelings of favor or disfavor toward inferior objects according as they shall from time to time, either accord or disaccord with this ultimate object; and also in making his subordinate purposes in respect to such inferior objects vary or change as they agree or disagree therewith;—then you will perceive a most beautiful consistency in those details of the Scriptures. As an example, look at the expression in Gen. 6:6, 7. "And it repented the Lord that he had made man on the earth, and it grieved him at his heart: And the Lord said, I will destroy man, whom I have created, from the face of the earth." It would seem that the revolt of Satan and his followers, and their consequent endless punishment, had so involved the divine character that a full development of himself had become indispensable to the preservation of those who remained in their first estate, and to the clear exhibition of his own righteousness, goodness, mercy, as well as the true nature of his justice, and the like. In other words, there was an imperative demand that he should make a complete development of his own glory; and in pursuance of it, the world was created to be the theater on which this grand work was to be accomplished. I admit that this is only an hypothesis; but it is one which will grow upon our credence the more it is pondered upon, and it affords a perfect exoneration of God for creating a world in which he foreknew sin and misery would exist, for if in so doing he acted under a *nĕcessity* if he would do right, he is to be applauded the rather. Whatever you may think of this hypothesis, the fact still remains that the world was created in order to promote his glory, and in pursuance of a prēpurpose therefor. In process of time, as men multiplied on the earth and their longevity enabled them to become great adepts in wickedness, they counteracted every provision he had made for their glorifying him, and they dishonored themselves as moral beings and disgraced him as their Creator by their stupendous crimes. "And God saw that the wickedness of man was great in the earth;" that they were hopelessly opposed to the great object of their creation. And, in view of the disappointment, what could be more natural or consistent than to grieve over their conduct, and to regret in view of *that*, that he had made man? If he had rejoiced at their conduct, and had felt pleased in view of *that*, that he had made man, it would have proved that he had lost his superior regard to the glory with which it had conflicted, and that he had become mutable. Whereas his grief, and his purpose to destroy men, although in seeming contradiction to his original purpose to create them, were created by the exigencies of his glory under such new circumstances, and were evidences of his immutable purpose to consult *that* under every change of circumstances. God is constantly dealing with his myriads of free moral creatures, and under every variation of circumstances you will find him firm in his general purpose; and will discover that every subordinate change whether of feeling or purpose (called in the Scriptures repentance) is still produced thereby, to the ultimate praise of his glory.

*I.* So far the subject seems clear. But in order to avoid the idea of mutability in God, I have supposed that from the beginning he always loved the elect, and always hated the non-elect. And my view seemed to be sustained by the declaration of the apostle (Rom. 9:13), "As it is written, Jacob have I loved, but Esau have I hated," when neither were yet born.

*P.* And when there was nothing of either to love or hate. As we have seen, God exercises toward sinners benevolence or the love of mere compassion, and toward believers complacency. The one regards their miserable condition irrespective of their character or deserts; the other their character only, or them on account of their good character. The former never determines him to reward, while the latter always does. Now, if the feelings of God toward Jacob previous to his conversion were those of complacency, or if displacency was absent,—that is, if he exercised toward him any feelings different in character from those toward Esau,—then he acted not only in contradiction to himself, but he favored unholiness, for there was then nothing but unholiness to be pleased with in him. But, as we have seen, the *present* character and conduct of a person is what elicits *present* feelings; and as Jacob's were then opposed to the divine glory, the feelings of God toward him were those of displacency; and these were not relieved by any foreknowledge of what he would *afterwards* become, on the principle we have before examined. But you will observe that it was not any regard whatever to Jacob personally that formed the motive to his election, as you have erroneously supposed, but the sole motive was his own glory which he foresaw could be promoted thereby; nor was it any hatred to Esau that produced his reprobation, but the same motive of his own glory, necessitated through the inimical course which he perceived Esau would irreclaimably pursue, prompted it in righteousness. All this the omniscient God could and did perceive before either was born, as clearly as when they subsequently developed their characters in their conduct; and his purposes were formed accordingly. It is just as if you should know beforehand that no proper means, used in consistency with the established rights of others (and which means only you would employ) would avail to bring that murderer of the child to repentance; you would still hate him, and in your own mind consign him beforehand to the fate of all incorrigible transgressors;—in other words, your love of justice would lead you to reject him in anticipation. And in like manner, if you could perceive beforehand that by the proper use of such means he could be brought to repentance, considerations of the glory of God, mercy, and the like, might induce you, even while you hated him for his evil conduct, to determine beforehand to employ effectually those means for his repentance. Thus, if personal considerations did not exert any influence on the subject, you would come to understand practically how God could elect some, not on account of any complacency toward them, or any personal merit or prēperceived works on their part, but solely on account of "him that calleth"—namely, himself and his own glory.—Rom. 9:11, 12.

*I* I can see the full force of the objection that there

was nothing personal for God to love or hate in Jacob and Esau before they were born, and that therefore no actual good or evil pertaining to them could have then influenced his purposes; and also, that after they were born and after both deserved and received his disapprobation, nothing existed in Jacob previous to his conversion to elicit his approbation and love,—and indeed the history of Jacob abundantly shows this fact. Nevertheless the Scriptures seem to assert that God *did* love Jacob before he was born, and in such a sense as to reward him.—v. 11.

*P.* But they do not. The declaration, "Jacob have I loved, but Esau have I hated," was not made previous to their birth, or previous to the conversion of Jacob, and therefore does not indicate any such feelings toward him then. It was made over a thousand years after the death of both, through the Prophet Malachi (ch. 1 : 2, 3); and was uttered to prove, by a reference to his subsequent conduct toward them and their descendants, even to the days of that prophet, that his previous purposes of election and reprobation were *accomplished.* And this is the very object for which it is introduced by the apostle, "As it is written," [in proof of the fact of their election and reprobation because of the demands of the divine glory, it is recorded eleven hundred and eighty-six years after their birth] "Jacob have I loved, but Esau have I hated," and its truth is to be seen in my conduct during all that period.

*I.* Permit me to propose a question bearing upon the creative right of God over his creatures. I do it with reluctance, because of its polemical and seemingly presumptuous character; but it is one with which my mind has been somewhat perplexed. Should God command you to trench upon the happiness of another, would you be bound to obey him simply because of his creative right over you?

*P.* Certainly I should; and under divine grace, I would form the purpose of obedience, as did Abraham when commanded to sacrifice the life of Isaac, and whose obedience *in purpose* elicited the commendation, "Now I know that thou fearest God, seeing thou hast not withheld thy son, thine only son, from me."

*I.* Upon what principle would you be justified in such a breach of your obligations to a fellow-creature?

*P.* Upon the principle that the superior obligation must prevail. There are various grades in the relations of beings, which produce various grades of obligations and various grades of claims or rights resulting therefrom; and when these conflict, the less must yield to the greater, the inferior to the superior. Thus, the brute creation are in certain inferior relations, and possess certain claims upon us, to humane treatment, for example; our fellow-immortal beings stand to us in superior relations and possess higher claims, so that if they conflict with those of the brute creation the latter must give way, the surrender of their lives by our hand for man's necessary food, for example; and God stands to us in a still higher relation, that of our Creator, and possesses still superior claims arising therefrom, so that should his claims interfere with those of our fellows, the latter must give way. Children, for example, are under certain relations and obligations to their parents, but are under superior ones to God; and hence, while they are commanded to obey their parents, it is only *in the Lord*, when in accordance with their duty to God, and subject to his superior authority.—Eph. 6 : 1. Should God, therefore, command me to do an act which will interfere with the claims of a fellow-creature, I am bound by the superiority of his rights over me to theirs, to obey.

*I.* Certainly the creative right of God is of superior authority over us, to any claim a creature can present; and the most imperative must prevail. But suppose God should command you to do an act clearly wrong?

*P.* A thing which is utterly impossible; but as it is a supposition which some persist in making to the injury of the souls of men, I will answer it. In such a case I should obey him without the least hesitation.

*I.* But should we do wrong toward our fellows?

*P.* No; nor should we do wrong toward our Creator. If he should command, I am bound by his superior right to command me; and however much I might, like Abraham in the contemplation of the sacrifice of his son, regret the pain to be inflicted on my fellow-creature, or however much I might condemn the wrong I was about to perpetrate toward him, I would be left to no alternative but implicit obedience to my Creator.

*I.* But would you not be criminal in the act?

*P.* No. Being so bound to obey God at all events, the entire responsibility of the act would rest upon him, as the real author and cause; and it would be shifted from me, as being the mere instrument of my Creator. In morals, it would be imputable to him as his act, and not mine; my conscience would not condemn me as censurable for doing the wrong, however much I might regret it; and I would be left as free as yourself to form and express my sentiments respecting the propriety or impropriety of the whole transaction. Whereas, should I suffer the inferior claims of my fellow to prevail over the superior right of God to control my conduct, and refuse to obey his command, I could never reason my conscience into an approval of such a renunciation of his authority, or silence its condemnations for my disobedience.

*I.* But should an earthly sovereign mal-administer his authority in the same manner, would you obey?

*P.* No. His authority does not rest on the basis of the creation and ownership of his subjects, and therefore his rights are not superior in every sense, as are those of God. Should he make such a requirement, therefore, I should meet it with the superior authority of God over me, should point to his command to "do justly," and should refuse to obey the former. Whereas should God virtually repeal this command to do justly, as your former question prēsupposes, then I should observe the latest exercise of his authority. Absolute sovereignty implies that the will of the sovereign is, in all cases, to prevail in the last resort; and in this sense there is but one lawfully absolute sovereign in the universe—namely, God.

*I.* But is not God morally bound by right and justice?

*P.* Yes. He himself has settled the principles of right, either directly by promulgating them in his law, or indirectly by placing his creatures in such relations as that various rights would, as he foresaw, necessarily emanate from them. But he has not therefore deposed his sovereignty into our hands; he has not exalted us above himself, and made us the judges in the last resort over him and his conduct, so that, if we consider that his requirements are proper, we may obey, and if not, we may refuse obedience. As the absolute sovereign, his authority over us remains supreme, however he may choose to exercise it. But, in reality as mankind have, by sin, forfeited every claim upon God, he cannot by any means treat them unjustly; and as he never will repeal his holy, just, and good law, this entire objection is foreign to any good purpose, while it tends unnecessarily to shock the sensibilities of the good.

*I.* My judgment and conscience coincide with these positions. But where there is no actual submission of the will to the creative authority of God, and consequently no appreciation of the dignity, power, and loveliness of the principle, the conscience will approve and urge its adoption indeed, but the natural heart will still revolt, and will, perhaps, decide the question against God in favor of the creature's happiness.

*P.* The very purpose, doubtless, which some have in view, in raising the question at all. They wish to add some other element to the creative right of God, and, by yielding thereto, persuade themselves that they have also yielded to such right; but their attacks upon it as an independent and all-sufficient basis of authority evince that they have never adopted it. They are never content with the mere command of God, but always want some other and further reason in order to obey; which shows that they do not obey *God* at all.

*I.* "The Lord reigneth, let the earth rejoice!" and may we hereafter rejoice in him, standing in his presence-chamber clothed in righteousness as with a garment, and ever casting our crowns before him there!

FINIS

www.ingramcontent.com/pod-product-compliance
Lightning Source LLC
LaVergne TN
LVHW020103110826
845151LV00001B/50